DATE DUE

APR 2 1 1985		
MAY 2 2 1988		
NOV 2 1 1988		
MAR 3 0 1994		

DEMCO NO. 38-298

Public Opinion:
Coalitions, Elites, and Masses

Public Opinion

Coalitions, Elites, and Masses

HARRY HOLLOWAY

JOHN GEORGE

St. Martin's Press • New York

ACKNOWLEDGMENTS

Monica Blumenthal: From *Justifying Violence*, copyright 1972 by University of Michigan.
Reprinted by permission of the publisher, the Institute for Social Research.

Lloyd A. Free and Hadley Cantril: From *The Political Beliefs of Americans: A Study of
Public Opinion.* Copyright © 1967 by Rutgers, The State University. Reprinted by permission of The Rutgers University Press.

The Gallup Opinion Index: Figures from The Gallup Opinion Index are reprinted by permission from Vol. 123, September 1975, Vol. 128, March 1976, Vol. 141, April 1977,
Vol. 153, April 1978, and Report #130 "Religion in America 1976."

Acknowledgments and copyrights continue at the back of the book on page 286, which
constitutes an extension of the copyright page.

To Carol and Treva

Preface

This book grew out of our desire to fashion a textbook on public opinion that would be interesting, readable, and wide-ranging. The subject interests many people, in and out of academia, but is elusive and not easily summed up. We use three major concepts as organizing themes: political coalitions (like the old New Deal), elites, and masses. The term "masses" is not very satisfactory, but we have been unable to provide a better one. By masses we mean simply the bulk of the population that is not normally highly involved politically. As it turns out in our analysis of public opinion, the masses matter a good deal. We only wish that they were more involved than they are.

The creation of a manuscript for publication is an arduous process punctuated from time to time by deadlines and bouts of frenzied activity, involving a number of people besides the authors. The typing was done with much care and patience by Geri Rowden, Dianne Handley, and Beci Weber. The editorial staff at St. Martin's was enormously helpful and understanding. We wish to thank particularly Bert Lummus, Carolyn Eggleston, and Mary Heathcote. Our wives, Carol Holloway and Treva George, helped in ways that can be acknowledged but not adequately described. For a time at least, "that book" will no longer be a part of family life.

H. H.
J. G.

Contents

Part One
THE SETTING

1 · Introduction

Anyone teaching a course in public opinion is likely to face perplexed students who want to know what "public opinion" means and what the course covers. The teacher, who presumably knows what he or she is doing and does so with gusto and pleasure, may feel a twinge of annoyance. But the question makes more sense than many of the questions people ask, and a good question, annoying or not, deserves an answer. Socrates, for example, made quite a name for himself by asking good questions, although it is not recorded that he taught much in the area of public opinion.

A Socrates who asked what public opinion means could be told that it means a variety of things. Some years ago one respected author of a text on public opinion, V. O. Key, Jr., defined it as "those opinions held by private persons which governments find it prudent to heed." This definition is broad enough to encompass almost everything but the proverbial kitchen sink; it may satisfy those familiar with the subject but is apt to leave others in the dark. Socrates would have had a field day with it.

To be more specific, we might explain that public opinion deals with those issues of the day to which the public reacts by forming groups of those who are for, those who are against, and those who are undecided. Given the vast array of polling results available—and the volubility of most professors—a book-length presentation of such information could easily be managed. But this definition is too narrow, and would be likely to leave the student with little more than a grab bag of assorted facts based on current polls. Socrates would probably retch.

What To Expect

Our own conception of public opinion is cast in broad terms, to encompass much of American life. As our title suggests, we look at coalitions, elites, and masses. By coalitions we mean basic political groupings that have shaped the American polity. The New Deal coalition, for instance, was much more than a public opinion poll or a collection of them somehow strung together. For a generation the New Deal coalition was the majority coalition and shaped much of the legislation that governed the country. Public opinion in the sense of a governing majority that shapes public policy provides a framework that helps us to organize and make sense of the wealth of polling information available. From this perspective we can also analyze change, since the fading of the New Deal has led to argument over its successors and to alternative concepts of the governing majority. Therefore one of our major concerns is with concepts of governing coalitions and their components.

But a Socrates might wonder if such majority coalitions do exist or make much difference if they do. There are those who believe that a small group of people, a group that stands apart from the mass of the population, really runs things. This small group, an elite, is seen as dominant, whatever the appearance of majority rule may be. Political coalitions based upon appeals to the broad mass of people would then matter very little. The public and its opinions become creations of skillful, manipulative elites. This perspective obviously has chilling implications for anyone who believes in popular rule, but it is an alternative that we cannot dismiss out of hand. The subject of elite control is a major issue that merits attention along with the analysis of political coalitions.

But public opinion, as we use the term, encompasses even more than this. The elite perspective necessarily focuses on what one social scientist has called the "higher circles" in the system. But what of the rest of the citizenry, those outside the "higher circles"? We need to know as well about the mass of people living out rather ordinary lives. Most people are not members of an elite nor leaders of political coalitions, yet they may be members of groups that contribute importantly to coalitions. We therefore need to look at mass opinion as it contributes to major blocs in the nation's political makeup. For example, the Democratic coalition has long depended heavily on the Catholic vote, but American Catholics matter more than as a contribution to a bloc of votes on election day. Religion is important to the mass of Americans in ways that are not necessarily associated with party politics and current events. For that matter, most Americans are not highly political. They have their problems but the majority are not badly exploited or heavily oppressed. Most Americans can lead a pretty good life with a minimum of political involvement. This analysis of mass opinion—an expression we use for want of a better one—carries us beyond the "higher circles" occupied by coalition leaders and the elite. Thus to the inquiring student—and to those who follow in the footsteps of Socrates—we say that public opinion encompasses the coalitions, elites, and masses of modern America.

The presentation of these themes and their implications occupies much of this book. However, before introducing the overall themes we think it worthwhile to discuss those troublesome terms "liberalism" and "conservatism" later in this introduction. The terms often confuse as much as they clarify, but they are so widely used in the United States that they are inescapable. We hope our explanation will help the reader understand the concept of political coalitions that is presented in Chapter 2, but we do not anticipate that our explanation of these ideological terms will satisfy everyone. (Readers who want further elaboration will find in Chapter 9 a subsection that deals specifically with the nation's confusing "radical-conservative" ideology.)

Chapter 2 picks up the central themes of our subject matter. Here we examine alternative coalition concepts and the elite perspective. After analyzing the New Deal coalition and its components, we turn to an account of several suggested alternatives proposed by authors who see the old New Deal coalition as largely a thing of the past. Alongside these coalition concepts we also outline the elite perspective as presented by two political scientists who have authored a popular text on American government. Our analysis of governing coalition concepts and elite theory we characterize as "perspectives on those in charge." The posing of these alternatives sets the stage for Part Two, in which we turn to extended analysis of mass opinion.

The importance of the opinions of ordinary people in America is a recurring theme of our analysis, so this section has implications for understanding the concepts of coalitions, elites, and the system as a whole. One of the most useful ways to begin an analysis of mass opinion is with a bit of the past and its powerful influence in the present. As the celebration of the nation's bicentennial in 1976 reminded us, this nation and its political system have been around a long time. This legacy and what it means in the present for our peculiar combination of political stability and social turmoil is discussed in Chapter 3.

Chapter 4 is about a fundamental matter on which much else depends, that is, mass participation. Here we explore contemporary political attitudes as well as behavior. The relatively nonpolitical attitudes that we have found are, we think, of basic importance. Having related past to present and outlined the degree of political involvement of the mass of ordinary Americans, we then focus, in Chapter 5, on the individual and early socialization, examining not only the family but some implications for later life and for different patterns of socialization. We find the family to be surprisingly strong in spite of the cries of alarm from some worried observers of family stresses. In Chapter 6, our discussion of education, we challenge the social scientists who highlight the contrasts between the well educated and the "unwashed" masses. Our examination of religion in Chapter 7 leads us to conclude that it is still quite powerful in its hold on Americans and is perhaps gaining strength, although, oddly enough, it seems to be of declining importance to party politics and the coalitions.

Ethnic influences, the subject of Chapter 8, overlap those of religion but are not the same thing. We concentrate attention upon black-white differences and their relationship both to the New Deal coalition and to the system's concepts of assimilation. Chapter 9 deals especially with economic differences and their political implications. Here one of our themes, the inadequacy of socialist perspectives in understanding America, illuminates both the weakness of socialism in the United States and some important characteristics of the nation. We argue for the declining importance of social class differences, viewed in terms of the struggle between the haves and the have-nots, in contributing to party politics and the persisting coalitions. This chapter is not likely to cause Marx to turn over in his grave but does provide much evidence to account for the nation's limited acceptance of the welfare state and the powerful strain of conservative, individualistic rhetoric that persists.

Part Three returns to the opening themes, and we must deal again with the theory of governance by an elite. For if elite theory holds, then mass opinion and its formation matter little. This encounter with elite doctrine takes us in Chapter 10 into a fairly extended treatment of the evidence for elite domination. To many Americans who are turned off and cynical, an elite perspective has considerable appeal and plausibility. But in Chapter 11 we marshal evidence to counter the elite perspective. Here we draw upon some of our analysis of mass opinion to argue the case for a system that is heavily middle class and relatively nonpolitical. The concept of a single, dominant—and domineering—elite is contrary to our conclusions. Although ambiguities abound, we argue that ordinary people's opinions really do matter. What we call the "view from the middle" better explains our political system, we believe, than the concept of a single controlling elite.

Once we have shown the limitations of the elite perspective, we turn to examination of the processes that channel public opinion into the system. Chapters 12 and 13 analyze the political parties, the politics of interest groups, the role of the media and the campaign managers in the political process. As the parties have decomposed, interest groups and the mass media, especially the latter, have come to the fore. The media in general and the campaign experts in particular have grown in importance. But it still appears to us that the voters are not mere puppets jerked into action—or inaction—by cunning elites.

Chapter 14 sums up the themes of our opening chapter on coalitions, elites, and masses. Here we try to spell out the relationships between elites and masses and, in addition, the theory of the dominant coalition, which we consider the most persuasive interpretation. Unfortunately, the American system is too complex for simple, unambiguous conclusions. We think the elitists exaggerate but are not entirely wrong. As for the coalitions, the Democratic coalition of 1976 was by no means a complete break with the past but nonetheless differed significantly from the New Deal coalition of earlier years. Furthermore, in reviewing the system as a whole we find that there are significant injustices present, as critics have frequently pointed out. Perhaps most worrisome is the tendency of many Americans to divorce their personal satisfactions, which tend to be considerable, from the public sector. A certain insensitivity and callousness toward the public sector may be the greatest fault of all. Surely a modern Socrates could raise some serious questions about this trend.

As authors, we readily acknowledge that our own values affect the book from start to finish. This is true of all books, of course, whether the influence is conscious or not. But our approach is different from the usual and our values color and shape the analysis throughout. A brief account of our own experiences is therefore in order. Originally, like most political scientists, we were on the liberal side of the political spectrum and generally voted Democratic. In 1964 it was easy to oppose Barry Goldwater and to support Lyndon Johnson enthusiastically. But by 1976 the answers no longer seemed so clear and enthusiasm had given way to considerable skepticism and uncertainty. At times government action has appeared, as conservatives warned, to make things worse, not better. Both of us feel the need for solutions that transcend established party and coalition leadership on both left and right. We hope that our own ambivalence—even confusion—has enabled us to bring a rounded perspective to our subject matter and to avoid the predictable posturing of the strong partisans of left and right.

Readers will understand that we cannot be experts in everything that we cover. In addition, we have sought to avoid encumbering the text with lengthy and detailed references. But we have sought to use major sources and recent ones, both to provide evidence for our views and to offer convenient starting places for students who want to pursue aspects of the subject. For our part, we enjoy teaching this subject and hope readers will enjoy our presentation of it. They may disagree with us but that is part of teaching and learning, ours as well as theirs. Politicians, ever mindful of the quest for votes, may kiss every baby in sight. As authors and not politicians, we hope we can afford to skip a few.

Liberalism and Conservatism Untangled

The terms "liberal" and "conservative" are much used and are almost as frequently abused. To define them is not easy but to avoid them is impossible. We will not try to account for the whole spectrum of political ideologies from left to right, a task that would take us far afield. We simply want to shed some light on opinions of garden-variety liberals and conservatives of today.

That confusion exists is clear enough. In 1964 Barry Goldwater, long a Republican senator from Arizona, ran for president against Lyndon Johnson. Goldwater was the author of a well-known book, *The Conscience of a Conservative*, and was widely recognized as one of the major spokesmen for conservative principles. Yet surveys of public opinion revealed that a surprising percentage of the public saw him as "radical."

Tom Braden, a respected columnist, in a column of February 1975 attempted to clarify his own understanding of these terms. He defined a liberal as one who held "the belief that men should have freedom and equality of opportunity in order to reason toward truth, and that under such conditions, they will try." He admitted that "by my definition, many whom we call conservatives are liberals." Braden then confessed that, having arrived at his own definition of liberalism, he was giving it up because no one else understood his usage.

Such confusion spawns political humor from time to time. One of the most delightful appeared in *Mad* magazine as its "Guide to Political Types." Conservatives the guide defined as those with traits such as the following: have pride in their penmanship, sleep in twin beds, waltz, are reliable pallbearers, mail in warranties, call Muhammad Ali Cassius Clay, drive cars with low license plate numbers, undertip, take pride in regularity, are on a first-name basis with bank officers, wear vests, and hate being called reactionaries. Liberals, on the other hand, were defined as those with the following traits: feed their pets organic food, use bicycles, support nonprofit TV, secretly wish the conservative publicist William F. Buckley were a liberal, sign petitions, prefer cremation to a burial plot, subscribe to *Consumer Reports*, grind their own coffee, and hate being called leftists. This satire tells little we really need to know about our political ideologies, and yet, so great is the confusion, it is hardly less informative than Braden's ill-fated struggle with the terms.

A good place to start a serious attempt at a definition of liberalism is with the New Deal coalition, which is a basic referent throughout our own analysis of public opinion. New Dealers believed in using the power of government, including a strong presidency, to curb big business and

*"I guess I'm a conservative, if you mean do I
put up a lot of jams and jellies."*

to help the underdog. They did not object much to taxes, especially those
on business, and did not mind government spending even if it meant possible deficits. They tended to favor labor, often invoked the virtues of the
workingman, and tended also to favor minorities. Major New Deal policies included government action to foster full employment and a series of
programs designed to help those unable to help themselves. The Social
Security system was one of the major New Deal achievements. New
Dealers also tended to be internationalist in outlook and usually felt that
American influence could be used abroad with good effect. In the 1960s
Lyndon Johnson's Great Society legislation, which vastly extended the
welfare state, stood in a direct line from the New Deal. For a time his
willingness to use American forces in Indochina fit this tradition of activism abroad, although it also led to strains within the coalition. Hubert

Humphrey, long a Democratic senator from Minnesota and vice president under Lyndon Johnson, ably represented this evolving New Deal tradition well into the 1970s.

Traditional New Deal liberals were largely oriented toward economic programs, welfare state policies, and unions and workers. During the 1960s and afterward other issues arose that fell somewhat outside traditional New Deal concerns. Simply to list these issues dramatizes the baffling complexity of the times and the diversity of possible reactions: civil rights protests by blacks; demonstrations by students; the war in Indochina; the rise of the environmental issue; mounting concern with women's claims to equality; demands for greater sexual permissiveness and new styles of living; Watergate; persistent problems of both inflation and unemployment that seemed to resist New Deal remedies; and the growing energy crisis. On the national scene Senator George McGovern of South Dakota, as the Democratic presidential candidate in 1972, represented to many an extension of New Deal liberalism tinged with radicalism in his attacks on the war, appeals for amnesty, and welfare reform proposals. On the other hand, Senator Henry Jackson of Washington, who sought the nomination in 1976, was thought by many to represent a moderate-to-conservative strand of the modern liberal tradition. He retained the New deal identification with the welfare state and the unions but also had a reputation for hawkish attitudes on foreign policy and military spending. Well out on the left are social critics like the economist and diplomat John Kenneth Galbraith and the socialist Michael Harrington. They might best be described as democratic socialists but are not far removed from liberal welfare state supporters and have certainly influenced liberal thinking. Their willingness to alter capitalism basically, not just reform it, sets them apart from the main body of the liberal camp that shares the New Deal heritage.

Most liberals, in spite of their disagreements, will strongly back government programs to further full employment, extend Social Security, and otherwise enlarge the welfare state. Yet many liberals have a keen interest in the individual and in civil liberties issues and may often attack the government they otherwise favor for misuse of its powers. Liberal-minded civil libertarians have defended the rights of communists, socialists, even fascists and on occasion, a member of the Ku Klux Klan. Freedom of expression publicly, whether in print or in speech, is highly valued, as is the right to privacy and the avoidance of governmental intrusion. Another brand of individualism arose out of the student protest of the 1960s and was more interested in "liberal" styles of living pertaining to sex, drugs, and styles of dress and hair than with welfare state policies.

Given the range of issues available, liberals have much to differ about—and do. It is also readily apparent that one can be "liberal" on some issues but not on others. While some liberals thought McGovern a bit radical, many on the left saw Jackson as really rather conservative. Union leaders such as George Meany, president of the AFL-CIO, saw organized labor as the leading force for progressive legislation, but many others who took pride in their liberal credentials saw the unions as a conservative establishment. Blacks have long had an intense interest in civil rights issues, but during the 1960s other groups usually supportive of New Deal legislation voiced mounting concern with crime and violence and criticized manifestations of reverse discrimination that they believed tended to favor blacks over whites. Some liberals could support the Concorde or an American SST and the jobs it would mean; other liberals saw the SST as an ecological disaster and an evil not to be borne. And so it goes. No wonder there is confusion when "liberalism" is mentioned.

As we move across the spectrum from the left, we encounter the right, the amorphous conservative camp. In the heyday of industrial capitalism in the nineteenth century, liberals believed in laissez-faire principles. They wanted government to do little; they believed in private property, the free market, and the virtues of a free-wheeling competitive system. But the liberalism of a century ago has become the conservatism of an America living with a New Deal legacy. Those who would turn back to the laissez-faire capitalism of the past and the stern individualistic values associated with it are usually described as reactionaries. On the other hand, ordinary conservatives may continue to express longings for a return to simpler times but try to live with the welfare state. In 1964 Barry Goldwater expressed much of this conservative impulse. At the time he came under attack from some quarters as a dangerous extremist who would lead us into war and destroy Social Security. Much of this intense hostility later died down, and in time Goldwater came to be seen as a conservative who merited respect for his integrity and forthrightness. Prominent among conservative leaders of the 1970s were Gerald Ford and Ronald Reagan.

In general, conservatives tend to be skeptical of what government can do and prefer to allow "free enterprise" to solve problems such as unemployment. Government solutions, they argue, add to government costs, create deficits, and spawn a government bureaucracy that makes things worse, not better. Conservatives often invoke the values of individualism, private property, the free market, and competition. They also tend to stress patriotism and national honor and support a strong national defense system. And whereas liberals usually value a strong presidency, conservatives tend to value a strong Congress and a vigorous federal system. One of the ironies of the Watergate affair was the tension created over just these values, for both liberals and conservatives, with Republican Richard Nixon in the White House defending a strong presidency. As often happens, partisanship outweighed principle: liberals attacked Nixon and conservatives tended to defend him.

In the main, liberals are Democrats and conservatives are Republicans, but there are prominent exceptions and a large middle group who are hard to classify. Jacob Javits, long a Republican senator from New York, could be classified as a liberal in many areas. On the other hand, James O. Eastland, a Democratic senator who represented Mississippi for many years, could easily be described as a conservative. There are those who would like to see American political parties reorganized as clear-cut groups of liberals versus conservatives, but the nation's voters on the whole do not seem to care. A figure such as Richard Nixon is not as easy to classify as might appear at first blush. He seemed to think himself a conservative and cordially disliked many liberals, a distaste they returned in full. But Nixon broke the mold of the Cold War of the 1950s and 1960s with his approaches to Peking and to Moscow. And at home he proposed welfare reform that included a form of a guaranteed minimum income and introduced peace-time wage and price controls in 1971. These are not actions calculated to win acclaim from conservatives.

For that matter, where do we put Jimmy Carter as a candidate and then as president? At times he talked the liberals' language of national health care and other New Dealish programs, but he also committed himself to a balanced budget by 1980. He combined both liberal and conservative elements and they varied somewhat from issue to issue. In this Carter was like much in American public affairs, with its complex and rapidly changing political scene. We cannot seem to live without those ambiguous terms "liberal" and "conservative." But in using them we should exercise care and be ready, like Tom Braden, to modify them or even cast them aside for other terms when necessary.

Restatement of Some Basic Ideas

We have set out our meaning of public opinion as rooted in three major concepts: political coalitions, elites, and masses. By political coalitions we mean major political groupings, like the old New Deal alliance, which have come together and persisted as an influential body of opinion. By elites we mean those who are set apart from the bulk of ordinary mortals in positions of leadership and authority, whether in politics and government or in some sector of the nation's social and economic system.

We use the term "masses" to refer to the ordinary mortals who make up most of a society's population. The term is not an attractive one and we use it for want of something better. We do not use it to suggest that most people are a bit dim and cannot be trusted, nor to imply a lack of individuality. At its worst the term arouses images of people who suffer harshly from poverty and oppression and who may explode in spasms of resentment. But as we think of most Americans they are neither poor nor radical and they enjoy a good many democratic rights. What we mean by "the masses" is much like what the politician means when he refers to "the public." They are not the leaders, usually, but they are not dimwits either.

New Deal liberals felt that government, led by a strong executive, could do much to solve the nation's problems. They favored the working people, unions, and the minorities and were apt to be suspicious of big business and concentrated wealth. This kind of liberal also tended to be an internationalist and a civil libertarian.

Conservatives, on the other hand, have tended to favor capitalism and to be suspicious of heavy reliance on government intervention. They have long spoken glowingly of the free market, private enterprise, and individual initiative. Balanced budgets have much appeal. National honor and a strong defense establishment have long figured in the conservative creed.

As to the organization of these groups into political parties, the New Deal laid down the main lines of liberalism and conservatism and deeply colored the Democratic and Republican parties. Democrats have usually leaned to the left and Republicans to the right. But the basic New Deal struggle that focused chiefly on domestic economic issues was overtaken by events. War abroad and issues at home of race, crime, ecology, inflation, Watergate, energy—and other issues as well—required responses that went beyond the New Deal mold. We have already seen that liberalism took on many forms, and conservatism too. These variations on liberalism and conservatism serve as a reminder that political ideologies are not set in concrete—and sometimes never seem to "set" at all. The same is true for terms and definitions. We cannot avoid using them but must do so with caution and with a willingness to change them as our society changes.

With this caution in mind we may now begin our analysis of public opinion and our exploration of the many ways in which ordinary Americans act upon the system and are in turn influenced by it.

SUGGESTIONS FOR FURTHER READINGS

Richard J. Barnett. "No Room in the Lifeboats." *The New York Times Magazine,* April 16, 1978, pp. 32 ff. A discussion, from a liberal point of view, of the conservative implications of the Age of Scarcity and its "lifeboat ethics."

John P. Diggins. *The American Left in the Twentieth Century.* New York: Harcourt Brace Jovanovich, 1973.

———.*Up from Communism: Conservative Odysseys in American Intellectual History.* New York: Harper Torchbooks, 1978.

Kenneth M. Dolbeare and Patricia Dolbeare. *American Ideologies: The Competing Political Beliefs of the 1970s.* 3rd ed. Chicago: Rand McNally, 1976.

Henry Etzkowitz and Peter Schwab. *Is America Necessary? Conservative, Liberal and Socialist Perspectives of United States Political Institutions.* St. Paul, Minn.: West Publications, 1976.

M. Stanton Evans. *Clear and Present Dangers: A Conservative View of America's Government.* New York: Harcourt Brace Jovanovich, 1975.

Leonard Freedman. *Power and Politics in America.* 3rd ed. North Scituate, Mass.: Duxbury, 1978.

Robert A. Goldwin, ed. *Left, Right and Center: Essays on Liberalism and Conservatism in the United States.* Chicago: Rand McNally, 1967.

"Is America Turning Right?" *Newsweek,* Nov. 7, 1977, pp. 34–44. Discusses the neoconservative trends of the 1970s and identifies some of their leading exponents.

Irving Kristol. *Two Cheers for Capitalism.* New York: Basic Books, 1978. One of the leading neoconservative writers defends capitalism—up to a point.

C. B. Macpherson. *The Life and Times of Liberal Democracy.* New York: Oxford University Press, 1978.

Clinton Rossiter. *Conservatism in America.* New York: Random House Vintage Books, 1962. A bit dated but still useful and readable.

William Rusher. *The Making of the Majority Party.* New York: Sheed and Ward, 1975. A conservative argues his case.

2 · Perspectives on Those in Charge: Coalitions and Elites

When Franklin D. Roosevelt won the presidential election in 1932, he laid the basis for a coalition that was to dominate the national political scene for decades. Commentators will long dispute the exact duration of the FDR–New Deal coalition. Certainly by the 1970s it was badly frayed, and observers were disputing possible alternatives. Some claimed that an emergent Republican coalition with a conservative bent had displaced the old New Deal coalition. Others thought that the "real majority" was a centrist or moderate grouping, that the people did not want to forge ahead along New Deal lines but neither did they wish to turn back. Many voters were splitting their tickets instead of voting for a single party, and other observers saw the ticket splitters as dominant. Politicians responded by stressing personality and issue concerns more than their party ties. A pattern of fluid, shifting alliances developed that was hard to describe as either liberal or conservative.

In addition, it was possible to argue that those in charge were an elite who controlled opinion from on high. In this view public opinion does not matter much. Mostly, influence extends from the top down. A small group at the top really makes the difference, not the wishes of the great mass of people. Often this elite is seen as a manifestation of a military-industrial complex. The theory of the elite is important enough to deserve our attention when we examine conceptions of the dominant group, large or small, that is said to prevail in the America of the 1970s.

The New Deal Coalition

At the outset we need to examine the first of these alternatives, the old New Deal coalition, which encompassed and shaped so much of the liberal left. What were the components of this coalition and what has happened to them?

For our purposes the best analysis is one by the political scientist Robert Axelrod, who analyzed the basic voting coalitions for Democrats and Republicans over the years from 1952 through 1968.[1] Admittedly the New Deal coalition was past its prime, but this analysis still tells us much about the coalition and its basis, then and earlier. Six major groups were examined as possible contributors to the underpinning of the Democratic coalition: the poor, blacks, the unions, Catholics and Jews, the South, and central cities. Even though these groups overlap somewhat, we can get a rough estimate of their importance as national voting blocs.

During the period 1952 to 1968 the poor declined in number from about one-third to about 12 percent of the population. Rising living standards reduced the number in poverty, and in any case their contribution to the Democratic coalition was not great. First, voter turnout was low. Second, surprisingly enough, the vote was not heavily Democratic; it tended to divide in much the same way as the rest of the country. Axelrod concluded that the poor were *not* a part of the coalition.

Blacks were another matter. In the early 1950s their turnout was low. Barriers to black voting, especially in the South, held down their contribution. But over the years turnout greatly increased, and the vote for the Democratic candidate was heavy most of the time, particularly in the 1960s. By 1968 blacks were nearly 20 percent of the coalition vote.

One would expect the union vote to be of major importance to the coalition, but its contribution to the Democrats fell from about one-third in 1952 to 28 percent in 1968. This decline Axelrod attributes chiefly to a decrease in loyalty, the willingness to favor a Democrat over a Republican. Still, organized labor contributed a larger share to the Democratic vote than the more loyal blacks.

Catholics, the forth group, have traditionally been associated with the coalition. Throughout the period this group consistently made up more than a third of the coalition vote. With their good turnout and loyal Democratic vote, Catholics were the largest single bloc in the coalition. The much smaller Jewish vote (which Axelrod included with the Catholics) also supported the coalition.

A fifth group, the southerners, once famous as the "solid South" in the Democratic camp, were originally about one quarter of the Democratic vote. Their turnout improved during the time of the study, because of increased voting by both blacks and whites. Axelrod concluded that the South appeared to be moving away from the Democrats. A vote that was once solidly Democratic dropped steadily to become much like the average Democratic vote nationally. Nor did Republicans necessarily gain, since in 1968 George Wallace drew many of their ballots. The South, then, was no longer a faithful part of the coalition.

The sixth group, the central cities, did indeed tend to favor the Democrats throughout. But they had only slightly above average turnout and were in any event a declining population group. Their share of the coalition vote fell from about 20 percent in the beginning to about 15 percent by 1968.

The upshot of Axelrod's analysis is not reassuring to coalition supporters. One major bloc, the South, was moving away. Another group, the poor, was declining and did not really favor the Democrats. Of the remaining four components, only the blacks displayed strong Democratic loyalties. Catholics and Jews showed signs of decreasing loyalty, as union members did also. And the central city voters, who of course also overlapped the other groups, were a declining share of the population, even if still tending toward the Democratic party. Nor did the election returns of 1972 offer any comfort to coalition loyalists. George McGovern not only lost to Richard Nixon by a landslide, he ran so badly that Nixon carried 2,963 of 3,091 counties in the United States. Two major groups long associated with the Democrats, union members and Catholics, split their vote, with more of it going to the Republicans than to the Democrats.[2]

The Conservative Coalition

Academic analysts were not the only ones to notice signs of the weakening of the old New Deal coalition. In the late 1960s Kevin Phillips, a conservative Republican activist, published a widely reviewed book that proclaimed the emergence of a new Republican majority.[3] The election of Richard Nixon in 1968 and Phillips' connection with this election and the new Republican administration, albeit somewhat below the top policy-making levels, led many to see him as a party spokesman. Phillips was probably never as influential as many observers thought him to be,[4] but he did serve as an effective spokesman for hopeful conservatives.

Phillips thought that the 1968 election quite possibly marked a turning point in the evolution of the party system, at least at the presidential level. The dominant Democratic group was in decline and a more con-

servative alignment of forces was emerging. Part of the decline he ascribed to the pressures of the civil rights groups in advancing the cause of
blacks. Many white middle-class Americans, Phillips thought, resented
the violence and lawlessness they associated with black protest. And
there was also resentment over the demands for change that whites felt
forced them to bear unfair burdens and at times suggested favoritism toward blacks. Democratic leaders who appeared to cater to blacks, to the
neglect of whites and *their* burdens, fed this resentment, Phillips implied.

Phillips also projected a growing white middle-class spread across
much of the South and Southwest—the so-called Sunbelt—and up into
the Midwest "heartland." These were people who were beginning to enjoy a measure of affluence. They resented high taxes, government inter-
ference, and the proliferation of government bureaucracy in programs of
questionable value. These people had worked to advance themselves and
felt others should do so as well. As Phillips saw it, the big cities, especially in the East, represented the heart of the liberal coalition. But they
were aging and decaying cities with declining populations. On the other
hand, the emerging conservative group was a vigorous and growing population. The Republicans had the opportunity to build a new coalition
that could draw upon disaffected white southerners and similarly disaffected white northerners, especially Catholics, to create a new and dominant majority of the future.

Phillips' ideas caught the public eye. There was also much criticism,
and Phillips himself seemed to modify his basic thesis in later pronounce-
ments, but he did speak for what seemed to be a more conservative public mood. Voters were becoming disenchanted with government activism
and social programs in particular. There was growing concern with lawlessness, with taxes, and with growing governmental bureaucracy. Phillips supplied the rationale for a more conservative government administration, for a "southern strategy" of catering to the South, and for
attacks by administration spokesmen upon the "liberal media elite."

The Moderates as Dominant

But was it possible to accept the demise of the old New Deal coalition
and at the same time reject Phillips' thesis of a conservative Republican
coalition taking its place? Two knowledgeable political activists and
writers believed that it was. They did so in a book arguing that the "real
majority" was a centrist or moderate group. Liberalism was no longer
dominant but neither was conservatism. The authors, Richard Scammon

and Ben Wattenberg, challenged misconceptions on both left and right to argue for the essential moderation of Americans as the decade of the 1960s closed and the 1970s began.[5]

At the outset they stated several basic theses designed to set the record straight. They first insisted upon the reality of the social issue. To many Democrats on the left the social issue was a code term for racism. In voicing a concern with crime and violence, people were really voicing anti-black sentiments. Scammon and Wattenberg insisted, however, that there was a genuine issue of crime, social turmoil, and relaxed moral standards, and that Democrats must face it, not ignore it or treat it as sheer prejudice. The issue, they argued, was real and it was also new. It did not fit into the pattern of economic interests associated with the New Deal. Thus one could not meet the issue simply by trying to focus on economic problems and upon improvements in the well-being of the common man. The social issue had to be recognized and dealt with on its own terms.

A second basic thesis was aimed at Democrats who inclined to see their natural constituency as consisting of the young, the black, and the disadvantaged. The attention focused on the protests of blacks, students, and others who were unhappy with the system during the 1960s had created a misconception, Scammon and Wattenberg believed, as to the true character of the electorate. For the electorate or voting-age population, as distinct from the population of all ages, was pretty much in the middle. The median age of the population might indeed be in the late twenties, but the median age of voters alone was in the mid-forties. They were people of roughly middle age. They also had a middling education; they were *not* typically college educated. They fell in the middle range of incomes and held rather ordinary jobs. And the typical voter was apt to live in a middle-sized city, not in a large city or in the country. Scammon and Wattenberg summarized this "Middle Voter" as "forty-seven-year-old housewife from the outskirts of Dayton, Ohio, whose husband is a machinist. She very likely has a somewhat different view of life and politics from that of a twenty-four-year-old instructor of political science at Yale."[6] If Scammon and Wattenberg were right, then Democrats who pitched their appeals heavily to the young and the blacks and the college educated were overlooking the main part of their constituency.

Alongside this analysis of the typical voter type, Scammon and Wattenberg also argued a third basic thesis, about the nature of the election process. Elections, they insisted, were really won by those able to appeal most successfully to the voters in the middle. Appeals gauged chiefly to the ideologies of either left or right were not likely to win elections. In the end the successful candidate had to swing the largest part of the group in the middle, the group that could go either way and thereby determine the outcome. This process of course tended to narrow the differences between the contending parties and their candidates in their competition for the middle. Successful parties therefore tended not to differ sharply in their ideologies, according to Scammon and Wattenberg. Rather, they tended to sound much alike in their appeals and had to do so to remain in contention for that vote in the center.

Scammon and Wattenberg's fourth point reinforced the third. They noticed that each party contained ideologists who preferred ideological purity to compromise, and that the purists tended to split with those to whom they were closest politically. Such a split in turn tended to help the other side most of all. Thus leftist Democrats who rejected moderation and split with other Democrats tended to weaken the left altogether and thereby aid the Republicans. Conversely, conservative Republicans who split with Republican moderates tended in the end to aid the Democrats.

These openings theses argued a powerful case for moderation, a case directed mainly at the Democrats. Up to a point it was a hopeful statement, for they were challenging Phillips' statement of the case for conservatism. As Scammon and Wattenberg saw it, Democrats did need to address the social issue, plainly recognize the "middling" nature of the electorate, and make appeals to it that avoided extremes of left and right. But they challenged those like Phillips who saw the electorate as essentially conservative. Throughout *The Real Majority* they argued that the electorate had actually moved left during the previous decade or so. What had once been liberal, perhaps even radical, had more recently become largely accepted. The kind of conservatism represented by Barry Goldwater in 1964 was quite reduced in significance by the end of the decade, as much of President Johnson's Great Society legislation gained a large measure of acceptance. More specifically, Scammon and Wattenberg argued for the essential moderation of the public on basic economic and racial policies. They presented evidence that the public did *not* want to repeal the welfare state, even if they did not seek expansion. They also cited data to back their claim that the public was aware of the plight of blacks and supported programs directed at the improvement of their condition. At the same time the authors reminded readers of the importance of the social issue as a major part of the public's concerns. All in all, the public mood as portrayed by Scammon and Wattenberg could be summed up as one of moderation or caution but not conservatism. Certainly their analysis was not ignored, even by their political enemies. Thus Jeb Stuart Magruder, writing about the planning in Richard Nixon's administration for the election campaign of 1970, reported respectful references to the analysis by Scammon and Wattenberg.[7]

Ticket Splitters and the Decay of Coalitions

Besides the liberal, conservative, and moderate interpretations of the public mood as the 1970s opened, there was a fourth, offered by those who saw the primacy of the ticket splitters. This interpretation is seemingly not ideological. It looked at the voters without much regard to political content. Yet there are ideological implications, since a ticket-splitting electorate would appear to have no cohesion and no coherent direction toward either left or right.

The authors of *The Ticket-Splitters*, Walter DeVries and Lance Tarrance, insisted that the ticket splitters were *not* independents and challenged the usual analysis of the latter.[8] The independent portrayed in other studies was one who *said* he was "independent"; in other words, the definition depended upon self-identification. But DeVries and Tarrance presented evidence that this self-identification was inaccurate. According to their information, some independents voted a straight party ticket and some self-identified Republicans and Democrats in fact split their tickets. Thus it was necessary to inquire into the actual pattern of voting. As against self-identification they argued the need to examine the actual behavior of the electorate in casting ballots.

Second, DeVries and Tarrance saw the ticket splitter as a growing force in American politics. As one example they cited a Gallup survey of the 1968 national election in which 54 percent of the voters claimed to have split their tickets. In general this point is probably the least challengeable of their basic claims. The deterioration of the political parties as organizations and the decline of party identification as an influence in voting, especially in presidential elections, have been widely noted. And since ticket splitters are increasingly the decisive element in the successful candidate's campaign, their influence extends well beyond their numbers.

A third point DeVries and Tarrance made is that the ticket splitter is no dummy. They examined the demographic characteristics of ticket splitters and also the influences on their voting decisions. In general ticket splitters come through as relatively well educated and informed. In their words, the "ticket splitter is slightly younger, somewhat more educated, somewhat more white collar, and more suburban than the typical middle class voter. In addition, the ticket splitter tends to consume more media output about politics and is more active politically than the straight Democrat (but less than the straight Republican)."[9] The ticket splitter is not the nonexistent ideal rational voter of civics texts but is a good deal better than the ill-informed and wishy-washy independent portrayed in most earlier analyses.

As one would expect of the ticket splitter, influences on vote decisions are complex. In the past, party identification was the basic variable: Democratic voters voted for Democratic candidates and Republican voters voted for Republican candidates. For the ticket splitter DeVries and Tarrance projected a different pattern. In general ticket splitters made up their minds on the basis of candidate and issue concerns, followed by party identification and group affiliation. Images and impressions projected by the candidate were primary, although party ties and other group affiliations were not without influence.

Furthermore, the ticket splitter was not easily reached or swayed by media advertising. One of the most telling pieces of evidence that DeVries and Tarrance cite is a table drawn from a 1970 election in Michigan.[10] This table summarized the responses of ticket-splitting voters who were asked about the factors that influenced their voting decision. Television advertising rated relatively low, but among the twelve factors rated "very important," the items that topped the list were TV newscasts, documentaries, and newspaper stories and editorials. The authors point out that only one item of the twelve, "contacts with candidates," was controllable by the candidate. The ticket splitter did pay attention to the media but not those aspects of the media that the candidate could influence directly. To reach and sway the watchful, wary ticket splitter was not a simple matter.

DeVries and Tarrance remark:

> The way voters see and use media is becoming one of the most significant factors in the way people make up their minds about candidates. The way to win elections is not through traditional television advertising that "sells" the candidate, but through an overall communications strategy linking the candidate and the target groups which constitute the "crucial minority" that will decide the election.[11]

What this approach means in application may be glimpsed through the authors' account of the election campaign of Governor William Milliken of Michigan against considerable odds. An initial theme devised for the campaign stressed the governor's experience in office. After this theme had been used for a time, a survey of reactions to it was run among ticket splitters. The results were a surprise. Milliken was the incumbent but had been in office only eighteen months. The ticket splitters viewed Milliken as a beginner. The theme stressing his experience was therefore dropped and a more prosaic but effective one adopted.

The electorate envisaged by DeVries and Tarrance is a relatively selective one, and it is one that is not set in its ways. The role of the party and the appeal to party identification still matter but are obviously not primary. This view not only assumes some interest and selectivity on the part of the electorate; it also assumes a dynamic and somewhat volatile set of voters with concerns and interests that change with time and circumstances. The campaign itself then becomes a process of constantly gathering information about the electorate which in turn shapes the candidate's communication with selected portions of the electorate.

These four concepts of the governing majority all leave us with a puzzle. None of them seems really adequate to account for the drift of public opinion in the 1970s, yet each of them contains some element of the truth. The old New Deal coalition was certainly frayed but was not necessarily beyond repair. Phillips' concept of an emerging Republican majority did speak for a shift in opinion away from support for the social legislation of the 1960s: voters seemed to be more conscious of the costs, especially in their antipathy to rising taxes, and there was certainly increased skepticism about the benefits of many governmental activities, a skepticism deepened by the Watergate revelations of governmental misconduct. On the other hand, voters did not appear anxious to repeal existing welfare state programs or to turn their backs completely on the claims of minorities. In spite of the emergence of the "social issue" and other apparently conservative reactions, there was also evidence of voter concern with social problems and the need to do something about them. In addition, it was clear that increasing numbers of voters were ticket splitting with a vengeance. New issues arose and cut across the electorate in baffling ways that created complex and shifting coalitions rather than a settled mandate for either left or right. It was a politics of candidates, issues, and interest groups tending to replace a politics of strong political parties drawing upon large blocs of party faithful, whether Democratic or Republican.

But does not this analysis conveniently overlook the election of 1976, when Democrats regained the White House and held onto their one-sided majorities in both houses of Congress? Faithful Democrats longing for a resurgence of a renewed New Deal had reason to cheer. But closer inspection raises significant doubts. In a careful analysis of the components of this election, political scientist Gerald Pomper concluded, "The Carter coalition, demographically, is a unique alliance. It is not simply the renewal of the Democratic majorities first assembled by Franklin Roosevelt."[12] There was a continuation of past patterns, but the coalition Carter assembled also included "some previous opponents of the party." Blacks and labor did as they usually do in supporting the Democrat. Catholics supported Carter, but his support among Protestants was better than usual for a Democrat. Southerners supported him, but it was a biracial vote, not the white vote that prevailed in the days of the solid South. The city vote was for Carter but was not very important. As Pomper saw it, Carter "could achieve victory only by bringing in new votes from suburbs, small towns, and rural areas." After further analysis which reinforced his initial conclusion, Pomper again insisted, "It is erroneous to see the Carter victory as simply a recreation of the alliance forged in the elections of Franklin Roosevelt. It is both like and unlike that dominant majority."[13] These comments warn us that perhaps not much was really changed by the elections of 1976. Phillips thought he saw a Republican and conservative majority emerging in 1968 with Nixon's victory. Democrats who read 1976 returns as the emergence of a renewed New Deal could be similarly mistaken. Much remained ambiguous and uncertain, and it was hard to be sure what coalition, if any, was in charge.

An Elite Perspective

The perspectives so far examined at least agree in assuming that public opinion matters a good deal in determining what happens politically. The elitist perspective challenges that assumption quite fundamentally, although there is often much ambiguity as to the role of the people or "the masses" in relation to the elite. Most elite theorists do not attempt a careful analysis of elites and masses in relation to the actual processes and institutions of American government. Because *The Irony of Democracy*, by Thomas R. Dye and L. Harmon Zeigler, does so, we shall focus upon it.[14] For now we shall simply sketch their concept of single elite theory. In Chapter 10, after we have reviewed mass opinion extensively, we shall elaborate more fully upon elite theory and briefly note some of its variety.

Dye and Zeigler attack the idea that the American political system is basically democratic, even if imperfect. They argue, instead, for a single elite, a small group of people who are different from the great mass of people. Members of this group tend to be much better off educationally, economically, and socially than the masses. They share a consensus on values that enable them to keep their differences within bounds and to rule as a basically unified whole. They are not closed; talented newcomers may win admission, although only gradually, as they accommodate themselves to the elite consensus. The elite need not be reactionary or necessarily hold any specific philosophy. In the past they were conservative. When FDR and the New Deal rose to power, elite philosophy shifted to a policy of noblesse oblige that entailed a willingness to look out for the well-being of the masses. Hence Dye and Zeigler see the elite from the 1930s on as a liberal establishment. Above all, whatever elite values may be, elitism is a structure of power, which means that influence flows from the top down and little mass influence filters up.

Throughout their exposition Dye and Zeigler maintain that what the elite does is little constrained by the masses. The elite rules, not the mass of people. Nor do these authors see any prospect for change. In their eyes, the masses are incapable of self-government and always will be. Besides, the looming fears of an age of scarcity with its attendant intensified competition for resources will probably enhance the need for elite governance. Unlike many elitists who write to condemn, Dye and Zeigler plainly state their preference for elite rule. Indeed, among elite theorists, Dye and Zeigler are noteworthy for their harsh assessment of the qualities of the masses. They see the masses as not only unfit for self-government but a threat to democratic values. Elite rule is necessary to protect the dignity of the individual and related democratic values. It is "the irony of democracy" that democracy exists for the masses but it is the elite which upholds democratic values. Dye and Zeigler do not see the elite as flawless. Indeed, they cite Watergate as a typical case of elite repression. But they see the masses as even more dangerous. One passage that summarizes their evaluation of the masses could hardly be more severely negative: "authoritarian, intolerant, anti-intellectual, nativistic, alienated, hateful, and violent."[15] This awesome list of undesirable qualities stamps the authors as anything but friends of the common man. For Dye and Zeigler the elite is both necessary *and* desirable.

The elite perspective so ably spelled out by Dye and Zeigler is provocative if it is nothing else. Later on we shall undertake a critical assessment of it and attempt to prove that public opinion does matter. For now we may look upon it as a major alternative model of public opinion.

The Alternatives Summarized

We have now examined five major "perspectives on those in charge" and Figure 2–1 presents them in outline form.

The old New Deal coalition long dominated the political scene. Its friends could even argue that it came to life again in 1976. The original coalition was thought to draw potentially from six somewhat overlapping groups: the poor, blacks, the unions, Catholics and Jews, the white South, and the central cities. But according to Axelrod's analysis, by the late 1960s neither the poor nor the South were firm elements of the coalition. The main components, in order of their strength, were the Catholics, unions, blacks, and the central cities. By 1976 other changes were evident. Blacks and labor supported Carter, but the Carter coalition differed in its appeal to Protestants, to the suburbs, to rural areas and to a biracial South.

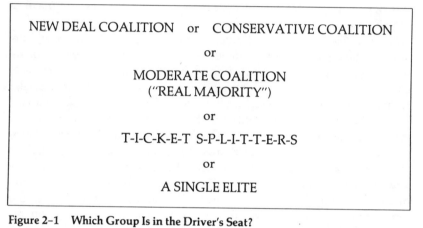

Figure 2-1 **Which Group Is in the Driver's Seat?**

In the light of Nixon's victory in 1968, Kevin Phillips argued the case for a splintered Democratic coalition and an emergent conservative majority. A growing white middle class drawn from the Sunbelt, the heartland, and urban ethnic groups resented the racial turmoil of the 1960s and the excesses of the welfare state. They were people who enjoyed a rising income and disliked seeing it taxed away to support a growing bureaucracy. A liberal big city elite catering to black pressures for social change could be seen as part of a declining liberal establishment.

Scammon and Wattenberg countered Phillips by arguing the case for a moderate majority. They held that Democrats had to confront the social issue that came to light in the turmoil of the 1960s. It was a new issue that arose outside of typical New Deal concerns, but Democrats could not afford to slight it. They also argued that much of the electorate was in the middle demographically in age, education, income, and outlook; it was not young, black, or disadvantaged. Candidates therefore had to avoid extremes and appeal to the middle group, and how that group divided would determine the outcome of elections. As for candidate appeals to left and right, Scammon and Wattenberg marshaled much evidence that people were not conservative, even if they did not want to rush ahead with expansion of the welfare state.

Another view, the rise of the ticket splitters, was developed persuasively by DeVries and Tarrance. They saw the electorate as moving away from the parties. The ticket splitters were a cut above the old-fashioned but misnamed independents, who were often not truly independent but were easily swayed. Ticket splitters were not dummies and tended to rely on sources of information in the media that candidates could not readily control. In making up their minds they looked more to candidates and issues than to parties, and their concerns could change during the election, so that candidates needed a continuous flow of information in order to address these shifting concerns. The electorate was complex and fluid, not firmly settled in a mold cast to right, left, or center.

Elite theory, the idea that a relatively small and homogeneous group dominated the system with little constraint from the masses, is the last alternative. As Dye and Zeigler outlined it, the elite was an unrepresentative group drawn from the upper strata of society. It was a limited group but one which admitted talented newcomers who accepted elite values. The elite shared a basic consensus on values. Disagreement was apt to be about means, not about ends. Among their values elites esteemed the dignity and worth of the individual, values the masses lacked. Given this structure of power, elites determined policy while the masses, ill-informed and unconcerned, amused themselves.

These "perspectives on those in charge" all pertain to those who attempt to mold public opinion, whether as spokesmen for competing coalition concepts or as members of an elite. But one of our major themes is that the mass of people and their opinions also matter, and quite importantly. To illustrate this we shall begin with a look at the nation's past and its impact on the present, since it created a political culture which has given the United States an impressive record of political stability and continuity.

NOTES

1. Robert Axelrod, "Where the Votes Come From: An Analysis of Electoral Coalitions, 1952–1968," *American Political Science Review*, LXVI (March 1972), 11–20.
2. "Vote by Groups in Presidential Elections Since 1952," *Gallup Opinion Index*, December 1972, p. 10.
3. Kevin Phillips, *The Emerging Republican Majority* (New Rochelle, N.Y.: Arlington House, 1969). Phillips' views have not remained static. A more recent version of them is given in his *Mediacracy: American Parties and Politics in the Communications Age* (New York: Doubleday, 1975).
4. Phillips later wrote, "And whereas back in 1968 Nixon's communications chief Herb Klein had distributed excerpts from "The Emerging Republican Majority," by autumn, 1969, the ostrichlike White House line was to deny having read it, as the President himself did at an October press conference." See Phillips' "How Nixon Will Win," *New York Times Magazine*, August 6, 1972, p. 36.

5. Richard Scammon and Ben Wattenberg, *The Real Majority: An Extraordinary Examination of the American Electorate* (New York: Coward-McCann, 1970).
6. Ibid., p. 70.
7. Jeb Stuart Magruder, *An American Life: One Man's Road to Watergate*, (New York: Simon and Schuster Pocket Books, 1975), pp. 135, 145.
8. Walter DeVries and Lance Tarrance, *The Ticket Splitters: A New Force in American Politics* (Grand Rapids, Mich.: William B. Eerdmans Publishers, 1972).
9. Ibid., p. 61.
10. Ibid., p. 77.
11. Ibid., p. 92.
12. Gerald Pomper with Ross V. Baker, Charles E. Jacob, Wilson Carey McWilliams, and Henry A. Plotkin, *The Election of 1976* (New York: David McKay, 1977), p. 64. The selection cited is written by Pomper.
13. Ibid., pp. 80-81.
14. Thomas R. Dye and L. Harmon Zeigler, *The Irony of Democracy: An Uncommon Introduction to American Politics*, 4th ed. (North Scituate, Mass.: Duxbury, 1978). In the second edition each author added a postscript containing further reflections on elites and democracy. Dye was forthrightly elitist, whereas Zeigler speculated that far-reaching reform might in time enlighten the masses and enhance the prospects for some self-government. Brief mention of this difference of opinion was also made in the preface to the third edition.
15. Ibid., p. 374.

SUGGESTIONS FOR FURTHER READINGS

Peter Bachrach. *The Theory of Democratic Elitism: A Critique*. Boston: Little, Brown, 1967. An important attempt to revise and counter elite theory.

Robert A. Dahl. *Who Governs? Democracy and Power in an American City*. New Haven, Conn.: Yale University Press, 1961. Dahl's book is often cited as the classic expression of the pluralist position.

John Kenneth Galbraith. *Who Needs the Democrats and What It Takes to Be Needed*. New York: New American Library Signet Broadside, 1970. A leading social critic argues that the Democrats should embrace socialism.

G. David Garson. *Power and Politics in the United States: A Political Economy Approach*. Lexington, Mass.: D.C. Heath, 1977. Reviews the clash between the elitists and the pluralists and attempts to move beyond it.

Barry Goldwater. *The Conscience of a Conservative*. 4th ed. New York: Manor, 1974. A leading conservative spokesman of the old school expresses his principles.

Floyd Hunter. *Community Power Structure: A Study of Decision Makers*. New York: Doubleday Anchor Books, 1953. Hunter's book led the way in power structure studies and is often cited as best representing the theory of a single elite.

Faustine Childress Jones. *The Changing Mood of America: Eroding Commitment?* Washington, D.C.: Howard University Press, 1977. A black assesses the national mood and finds a declining commitment to racial justice.

Everett Carll Ladd, Jr., with Charles D. Hadley. *Transformations of the American Party System: Political Coalitions from the New Deal to the 1970s*. 2nd ed. New York: W.W. Norton, 1978. Contains a good analysis of the changing New Deal coalition and the emergence of ticket-splitting voters.

Charles E. Lindblom, *Politics and Markets: The World's Political-Economic Systems*. New York: Basic Books, 1977. An economist not strongly identified with either left or right expresses doubts about the power of the business system in a democracy.

Seymour Martin Lipset, ed. *Emerging Coalitions in American Politics*. San Francisco, Calif.: Institute for Contemporary Studies, 1978. Contributions from an impressive array of observers, some academic and some active in public life, who present their perceptions of the potential for coalitions.

C. Wright Mills. *The Power Elite*. New York: Oxford University Press, 1956. One of the most famous and controversial statements of elite theory applied to the national political scene.

Richard M. Nixon. *RN: Presidential Memoirs*. New York: Grosset and Dunlap, 1978.

Geraint Parry. *Political Elites*. New York: Praeger, 1970. A readable account of elite theorists and their theories, past and present.

Kevin Phillips. *Mediacracy: American Parties and Politics in the Communications Age*. New York: Doubleday, 1975. The author of *The Emerging Republican Majority* revises and updates his ideas.

Kenneth Prewitt and Alan Stone. *The Ruling Elites: Elite Theory, Power and American Democracy*. New York: Harper & Row, 1973. A relatively brief and readable survey of elite theory in the American setting.

James L. Sundquist. *Dynamics of the Party System: Alignment and Realignment of Political Parties in the United States*. Washington, D.C.: Brookings Institution, 1973. Argues for the continuation of the New Deal party system in spite of the conflicts that emerged in the 1960s.

Michael Weinstein. *Philosophy, Theory, and Method in Contemporary Political Thought*. Glenview, Ill.: Scott, Foresman, 1971. An analysis of twentieth-century political theory and its relationship to political inquiry.

Part Two
MASS OPINION

3 · American Political Culture: Consensus and Conflict

The celebration of the bicentennial of the United States in 1976 was an eloquent testimonial to our country's longevity. Its political system has worn well, as the living reality of the United States Constitution, drafted in 1787, demonstrates. Such a record in itself suggests a people well steeped in the system's basic values. But although we may justly celebrate this heritage and its manifestations in the present, we should not overlook the darker side, our remarkable record of turmoil and violence. This lawlessness and violence is too much in evidence to be denied.

What we have to account for, then, is an unusual combination of stability and turmoil. In explanation we shall argue that Americans do accept the system's basic values but these take the form of broad generalities. Applying these generalities to specific situations is another matter. Principles are fine but applying them may lead to much contention. There may be strong disagreement over the application of general principles to particular cases. For example, everyone can agree that individual liberty is the ideal, but much conflict may arise when Communists, or neo-Nazis, or members of the Ku Klux Klan demonstrate publicly. Thus the system and its values survive even as Americans argue, sometimes violently, over the application of those values. Observers may find this combination disturbing, but the natives, the great mass of Americans and their leaders, have made it work for a long time.

The Historical Record of Stability

The Constitution has been amended and reinterpreted many times since 1787; but it is still a commonplace of political discourse, both among elites and among the people at large, to refer to the Founding Fathers and the "meaning" of the Constitution. For a country that has often displayed pride in its youth, the influence of the aging United States constitutional system is amazing. A basic framework of institutions and processes that is nearly two centuries old has remained extraordinarily "alive and well" as the nation moves into the final quarter of the twentieth century.

And in spite of the confusion that often characterizes American politics day by day, there is much that is assured and taken for granted. One illustration dramatizes this point. The United States began holding elections under the constitution in 1788. Since that time national elections have been held every two years as prescribed by the Constitution, in war and peace, in depressions and in prosperity. It would be difficult to find another government for which such a claim could be made. The resolution of the crises we term collectively "Watergate" is another dramatic example, for Richard Nixon left office—an office that is certainly one of the most powerful in the world—without upsetting the constitutional process. By way of contrast we might take a look at the behavior of the leadership of another democracy, India. That nation's duly elected executive faced a domestic crisis in 1975, the year after Nixon's forced resignation. Prime Minister Indira Gandhi declared an emergency, suspended civil liberties, and suppressed the opposition. Nixon may have *wanted* to jail some reporters, especially those on the *Washington Post*. But the mind boggles at the thought of an American president actually doing what Gandhi was able to do for a time in India. American elites and the public at large resolved the Watergate crises in the main through established constitutional procedures.

Clearly the influence of the nation's constitutional framework of institutions and processes is extraordinary. Critics may decry the exceptions and point to ominous signs of decay, but one wonders where they could find a similarly large and complex nation whose constitutional stability in sustaining an open, democratic process is any better.

Consensus on the Generalities

Given this record of political stability over a long period of time, an observer could reasonably conclude that *some* consensus on basic values has to be present. One major effort to probe such values is a study by the political scientist Herbert McClosky.[1] McClosky used two samples—a sample of adults taken in 1958 and a sample of the political elite drawn from delegates to the major party political conventions of 1956. The latter would tend to underrepresent certain segments of the elite as portrayed by many theorists, but given the serious problems of elite selection and of gaining access for interviews, McClosky's methodology is perhaps as good as any. He also dealt forthrightly with the problem of defining consensus, which is supposed to mean a level of agreement well beyond mere majority support. Fifty percent plus one is obviously not sufficient, but it is not clear just what further margin is essential. McClosky chose 75 percent because that is the margin required for special constitutional purposes; for instance, ratification of an amendment requires the approval of three-fourths of the states. Certainly this is an exacting standard even though it falls short of complete agreement.

McClosky's study encompassed several different areas of possible consensus. One was what he called "rules of the game." Presumably everyone must accept certain rules within which they ageee to operate in pursuit of their divergent goals. Certainly it is plausible to believe that there must be certain basic rules or guidelines which constrain the competition for political power and keep the system from flying apart. However, a set of questions designed to explore the acceptance of such guidelines failed to find much consensus. And some of the responses were shocking. A large minority expressed a willingness to accept astonishingly harsh methods in pursuit of certain kinds of objectives. For instance, more than 40 percent agreed with the statement that "We might as well make up our minds that in order to make the world better a lot of innocent people will have to suffer." Nearly a third agreed that "Almost any unfairness or brutality may have to be justified when some great purpose is being carried out." Because of these and other responses, McClosky concluded that "a large proportion of the electorate has failed to grasp certain of the underlying ideas and principles on which the American political system rests."

McClosky next examined a set of responses designed to explore support for "general statements of free speech and opinion." These, McClosky explained, he modeled on that classic defense of individuality, John Stuart Mill's essay *On Liberty*. Included were statements such as "No matter what a person's political beliefs are, he is entitled to the same legal rights and protections as anyone else." Another was "I believe in free speech for all, no matter what their views might be." Almost all these statements won such high levels of agreement that McClosky was able to conclude "that for these values, at least, a far-reaching consensus has been achieved."

This happy outcome was not reinforced by other findings, however. When respondents were asked about "specific applications of free speech and procedural rights," over 55 percent agreed that "Freedom does not give anyone the right to teach foreign ideas in our schools." Similarly, 50 percent agreed that "A book that contains wrong political views cannot be a good book and does not deserve to be published." Of these responses McClosky remarked that "the principles of freedom and democracy are less widely and enthusiastically favored when they are confronted in their specific, or applied, forms."

Cynicism was another subject McClosky investigated. The results were revealing. It would appear that cynical attitudes about politics were present long before Watergate, whatever further impact that scandal may have had. In response to the statement "Most politicians are looking out for themselves above all else," more than half agreed. Sixty-five percent agreed that "Many politicians are bought off by some private interest." More than half the respondents agreed that "No matter what the people think, a few people will always run things anyway," and they also agreed that "Most politicians don't seem to me to really mean what they say." These and similar kinds of responses predominated.

But another, contrasting theme emerged when nearly 60 percent agreed that "Most politicians can be trusted to do what they think is best for the country." And almost 90 percent could agree that "I usually have confidence that the government will do what is right." It would appear that about half of the population takes a darkly cynical view of the political process and personnel. Yet faith in the system somehow prevails overwhelmingly, not just marginally. In McClosky's words, "They may be cynical about the operation of the political system, but they do not question its legitimacy." It is plausible to believe that such attitudes have long been a pervasive feature of the American political tradition. After all, the separation of powers and the checks and balances among the executive, legislative, and judicial branches of government foster a system in which ambition is used to counteract ambition and no one is to be trusted with unchecked power. We may view the popular attitudes McClosky found as a common-sense version of the theory of checks and balances operating within a framework of values that accords legitimacy to the system. Indeed, one may argue that the two sets of attitudes go together and reinforce each other, that an ultimate faith in the system is possible just because we realistically recognize that politicians are suspect and checks upon their misbehavior are present. Faith is possible because its limits are recognized.

Another aspect of McClosky's study was the subject of political efficacy, the feeling that what one does can make a difference politically. Like most studies of mass political participation, McClosky's showed that the vast majority did not consider themselves to be politically effective. Not surprisingly, then, 60 percent of the respondents agreed that "The people who really 'run' the country do not even get known to the voters." Another statement, "Nothing I ever do seems to have any effect upon what happens in politics," won the endorsement of just over 60 percent. And just over half agreed that "It seems to me that whoever you vote for, things go on pretty much the same." As McClosky put it in analyzing the responses about both cynicism and political efficacy, "Many feel themselves hopelessly ineffectual politically." Still, as he also pointed out, in spite of the feelings of cynicism and lack of efficacy, people did not seem to lack faith in the system.

In the end McClosky was able to find consensus only on the broad generalities of individual freedom. In other matters there was a notable lack of consensus accompanied by much cynicism and lack of efficacy. And the fact that a sizable minority was willing to accept harsh methods as necessary to achieve certain kinds of goals offers powerful evidence of the strain of lawlessness and violence in American culture.

Consensus on a Lockean Liberal Tradition

McClosky's study is fascinating as a look at the public mind but provides limited support for the notion of a national consensus. Fortunately there is a further study which does provide strong evidence for consensus. This study, by Donald J. Devine, is book length and is not easily summarized in a manner that does justice to it. At the outset Devine recognized that the United States political regime is characterized by outstanding stability.[2] He argued, and we believe quite rightly so, that this historical fact in itself requires explanation. His analysis is therefore in part an attempt to account for this stability.

Unlike McClosky, Devine did not construct a survey to sample the public, but his approach in analyzing the political culture of the United States draws upon a large body of survey data. First he examined the United States political tradition to determine what could be considered the core values of the political culture. This examination led him to peruse a wealth of historical literature. Two main sources were of special importance, John Locke's *Second Treatise* and the *Federalist Papers*, written by Alexander Hamilton, James Madison, and John Jay to explain and urge adoption of the Constitution. These, supplemented by other sources, both past and present, provided Devine with a set of fundamental values. He then examined a large body of survey data from the mid-1930s through 1968 to find evidence for and against public support of the key values. In the process he modified McClosky's definition of consensus as a three-fourths margin of support. Instead, Devine specified majority support for the values plus a difference of at least twenty percentage points between majority and minority opinions.[3] This standard is in itself less rigorous than McClosky's, but Devine explored the application of the core values quite thoroughly. Using a time span of about a generation, he examined literally hundreds of surveys and probed the application of these values via many subgroups of the population. Furthermore, he examined the persistence of the core values under conditions of stress, finding that under such conditions the values were modified but not rejected. And when modification occurred, as in wartime or during the Cold War, the values continued to be a shaping influence.[4]

Although it is difficult to convey fully the cumulative impact of Devine's study, a passage from it suggests its scope and detail:

> *For the major values,* 307 tests have been performed to find the extent to which Lockean values were supported by thirty-seven major political cleavages. Only 3.5 percent of these tests did not show majority support for the traditional values. The data may also be viewed chronologically. If the values are divided into four time groups—1940–1948, 1958, 1960, and 1967–1968—support does not differ significantly for the four periods. That is, there does not seem to be any trend over time, at least with these indicators, in support for the tradition. Even if we look at the single value indicator which has the least widespread support . . . the data show that it is supported by 80 percent of the groups. Since, overall, 96 percent of the tests showed that the values were supported, it must be concluded that the liberal tradition has the widespread support necessary for a consensual political culture. The data which have been presented suggest that the liberal tradition is strongly supported by the politically relevant groups.[5]

To this we might add Devine's observation as he concluded his study: "For a considerable period of time the regime tested [the United States political system] has survived substantial stress. Over two centuries of conflict have not very substantially changed either its values or its regime structure." Devine's study offers convincing evidence that the persistence of a Lockean liberal tradition of values as the core of the political culture best accounts for the remarkable stability of the United States.

The Violent Past

But accounting for the system's stability still leaves us with the problem of accounting for the turmoil which is so often at odds with the stability. During the 1960s there were riots in the cities and disruptions on the campuses. There were also the tragic assassinations of the two Kennedys and of Martin Luther King. In the decade that followed the nation found itself caught up in the Watergate scandal, with revelations of another brand of lawlessness. In the words of two scholars who carefully examined America's violent ways, "Paradoxically, we have been a turbulent people but a relatively stable republic."[6]

The explanation of this paradox will tell us a good deal about the nation's values, and we believe that the explanation runs something like this: A core of shared values persists and accounts for the system's amazing stability. But these values are interpreted and applied with much elasticity and variety. The system's elasticity probably contributes to its stability, and its elasticity extends even to lawlessness and violence.

The evidence for United States violence is partly historical and partly contemporary. For the historical record we could hardly do better than to cite *American Violence*, by the respected American historian Richard Hofstadter and his collaborator, Michael Wallace.[7] Hofstadter and Wallace surveyed the long national record of violence and arranged the results under subheadings. In his preface, Hofstadter warns readers not to take these attempts at classification "too literally," but the categories do illuminate the scope and variety of the subject. Opening sections include "Political Violence" and "Economic Violence." Then comes "Racial Violence," which includes slave revolts, ghetto riots, and violence visited upon helpless victims. Other headings are "Religious and Ethnic Violence" and "Anti-Radical and Police Violence." The entries in "Personal Violence" range from the Hamilton-Burr duel to the feuding between the Hatfields and McCoys. "Assassinations, Terrorism, Political Murders" is followed by "Violence in the Name of Law, Order, and Morality," which deals with various vigilante groups. The Revolutionary War and the Civil War do not receive special attention, but we should not forget that the United States was born in violence and its union was sealed by perhaps the bloodiest war of the nineteenth century. Nor are we allowed to forget the violence of the frontier.

One of Hofstadter's comments on labor violence adds to the reader's feeling for the prevalence of violence in general:

> The rate of industrial violence in America is striking in light of the fact that no major American labor organization has ever advocated violence as a policy, that extremely militant class philosophies have not prevailed here, and that the percentage of the American work force organized in unions has always been (and is even now) lower than in most advanced industrial countries. With a minimum of ideologically motivated class conflict, the United States has somehow had a maximum of industrial violence.[8]

This peculiar situation reinforces the view that Americans tend to be a distinctively violent people, whatever form their disputes may take.

From this record Hofstadter concluded that a number of characteristics stood out. First, there was the pervasiveness of violence, its "extraordinary frequency, its sheer commonplaceness in our history, its persistence . . ." Second, it was usually limited in scale, although the Civil War was a major exception. Still, most American violence, for all its commonplaceness, did not involve huge numbers of people at the same time. Third, American violence tended to "lack cohesion," to be "various" and "diffuse"; there was no center ideologically or geographically. This trait is important. It means that American violence cannot be explained as rooted in a single basic division, such as class conflict, cutting through the entire population. Two other characteristics of this record are somewhat related. One is that Hofstadter thought most of the violence to be conservative; that is, the violence usually consisted in measures taken by top dogs or middle dogs against the underdogs. Violent measures taken by employers against their workers are an example. A related characteristic of American violence also reflected a conservative bias; for, according to Hofstadter, "very little of it has been insurrectionary."[9] Most violence consisted in actions taken by one group against others, rather than by citizens against the state. In sum, Hofstadter found violence to be commonplace, limited in scale, diffuse, and conservative in that it was usually not insurrectionary and was used by those on top against those on the bottom. These characteristics enable us to see why the United States could have both a stable political system and a "culture of violence." Certainly our system has tolerated lawlessness and violence throughout its history.

Contemporary Violence

In addition to probing the past, writers have sought to devise objective, quantitative measures of violence in its various forms that could be used in comparing different nations. Thus in 1969 the authors of the Introduction to the Final Report of the National Commission on the Causes and Prevention of Violence stated:

> Violence in the United States has risen to alarmingly high levels. Whether one considers assassination, group violence, or individual acts of violence, the decade of the 1960s was considerably more violent than the several decades preceding it and ranks among the most violent in our history. The United States is the clear leader among modern, stable democratic nations in its rates of homicide, assault, rape, and robbery, and it is at least among the highest in incidence of group violence and assassination.[10]

Hofstadter, the somewhat skeptical historian, was not inclined to accept these quantitative analyses without question but still concluded:

> Nonetheless, the figures compiled by the National Commission's experts constitute the only check we have thus far against arbitrary impressions, and they confirm our sense that the United States is far from being the most peaceful among the Western or other industrial nations with which comparison seems most appropriate. These experts find in the United States of recent years a magnitude of civil strife that compares very unfavorably with most other nations of a high level of economic development, and somewhat unfavorably even with some nations of a medium level of economic development.[11]

In addition to the historical record and recent quantitative analyses we have evidence from the late 1960s of a survey of American males, ages sixteen to sixty-four, and their attitudes toward violence. The survey was designed to get at the willingness of these men to justify violent actions, and the questions explored contrasting perspectives. One perspective centered on violence for social control, the other on violence for social change. The first dealt with actions by the authorities, such as police, in putting down a disturbance; the second with actions aimed at bringing about change in the status quo. As psychologist Monica Blumenthal and her coauthors described their findings:

> There was widespread consensus among American men that disturbances such as those caused by hoodlums, student demonstrations, and inner-city upheavals should be handled by minimal amounts of police force whenever possible. From 80 to 87 percent of Americans agreed that police ought to make arrests in such disturbances without using clubs or guns "almost always" or "sometimes." Seventy-six to eighty percent thought that such arrests should be made using clubs but not guns "almost always" or "sometimes." There was considerably less agreement about the appropriateness of the use of guns in such disturbances. From 48 to 64 percent of American men, depending on the specific situation, felt that the police should shoot (but not to kill) "sometimes" or "almost always" in controlling such situations, while from 19 percent to 32 percent felt that the police should shoot to kill.[12]

In other words nearly half of the respondents, at a minimum, felt that in certain circumstances the police should use their guns in controlling disturbances. A smaller percentage felt that the police should shoot to kill. These people were voicing support of violence when utilized for social control. The other group, those willing to advocate violence for social change, was smaller but still significant. About 20 percent believed that "Protest involving some property damage or personal injury is necessary to bring about change at a sufficiently rapid rate." Within this group about 10 percent believed that protest involving "extensive property damage and some deaths is necessary" to achieve the social changes desired.

If we add these two groups, we have a large percentage, almost 70 percent, who are willing to support some violence for either social control or social change. In the end the authors of this study concluded that "violence is widely regarded as instrumental by American men,"[13] that American men widely accept violence as a way of getting results. The authors did *not* find that attempts to explain violence as arising from emotions or passions accounted for much: "It seems unlikely to us that major variations in attitudes toward violence will be explained by further measures of hostility or anger."[14] American men were willing to resort to violence because it could get results, not because they were seething with emotions they could not control.

To this evidence we can add an even more recent example, the Watergate scandal. The Watergate misdeeds were quite unlike those associated with the turmoil of the 1960s. They were the misdeeds, not of the powerless who use direct action to call attention to injustices, but of the powerful who have access to the authority of government set up to insure order and national security. We may therefore quite appropriately describe this series of crimes as a form of violence for social control. And they bear comparison with lawless, violent actions by elites at other times, as when in the 1950s the late Senator Joe McCarthy used his senatorial powers ruthlessly in pursuing Communists and those he thought subversive. In thus classifying Watergate we have the authority of Archibald Cox, the distinguished lawyer who was for a time directly caught up in the unraveling of Watergate as the Special Prosecutor under the Attorney General. Cox has since written of Watergate and its implications by explicitly drawing parallels between it and the events of the 1960s. As Cox viewed it, Egil Krogh, who was directly implicated in the Watergate misdeeds of the Nixon administration, warranted comparison with Dr. Daniel Ellsberg, who bears much of the responsibility for revealing the Pentagon Papers. Overall, according to Cox, the lawlessness of Richard Nixon's administration bears comparison with the protests on college campuses during the 1960s. This perspective is not, to put it mildly, the typical one. But Cox insists that the basic issue is one of constraints on the means used by those who seek to accomplish their goals:

> It is the forgetting of constraints upon methods of working our wills that counts because, despite short-run frustrations, such constraints furnish . . . the best hope of combining liberty, change, and progress. . . . Those who assert freedom to override the constraints in attacking the government cannot seri-

ously suppose that government will observe the constraints if frightened; nor that they themselves will suddenly observe the constraints if, as they hope, they come to power.[15]

On this basis, then, Watergate belongs with other forms of lawlessness and violence in America's checkered record.

The United States is not altogether unique. Indeed, violence seems to be on the increase everywhere. But the evidence from a variety of sources clearly indicates that in its degree of violence and lawlessness, past and present, the United States does stand out in comparison with other developed Western nations.

Core Values and Perspectives on Violence and Legitimacy

Part of the explanation for our peculiar combination of stability and turmoil emerges in another portion of the study of attitudes toward violence in American males, an analysis of the "meanings of violence." Some variations in these perceptions may be seen in Table 3-1. For example, most of those responding saw "looting" as violence clearly enough, but less than one-fifth saw "police stopping to frisk people" as a form of violence.

Table 3-1   Percentage of Respondents Defining Certain Acts as Violence (all respondents; N = 1,374)

	Yes	Both	No	Total
Do you think of looting as violence?	85%	3%	12%	100%
Do you think of burglary as violence?	65	5	30	100
Do you think of draft card burning as violence?	58	4	38	100
Do you think of police beating students as violence?	56	14	30	100
Do you think of not letting people have their civil rights as violence?	49	8	43	100
Do you think of student protest as violence?	38	15	47	100
Do you think of police shooting looters as violence?	35	8	57	100
Do you think of sit-ins as violence?	22	9	69	100
Do you think of police stopping to frisk people as violence?	16	10	74	100

Source: Monica D. Blumenthal, Robert L. Kahn, Frank M. Andrews and Kendra B. Head, *Justifying Violence: Attitudes of American Men* (Ann Arbor: Institute for Social Research, University of Michigan, 1972), p. 73.

Blumenthal and her collaborators carried this analysis a step further by breaking down their respondents into five distinct groups within the total sample representing males sixteen to sixty-four years old. These were: college students; those with a college education or higher; white union members; whites who believed there was reverse discrimination, that is, discrimination that favored blacks over whites; and blacks.

When these groups were asked about the meanings of violence, the differences from group to group were striking.[16] When respondents in this survey were presented with the statement "Police beating students is violence," 79 percent of the college students agreed but only 45 percent of the white union members. To the statement "Police shooting looters is violence," 59 percent of the blacks agreed but only 23 percent of the white union members. The statement "Student protest is violence" won the agreement of only 18 percent of the students but 54 percent of the reverse discrimination whites. Only 4 percent of the students agreed that "Sit-ins are violence," but among the reverse discrimination whites, 40 percent agreed. To the statement that "Draft card burning is violence" only 26 percent of the students agreed but 74 percent of the reverse discrimination whites agreed. And the statement that "Denial of civil rights is violence" won agreement of only 40 percent of white union members but 70 percent of blacks.

From these findings the authors concluded, "These data imply that American men differ greatly in what acts they call 'violence,' and that many people do not use the word as a description of forceful action which leads to injury or abuse." To account for these results they suggest:

> People use the word "violence" as a term meaning illegitimacy. The logic underlying such usage might be something as follows: The state alone can exercise major force within the law. This is "legitimate violence," and legitimate violence is not really violence. The police are agents of the state; therefore not violent. Protest, dissent, burglary and the like are forceful actions against the state, illegitimate and hence violent.
>
> This line of reasoning may be equally convenient for those who question the legitimacy of the state. For them it might run something as follows: The state (for whatever reason) is not legitimate to me; the police are agents of an illegitimate state, therefore their acts are violent. Moreover, dissent is an attempt to change the state in such a way that it becomes more responsive to the disfranchised elements in the population. Thus dissent is legitimate, and it is therefore not violent.[17]

After some further discussion of these results the authors returned again to the view that "it appears that labeling an act 'violence' is a statement that the act in question is not legitimate, good or necessary," and "whether or not a particular act is called violence can be explained in part by attitudes toward the group performing such acts." Thus, "Those who tend to sympathize with student demonstrators and black protesters are less likely to call acts of protest violence than those who do not." On the other hand, those who tend to sympathize with the police in putting down disturbances are less likely to see police actions as violence than those who do not sympathize with the police.

These tendencies toward selective perception and the rationalizing of violence for purposes one approves of raise a further question. Do people tend to approve of violence in general? The investigators found that "On the whole, Americans view violence as fierce, strong, necessary, avoidable, and bad." But then they add, "One could infer that when behavior is seen as not having such qualities, it is not defined as violence." Thus when police shoot looters it is "defined as not being violence by the majority of Americans." Furthermore, these same Americans might think of such actions as "fierce and strong, but neither avoidable nor bad, and certainly necessary." And they concluded that "violence committed by a legitimate power . . . is not seen as violence."[18] Similarly, those who advocated violence for social change tended to view what was done as not violent. This analysis of the semantic meanings of violence shows us that Americans do approve the *language* of nonviolence and the minimal use of force. But they do so in part by reinterpreting some forms of violence to explain them away. The language of peace is preserved literally by misperceiving some of the violence that occurs. No wonder, then, that Hofstadter, the historian, found that Americans have by and large seen themselves as peaceful.

Blumenthal's study is extremely important because of what it says not just about violence but about standards of legitimacy and the core values of a stable political system. It suggests some important tendencies.[19] One is that the language of peaceful, nonviolent behavior is pervasive and widely approved. People tend to see themselves and the system, normally, as relatively nonviolent. Second, and in some opposition to the first trait, there is a widespread tendency to perceive violent behavior selectively in accord with the observers' evaluation of the objectives at issue.[20] Harsh measures taken by the police to quell disturbances will be seen by many as not really violent behavior. These people will tend to discount the violence to view what is done as desirable, necessary, and legitimate. And, of course, those who advocate violence for social change will tend, albeit in the other direction, to view the conduct of protesters as not violent and as desirable, necessary, and legitimate. Americans can maintain peaceful ideals *and* at the same time support instrumental violence by such rationalizations. The system therefore retains its legitimacy in spite of the turbulence that occurs.

Now we are in a better position to see why McClosky found such massive one-sided support for general statements in support of freedom alongside the sizable percentages willing to endorse strong measures that include violations of the rules of the game. Americans can endorse considerable lawlessness and violence in behalf of certain goals and at the same time sincerely affirm their support of the system's core values. This tendency may be dangerous, even "Orwellian" in its capacity to alter the meanings of plain words.[21] But it seems to be widespread.

Civil Liberties and the Rationale for Violence

To understand the contemporary application of the core values we turn again to the statement by Archibald Cox in which he explicitly compared the misdeeds of Watergate with the protests of the 1960s. This perspective puts those who advocate violence for social change on a par with those who support violence for social control. It sees as a common factor in both the reluctance to accept constraints on ways of working one's will. In effect, it condemns the tendency to resort to instrumental lawlessness and violence on behalf of goals believed to be of special value, however sincere the beliefs of those who engage in such actions. Interestingly enough, Cox reported resistance to this perspective from those inclined to sympathize with the war protesters and with Daniel Ellsberg. In our view, this resistance is itself a characteristic response. Those who rationalize their methods do not like to see their rationalizations attacked.

Further examples from two quite different authors illuminate these tendencies. One writer is Jerome L. Skolnick, a prominent sociologist who has taught at some of the nation's most respected universities. With the help of a team, he wrote an analysis of the turmoil of the 1960s as part of a larger study of this subject by the National Commission on the Causes and the Prevention of Violence. Skolnick's own words in the preface and in the résumé of the volume's findings tell us much about his attitudes toward violence as it relates especially to student and black protesters during the 1960s.[22] The preface describes the author's values and tells us frankly that what follows is not value free. Specifically, Skolnick concedes a partiality to the values he associates with "constitutional democracy" and "due process." He also believes that social analysts must recognize "that violence has often been employed in human history" in achieving various goals, "social, political, and economic." He adds, "It is not enough to deplore violence—we must seek to understand what it is and what it is not." Already, then, we have an avowal of the value of constitutional democracy and due process combined with a plea to recognize the role that violence has played in history in furthering the goals of certain groups.

Now let us look at his treatment of the study's main findings as presented in his summary in the opening section. First Skolnick tells us that there has been "relatively little violence accompanying contemporary demonstrations and group protest." Another "critical point" made is that mass protest must be analyzed "in relation to crises in American institutions." As a further finding within this context Skolnick remarks that mass protest is essentially "political" and "engaged in by normal people." He also finds that violence has frequently accompanied the efforts of deprived groups to achieve status in American society. He ends this brief summary with a statement that the prevention of violence must address "the issue of fundamental social and political change." Of course we have quoted selectively from Skolnick's remarks, but we do not believe that fuller citations would change matters much. In the first place, we should notice that Skolnick tends to justify instrumental violence when committed on behalf of goals with which he is in sympathy. Second, Skolnick also tends to rationalize away the extent of the violence that has occurred. In the end, then, Skolnick's affirmation of faith in due process and nonviolent change has its limits, just as it does for most Americans, whether they are members of the academic elite or ordinary citizens.

Now let us turn to a quite different example, that of Jeb Stuart Magruder of Nixon's White House staff. Magruder, in writing an insider's account of Watergate-related events, describes how at one point he sought to face questions he anticipated in his appearance before a Senate investigating committee. He offers us an insider's rationalization of Watergate as a counterpoint to Skolnick's rationalization of the turbulent protest of the 1960s. As Magruder explains it:

Senator Howard Baker had tried, in his questioning of the various witnesses, to probe their motivations. I anticipated his question, and in my answer I tried to point out the frustrations we in the White House had felt in trying to cope by legal means with antiwar people who resorted to illegal acts—the draft-card burning, the leak of the Pentagon Papers, the May Day attempt to shut down Washington, the bombing of the Capitol and so on.

I specifically mentioned the case of William Sloane Coffin, who had been indicted for counseling young men to resist the draft—in effect, to break the draft law. I went on to say:

Now, here are ethical, legitimate people whom I respected, I respected Mr. Coffin tremendously. He was a very close friend of mine. I saw people I was very close to breaking the law without any regard for any other person's pattern of behavior or belief. I believed as firmly as they did that the President was correct in this issue. So, consequently—and let me just say, when these subjects came up and although I was aware they were illegal, and I am sure the others did—we had become somewhat inured to using some activities that would help us in accomplishing what we thought was a cause, a legitimate cause.[23]

Magruder then hastened to add a demurrer to the effect that two wrongs do not make a right. Nonetheless, we have a glimpse here of a rationale for Watergate. And it certainly looks as though the same tendencies toward selective perception and the rationalizing away of lawless, violent conduct on behalf of approved goals are present. Magruder's statement is, incidentally, a telling confirmation of the point made by Archibald Cox when he remarked that a lawless population tends to have its counterpart in lawless action by government. Skolnick and Magruder each represent, we believe, a reaction toward lawless, violent conduct that is widespread among Americans. This is true even though, of course, each would probably disagree strongly with the other, and each is likely to see himself as, for the most part, a good American who believes strongly in the system's values and normally deplores lawlessness and violence.

Another example of this kind of divergence in the application of system values is even more striking. This case does not relate to lawlessness or violence specifically but does illustrate nicely the way core values may be interpreted in divergent ways, even by elites. The problem in this instance involved a proposed speech for a fee on the Boston University campus by Ron Ziegler, former press secretary for President Nixon. Protesters argued that Ziegler was free to speak but should not be paid. To protesters the fee was the issue and not free speech. Tom Wicker, the well-known *New York Times* columnist, took essentially the same position: "A public personality offering himself or herself on the lecture circuit for a fee, can hardly claim that a Constitutional right has been violated if no one wants to pay the fee, or if only some are willing and others are not."[24] Yet on the facing page a *Times* editorial took an opposing position. The editorial, entitled "The New Censors," deplored the fact that some recent infringements on free speech had arisen from self-appointed censors from the liberal end of the political spectrum. The editorial then cited the Ron Ziegler incident specifically and added that "there is little doubt that efforts to cancel his appearance in both Massachusetts and Michigan stem from motives other than financial." To the editorialist the major issue was not the fee but the "free exchange of ideas, particularly unpopular ideas . . ." Both Wicker and the anonymous editorialist accepted the core values relating to free speech, but the application of general values to this specific situation led them to quite different conclusions. What one writer perceived as merely a question of fees to be paid for a talk by a controversial figure the other perceived as a matter of First

Amendment rights. Clearly such examples could easily be multiplied. Our core values, including the Constitution, are widely accepted but their application normally leads to much diversity of opinion, a diversity not confined to nonpolitical masses.

This diversity in the application of general principles is important to recognize but conclusions from it can be overdrawn. The observer who accepts this line of thought may conclude that the generalities mean little and that the rights of Americans supposedly guaranteed by the system are not effectively realized. Some students of the matter have drawn such conclusions. The editor of a professional journal which devoted one issue entirely to the subject of civil liberties sounded a pessimistic note in his overview: "One regrettably common message from a number of papers [published] in this issue is that there is no solid consensus to support specific applications of the Bill of Rights, despite the increase in the last 20 years in the United States public's stated willingness to support the liberties of some dissenter groups."[25]

This conclusion is not surprising but is far from the whole story. The political scientist David G. Lawrence presents a different and more complex assessment. We have already cited Lawrence's findings (in footnote 20) as supporting the argument that perspectives on what is legitimate are issue related. Lawrence, who used a 1971 sample of adults, did find that tolerance was "highly issue-related," but he also concluded that the public was more tolerant than one might expect from earlier studies: "Large majorities of respondents with tolerant general norms apply them consistently in specific situations, even on the hardest issues and groups."[26] In other words, tolerance prevailed even when respondents were called upon to judge some ticklish hypothetical situations that Lawrence posed in his study. And in spite of the tendency for tolerance to be issue related, Lawrence found the general norms of tolerance to be more powerful than specific issue orientations related to a specific case. The norms fostered tolerance, and countered the tendency for people to be intolerant of those with whom they disagreed. His study offers significant assurance that the core values of the system are not simply glittering generalities that, when applied, shatter ineffectually into a welter of divergent interpretations. The generalities do make a difference in behavior. American civil liberties would be a good deal less without them.

The Core Culture and Its Impact

What may we conclude, then, as we review what we found out about American political culture? In the first place, there is powerful evidence for the conclusion that a core of values does exist and shape the system.

The political system has lasted a long time in serving a nation that has grown and changed enormously since the 1780s. Recent survey studies lend support to this conclusion. McClosky found support for the generalities associated with individual liberty, even though consensus was lacking in other areas; and Devine's study certainly offers support for the existence of a core of Lockean values. These values legitimize the system and explain its remarkable stability and continuity, in spite of much turmoil. Using the terms of analysts of political systems, we could say that the basic values of the system in the form of national community and regime values have widespread support among both elites and masses.[27] This successful rooting of the system in the people is an amazing feat and is often not sufficiently appreciated. The United States is a large and diverse nation, "a nation of immigrants." To have created a political system which has enjoyed such legitimacy—and stability—for so long for such a people is an enormous achievement. And in spite of the system's limitations, the behavior of elites during such crises as Watergate surely demonstrates that the system's values do permeate elites and serve as some restraint on their behavior. For all the scorn one may heap upon Richard Nixon, our system made his behavior under stress far more restrained and "constitutional" than that of other powerful leaders.

But we have also seen the other side, the dark side, of the political system, the prominent strain of lawlessness and violence. In explanation for this continuing tendency we have argued that acceptance of the generalities associated with core values does *not* mean that people agree on what those values entail in application to specific situations. We might expect the relatively nonpolitical ordinary citizen to be uncertain and ambiguous in applying general system values. But elites, too, show diversity in applying general values. People do not even agree about what is meant by violence: what some see as violent actions others do not, and much depends upon the aims of the actions in question. Those who approve the purpose of an action tend to see it as nonviolent and legitimate. We have seen this difference particularly in attitudes toward violence for social control on the one hand, and violence for social change on the other. Each group tends to "see" different kinds of violence and draw correspondingly different conclusions as to what is legitimate. The language of peace, due process, and nonviolence persists. But in practice large numbers of Americans support instrumental violence for one purpose or another and rationalize away much of the discrepancy. This elasticity in the application of the system's core values has long occurred and in a sense is the normal state of affairs. To the outsider it may seem hypocritical, but it has probably been an important factor in the system's long life. An eighteenth-century Constitution could not have survived as well as it has without such elasticity.

The core values that pervade the system and legitimize it have a further major consequence. It makes for a politics of consensus which limits extremes and pushes political discussion toward the middle. Extremists usually lose. Those who appeal to the middle are normally far more successful than those on the far left or far right. As many observers have noted, the United States has never developed a vigorous left wing or socialist party, nor has it produced a large bloc of ultrarightists. Instead, American political parties are much like Tweedledum and Tweedledee, differing far less on basic issues than their propangandists would imply. Protest parties that arise as an alternative tend either to die from lack of support or, if successful, to be absorbed into the mainstream.

Successful political coalitions, whether bent toward left or right, must function largely within this mainstream. And their rhetoric, too, must in the main draw upon the familiar terms of American political discourse. Americans could accept FDR's New Deal ideas, but the appeals of the really radical left did not make much headway then or later. The mainstream, rooted in a political heritage that reaches back to the Founding Fathers and the original Constitution, wins time after time. Nor is this heritage merely a matter of rhetoric, with its generalities having no meaningful application in support of civil liberties. On the contrary, the generalities generate popular support for civil liberties. These norms do tend to counter people's tendency to be intolerant of those with whom they disagree.

The political culture of the United States has been and continues to be a potent influence on the system and on the mass of ordinary Americans it governs. But how much do the mass of people actually take part in the nation's political affairs? We shall next examine mass political participation, then turn in later chapters to specific aspects of mass opinion related to family, education, and the like.

NOTES

1. Herbert McClosky, "Consensus and Ideology in American Politics," *American Political Science Review*, LVIII (June 1964), 361–382.
2. Donald J. Devine, *The Political Culture of the United States* (Boston: Little, Brown, 1972), Chapters 1 and 2.
3. Ibid., p. 70.
4. Ibid., pp. 298 ff.
5. Ibid., p. 284.
6. Hugh Davis Graham and Ted Robert Gurr, *Violence in America*, vol. 2 (Washington, D.C.: U.S. Government Printing Office, June, 1969), p. 629.
7. Richard Hofstadter and Michael Wallace, eds., *American Violence: A Documentary History* (New York: Random House Vintage Books, 1971).
8. Ibid., p. 19.
9. Ibid., pp. 3 ff.

10. *To Establish Justice, To Insure Domestic Tranquility* (Washington, D.C.: U.S. Government Printing Office, 1969), p. xv. This work was the Final Report of the National Commission on The Causes and Prevention of Violence, chaired by Dr. Milton S. Eisenhower.
11. Hofstadter and Wallace, *American Violence*, p. 8.
12. Monica D. Blumenthal, Robert L. Kahn, Frank M. Andrews, and Kendra B. Head, *Justifying Violence* (Ann Arbor, Mich.: Institute for Social Research, University of Michigan, 1972), p. 39.
13. Ibid., p. 243.
14. Ibid., p. 245.
15. Archibald Cox, "Ends," *New York Times Magazine*, May 19, 1974, p. 68.
16. Blumenthal et al., *Justifying Violence*, p. 76.
17. Ibid., p. 79.
18. Ibid., p. 80.
19. Here we are generalizing these tendencies to the population, although the study itself dealt only with males aged sixteen to sixty-four. Other studies show that women and men differ in their attitudes toward violence (see Chapter 5), but male values certainly predominate in the system.
20. Confirmation of this tendency to relate standards of legitimacy to ends or issue content may be found in a major study of attitudes toward civil liberties based upon a 1971 sample of respondents. The author concluded that "Tolerance is highly issue-related. Respondents who are sympathetic to the goals of the demonstrators are considerably more likely than those neutral or hostile to permit the demonstration to take place." See David G. Lawrence, "Procedural Norms and Tolerance: A Reassessment," *American Political Science Review*, LXX (March 1976), p. 99.
21. Ibid., 130.
22. Jerome L. Skolnick, *The Politics of Protest* (New York: Ballantine Books, 1969).
23. Jeb Stuart Magruder, *An American Life: One Man's Road to Watergate* (New York: Simon and Schuster Pocket Books, 1975), p. 364.
24. *New York Times Week in Review*, February 2, 1975, p. 15.
25. Sheldon S. Zalkind, "Civil Liberties: An Overview of Some Contributions from the Behavioral Sciences," *Journal of Social Issues*, 31: 2 (1975), 8.
26. "Procedural Norms and Tolerance: A Reassessment," *American Political Science Review*, LXX (March 1976), p. 99.
27. On the use of these terms see Easton, "An Approach to the Analysis of Political Systems," *World Politics*, 9 (1957), 383–400. We equate the national community with the American nation; regime values are those of U.S. constitutional democracy.

SUGGESTIONS FOR FURTHER READINGS

Gabriel A. Almond and Sidney Verba. *The Civic Culture: Political Attitudes and Democracy in Five Nations*. Princeton, N.J.: Princeton University Press, 1963. An examination of political culture in five nations, including the United States.

Albert H. Cantril and Charles W. Roll, Jr. *Hopes and Fears of the American People*. New York: Universe Books, Potomac Associates, 1971. A summing up of the nation's mood and some of its values based upon national surveys.

Lawrence Chenoweth. *The American Dream of Success: The Search for the Self in the Twentieth Century*. North Scituate, Mass.: Duxbury Press, 1974. A historian analyzes American values as revealed in articles and stories in popular magazines of the recent past.

Harry M. Clor, ed. *Civil Disorder and Violence: Essays on Causes and Cures*. Chicago: Rand McNally, 1972.

Edward S. Corwin and J. W. Peltason. *Understanding the Constitution*. 6th ed. New York: Holt, Rinehart and Winston, 1973.

Ovid Demaris. *America the Violent*. Baltimore, Md.: Penguin Books, 1970.

Roy P. Fairfield, ed. *The Federalist Papers*. Garden City, N.Y.: Doubleday, 1961.

Lloyd A. Free and Hadley Cantril. *The Political Beliefs of Americans: A Study of Public Opinion*. New Brunswick, N.J.: Rutgers University Press, 1967. An important study based on surveys of American political beliefs.

Louis Hartz. *The Liberal Tradition in America: An Interpretation of American Political Thought Since the Revolution*. New York: Harcourt, Brace, 1955. An important statement of the prevalence of the Lockean liberal tradition in American political thought.

Lawrence J.R. Herson and C. Richard Hofstetter. "Tolerance, Consensus and the Democratic Creed: A Contextual Exploration." *Journal of Politics*, 37 (November 1975), 1006–1032. An empirical study, based upon a group of Ohio adults, of tolerance and consensus.

Richard Hofstadter and Michael Wallace, eds. *American Violence: A Documentary History*. New York: Random House Vintage Books, 1971. Hofstadter's introduction is excellent and the range of readings drawn from American history is impressive and sometimes chilling.

Peter Laslet, ed. *Locke's Two Treatises of Government*. Cambridge, Eng.: Cambridge University Press, 1960.

Jethro K. Lieberman. *How the Government Breaks the Law*. Baltimore, Md: Penguin Books, 1973. A somewhat novel perspective that classifies and vividly illustrates forms of governmental lawbreaking.

John Stuart Mill. *On Liberty*. Chicago: Henry Regnery Co. Gateway Edition, 1955.

James W. Prothro and Charles H. Grigg. "Fundamental Principles of Democracy: Bases of Agreement and Disagreement." *Journal of Politics*, 22 (May 1960), 275–294. An important study of people's adherence to democratic norms.

Charles Rivera and Kenneth Switzer. *Violence*. Rochelle Park, N.J.: Hayden, 1976. A useful, well-written survey of the subject, including theories of violence.

Walter A. Rosenbaum. *Political Culture*. New York: Praeger, 1975. A comparative study with useful commentary on the United States.

Samuel A. Stouffer. *Communism, Conformity, and Civil Liberties: A Cross-Section of the Nation Speaks Its Mind*. Gloucester, Mass.: Smith, 1963. A fine study, well written and still quite valuable for its findings on attitudes toward Communists and others.

4 · Mass Participation in Politics: Citizenship Without Politics

One of the most basic values of the American heritage is the importance of popular participation in public affairs. Good citizenship as expressed through involvement in the community's affairs is on a par with mother love in the hierarchy of values. But the reality may be something different. Practice, as often happens, falls short of the ideal. And if the evidence points to mass apathy and ignorance, the argument for elite domination is manifestly strengthened. In any event, mass participation is obviously a fundamental aspect of mass attitudes and behavior.

We shall first review several basic studies that outline the extent of participation and note some possibly important changes, then look at popular values and attitudes. A major discovery through these observations is that the American political system tends to produce an individualistic "privatism." This privatism is at odds with the ideal of the citizen who plays an active role in the political system, but it seems to be the role the bulk of the population prefers. In some ways the system encourages a form of citizenship that we might call "rights without politics."

The Active Minority and the Inactive Mass

There are many studies of political participation, but perhaps the best place to start is with a study published in 1950 by Julian L. Woodward and Elmo Roper.[1] It is particularly good because it uses a fairly simple but graphic index of political activities on which it is possible to grade the entire adult population. The questions were pretested on a sample of 500 respondents before the researchers administered the finished product to a national sample of some 8,000 respondents representing the total adult population.

The index of political activities ranged from the simple act of voting in national elections through a variety of more demanding forms of activity, including working for the election of a candidate and contributing money to a party or candidate. The scoring ranged from zero for the completely inactive through a total of twelve points for the complete activist. A person who simply voted regularly could earn a score of three on the twelve-point scale. For this reason one might expect that many people could get pretty good scores even if not especially active.

The results, however, portray a citizenry that is strikingly inactive. Roughly 73 percent of the respondents scored no higher than 3 on the index. Of this group some 38 percent had a score of either zero or one. Another 19 percent had a score of two. At the other end a tiny group, only 0.1 percent, had a score of 12. As Woodward and Roper concluded, much of the public is "inactive" and some of these are, in their words, "very inactive." It may be argued that some error was present and perhaps there was. The national elections of the 1940s on which this study was based, had relatively low turnouts. In the presidential elections of the 1950s turnout rose appreciably. On the other hand, researchers in this field know that people questioned in surveys tend to overstate a bit when asked about their voting behavior. This source of error would tend to counteract the first. In general it is reasonable to treat findings like those of Woodward and Roper as crude but highly significant approximations and round off the figures accordingly. We may then conclude that roughly 70 percent of the adult population is inactive politically and the remainder, 30 per cent, is relatively active. It is more than coincidence that 31 percent of the respondents in Woodward and Roper's study claimed to belong to at least one organization that takes stands on public issues. We shall review further evidence on this score shortly, but at this point we wish to propose a basic division of the population, something like 30 percent being politically active and about 70 percent inactive.

Woodward and Roper made another important finding in this study. They subdivided their sample into groups based upon income, education, and other differences and measured the extent to which each of these subgroups was active politically. In general those who were better off economically, educationally, and in other ways were more active than those who were disadvantaged. Executives, professional people, the college educated, men, middle aged and older people, and whites tended to be more active than the poor, blacks, those with only a grade-school education, housewives, and young people. Still, there was a minority of the top group, the best off, that was quite inactive. At the other end of the scale a minority of the disadvantaged was in fact "fairly active" or "very active." We are dealing with tendencies, not absolutes.

A more recent major study, based upon a national sample queried in 1967, alters in some important ways the conclusion that roughly 30 percent are active and 70 percent are inactive. In this survey, by Sidney Verba and Norman Nie, the basic division holds up well: over 70 percent reported voting regularly in presidential elections, but only 32 percent claimed to be "Active in at least one organization involved in community problems."[2] Within this range of activism the authors classified 15 percent as "campaigners" and 11 percent as "complete activists." (These two groups total less than 30 percent but are close to it.) But within the 70 percent we have described as normally inactive, Verba and Nie found two groups overlooked by Woodward and Roper and categorized them as the "parochial participants" and the "communalists."

The parochial participants amounted to a mere 4 percent of the population and were those who participated only on a highly personal basis. They did not engage in campaign activities or civic affairs. They made direct contact with people in government but did so in a manner related to their personal lives. In effect they were people who wanted something for themselves and were *not* active because of an interest in public affairs at large. A constituent who writes to his congressman for help in straightening out a problem with his Social Security check would be a parochial participant.

The communalists, some 20 percent of the population, were a more significant group. They were described as people who prefer to avoid political conflict but who are willing to be active in community affairs. Typical political activities in which there is some contention or controversy over party, candidates, and issues were not for them. As described by Verba and Nie they "perform at least two of the five demanding communal activities but almost no campaign activity." They are active in community matters beyond their personal lives but avoid partisan contests. One can easily imagine a communalist working vigorously in a drive for blood donations or supporting the Heart Fund, all the while skirting the rough and tumble of politics.[3]

At this point we might portray the political participation of American citizens as follows: About 10 percent are complete activists and another 15 percent are campaigners. All told, some 30 percent, more or less, tend to be active and attentive on a sustained basis. Roughly 70 percent tend to be inactive normally in political matters other than voting. But within this group, which obviously includes the bulk of the citizenry, there are two groups that are active in some ways. The larger group, the communalists, engage in civic affairs but tend to shy away from partisan and controversial public affairs. A much smaller group, the parochialists, are active primarily on a personal basis relating to their own lives.[4]

One specific facet of participation that deserves further attention is the rate of voting in presidential elections. In 1948, just before Woodward and Roper made their study, the turnout of adults voting in the presidential election amounted to only 52 percent of the adult population.[5] In 1952 it jumped to 63 percent. In 1960 the highest turnout of all occurred, 64 percent. In succeeding elections the percentage decreased but remained through 1968 at over 60 percent of adults. Then in 1972 turnout fell to about 55 percent of the adult population, and in 1976 about 53 percent of adults voted. Thus in the two most recent presidential elections about 45 percent of the adult population was *not* willing to vote even in the nation's most important election. The voting public is likely to include most of the "actives" plus some of the "inactives." Among the normally inactive, about one-fifth do not vote at all; they are inactive at every dimension of participation.

Changes in Participation

These figures show that participation as measured by voting has fallen since 1960. But the changes in participation, if any, are a complex matter. In general, those of high socioeconomic status, as measured by income, education, and occupation, tend to participate more than those at the low end of the scale. But changes in black participation, for instance, cannot be explained by socioeconomic factors alone. At the time of Woodward and Roper's study many blacks in the South were effectively barred from voting by local law, custom, and intense white hostility. Over the years these barriers have largely crumbled. Furthermore, Verba and Nie concluded from their survey of participation in the late 1960s that blacks actually exceeded the rate of participation one would expect from a group with their demographic characteristics. As they put it, . . . "rather than the average black being an underparticipator, we find that he participates in politics somewhat more than we could expect given his level of education, income, and occupation, and more than the white of similar status."[6] This rather surprising result Verba and Nie attributed to group consciousness. Blacks who consciously identified with their race tended to be more involved politically than whites. Slogans such as

"Black power!" therefore probably had a positive effect in heightening group consciousness and levels of political activity. Of course much of this intensified political activity benefited the Democratic coalition.

What of women and their political participation? If we go back in time we find that for some decades after they got the vote in 1919, women participated decidedly less than men. In some families it was simply thought that "politics is a man's business." Many women did not try to vote and among those who did there was a tendency for married women to vote as their husbands suggested. In more recent years the difference in participation has narrowed. Thus Gerald Pomper concluded that "sex . . . does not determine turnout."[7] He did find lesser variations, however, due to region and the presence of young children in the household; in particular women who were more closely identified with southern culture, as measured by length of residence in a southern state, tended to vote less than others. He also found, however, that by 1972 this regional disparity was considerably reduced, and that factors such as the presence of young children no longer affected women more than men. Overall, he concluded that the trend was toward greater equality between the sexes and therefore a minimizing of distinctive political roles for the sexes.

In general, then, blacks and women have tended to increase their turn-out in elections. On the other hand, the reduction of the voting age to include those eighteen and over has operated in the other direction. As we have already noticed, turnout tends to be less among the young. Thus the reduction of the legal voting age incorporated into the electorate an age group with low rates of voter turnout as compared with those of their elders. This change in the suffrage probably contributed to the low turnout in the 1972 election. George McGovern's appeal to the young in 1972, whatever else may be said for it (he received less than half the under-thirty vote), was not an appeal gauged to the most active age group. The famous pollster George Gallup does not believe the young are uninterested in politics; his survey data show them no less interested than others.[8] He also finds, however, that young people move about a good deal and he believes this mobility has a marked effect on political involvement. Young adults have so much to manage as they begin their working life, start a family, and settle into a home that political activity assumes a low priority. In addition to this generational effect, the authors of one major voting study present evidence that some young people who would otherwise have entered the electorate during the 1960s instead were, as they put it, "turned off." Some of them became independents and some became nonvoters.[9] The normally low turnout of young people was therefore accentuated by their reactions to events of the 1960s and 1970s.

On the other hand, there is a variety of influences working in the other direction, toward increased participation. Readers will recall that those who have higher levels of education and better jobs and incomes tend to be more politically active. These socioeconomic measures of a people's well-being are widely considered fundamental correlates of activism, even though other factors also play a part. Over the decades since World War II these measures of well-being have on the whole risen in the United States. In addition, barriers to voting, such as those which once confronted blacks in the South, have largely eroded. The legal age of voting has moved down. Registration has been simplified and lengthy residence requirements have been curbed. All in all, then, the trends in recent decades that relate to population characteristics and to access to the political system appear to favor enhanced political participation.

But has participation in fact increased? One authority, Norman Nie, suggests a depressing conclusion:

> Time-series data for a number of measures of citizen participation in presidential campaigns indicate that there have been no statistically significant increases in this type of participation from 1952 through 1968. During this same period, however, many of the variables which we know to be highly correlated with levels of political participation have been rising, and rising rapidly. Median years of education have risen in this sixteen-year period from 9.5 to 12.1, and the proportion of the population who have completed college has just about doubled. Income, which opens the way for a greater variety of leisure activities, has risen dramatically, and the proportion of the population in white-collar occupations has increased by almost 10 percent. Yet levels of participation which are so highly correlated with these factors (income, occupation, and education jointly explain as much as 20 percent of the variance in rates of participation in the United States) have not been substantially altered.[10]

Nie speculated that watching television might possibly be the reason, because he found that it had, in the main, an adverse relationship to all political participation beyond the simple act of voting. This relationship prevailed at various levels of political interest, and those who reported high initial rates of interest were found to reduce the number of their political acts as they increased their TV watching time. Overall, increased television use dampened political activism, other than voting, at all levels of political interest.

Nie realized that TV was not by any means the only influence for or against political activism, but he found the relationship so significant and worrisome that he wrote very seriously about its future effects. Specifically, he was concerned about the elaboration of TV offerings in the homes of the future in the form of "Individualized Home Entertainment and Information Systems." He projected the probable development within the next decade of cable TV networks able to provide a large variety of entertainment and information. Instead of the fairly few channels available to most viewers now, a host of channels would be available at the flick of a switch. If TV fare on a limited basis had a dampening effect, then developments that enhanced the attractiveness of TV watching in the future would be likely to depress political participation, aside from merely voting, even further. And the effects would probably be greatest for those who would otherwise tend to be most active. Nie thought that "if new and attractive home entertainment and information systems substantially increase amounts of viewing, then the leveling effects are likely to produce a participatory stratum composed of large numbers of those who are currently underrepresented and smaller numbers of those who are presently overrepresented."[11] These changes in turn Nie believed would tend to produce a more representative system but reduce the *quality* of representation. Activists normally have higher levels of political interest and information than nonactivists. A reduction in their activities would tend to lessen the influence of these qualities. The quality of representation fed into the political system from the public would therefore tend to fall.

Whatever their limitations, Nie's observations offer a suggestive partial answer to the puzzle posed by the failure of mass political participation to increase in the seemingly favorable conditions of recent decades.

The Private World of the Ordinary Citizen

In addition to assessing trends in participation, we need to try to visualize how ordinary people perceive the political system. Elitists who see the masses as a pernicious influence are likely to welcome the inactivity of the population. Reformers condemn it and ponder ways to overcome it. Neither view altogether does justice to popular attitudes. When we argue that privatism prevails, we mean the prevalence of a set of values that center on the well-being and advancement of the individual. Public concerns and political involvement, possibly apart from some voting, are seen as peripheral and burdensome. The system itself tends to foster this outlook, since individuals and their families can, in the main, get most of what they want without political activity, or see no direct connection between such activity and getting what they want. Political activity does not "pay." For that matter, it may even be counterproductive for the ordinary person to spend time on political affairs that might otherwise be devoted to work or personal life.

Perhaps in passing we should make it clear that citizens who are inactive are not only a large but a diverse group. Some are highly educated and enjoy many of the advantages that high income in an affluent society make possible. One example is Joseph Heller, author of *Catch-22*. This novel is famous and successful: it is also in many ways a political novel and during the 1960s was widely read as an antiwar tract. But Heller's political attitudes as expressed in an interview in 1975 reveal him to be apathetic and even antipolitical. The interviewer noted that in 1972 Heller said he had not voted in twelve years but that year he voted for George McGovern. Heller regretted this lapse and exclaimed, "Now I'm *never* going to vote again—for anybody. The smartest people in Washington are the political reporters. They write about their inferiors."[12]

The public we describe as nonpolitical is, as Heller's retort reminds us, diverse and not necessarily irrational or unintelligent. Indeed, Anthony Downs, in applying basic economic assumptions of rationality and self-interest to democratic theory—and weighing the costs of getting enough information to cast an intelligent vote against the gains or payoffs from voting—concluded: "In general, it is irrational to be politically well informed because the low returns from data simply do not justify their cost in time and other scarce resources."[13] If Downs is right, the costs of political information outweigh the gains, and therefore to be well informed is to be irrational.

This conclusion goes against the grain of most democratic theory, of course. Nor does Downs, who was primarily concerned with the logic of his economic theory of democracy, make any effort to back up the theory with empirical data. One study that does provide us with such evidence is a national survey from the days of the Cold War and the late Senator Joe McCarthy. This study, by Samuel Stouffer, explored people's reactions to McCarthyism and civil liberties. One question asked of respondents was, "What kinds of things do you worry about?" At the time the whole country seemed to be in an uproar over McCarthyism. One might suppose that people would respond with some mention of either Communists or the violations of civil liberties associated with McCarthyism. In fact, such concerns as a major worry were almost negligible.[14] One example of the kinds of things people mentioned as what they were apt to "worry most about" was "paying bills. My husband has been in the hospital and may have to go back again." Another typical reply was, "My job. I'm just new at managing this chain store and I'm very concerned about it." Someone else said, "Security, we do not own our own place. We want to and hope to. And we want to educate our children." One of the best explanations was that of a veteran:

> I've served my time on Guadalcanal and now I'm home minding my own business. I work graveyard shift and put in a crop besides. The plant has cut down to a four-day week. That's what bothers me. I don't worry about world problems. When trouble gets here I can take it. I'm paying taxes for someone to do my worrying for me.

This hard-working veteran with two jobs was completely preoccupied with making a living and getting ahead. The problems of managing his own life loomed large. Stouffer found this kind of response pretty much the usual. Thus when he arranged the responses in categories, "personal" and "family" problems predominated. The problems of the world and the nation, including the national controversy surrounding Senator McCarthy, simply did not rate high in the personal priorities of the vast majority.

The focus on personal concerns emerges even more clearly in a survey of people's personal aspirations and fears that was made in the 1960s.[15] The personal aspirations most frequently cited clustered about several concerns that focused on standards of living, health, and the prospects for their children, including their education and their opportunity for advancement. (See Table 4-1.) Personal fears tended to be the other side of these same concerns, with one major exception, the fear of war. (See Table 4-2.) This study, made just before the Indochina war escalated, appears to reflect people's worry that a major conflict could jeopardize everything they might hope for. Otherwise the fears tended to overlap the aspirations, with fear of a falling standard of living and of unemployment, fear of poor health, and fear of inadequate opportunities for their children. As with the Stouffer study we notice the tendency of Americans to see their lives in a personal setting not much related to the political framework.

What these attitudes lead to is privatism, a self-centered individualism which tends to distinguish the personal from the social or public sector of national life. This outlook is echoed and summarized by the authors of a survey of the state of the nation in the early 1970s:

> This discrepancy between the evaluations people made of the conditions of their own lives on the one hand and of the general social situation on the other points up what some other societies would consider a curious divorcement in the thinking of Americans. In the United States, the country of individualism *par excellence*, there is a sharp distinction in people's minds between their own personal lives and national life. Believing that individuals not only should but

can take care of themselves and stand on their own two feet, Americans appear not to make a direct connection between their individual situations and the conditions of the nation—except in the case of war or severe national calamity. As a result, they find it possible to feel that they as individuals can fare well, even though they perceive the country to be faring poorly.[16]

We may deplore this "curious divorcement" between the private and the public sector in the thinking of most Americans. But it makes a good deal of sense in explaining the apolitical behavior of much of the population.

Table 4–1   Personal Aspirations (Specified by 5% or more of sample)

Improved or decent standard of living	40%
Children—adequate opportunities for them (particularly education); children themselves do well, be happy, successful	35
Own health	29
Health of family	25
Happy family life	18
Peace; no war or threat of war	17
Have own house or get better one	12
Maintain status quo	12
Emotional stability and maturity—peace of mind	9
Good job, congenial work	9
Employment	8
Happy old age	8
Resolution of one's own religious, spiritual or ethical problems	6
Recreation, travel, leisure time	5
Wealth	5

Source: Lloyd A. Free and Hadley Cantril, *The Political Beliefs of Americans* (Clarion Books [Simon & Schuster], 1968), p. 97.

Table 4–2   Personal Fears (Specified by 5% or more of sample)

War	29%
Health of family	27
Own health	25
Deterioration in or inadequate standard of living	19
Unemployment	14
Children—inadequate opportunities for them (particularly education); children themselves do poorly, be unhappy, unsuccessful	10
Can't think of any fears or worries	10
Relatives—separation from; not able to help or take care of them	8
Communism	8
To be dependent on others	6
Lack of freedom, including specifically freedom of speech, religion, etc.	6

Source: Lloyd A. Free and Hadley Cantril, *The Political Beliefs of Americans* (Clarion Books [Simon & Schuster], 1968), p. 97.

We noticed earlier that alongside a consensus on the core values of the system there were also feelings of cynicism and futility. People had faith in the system but expressed much doubt about politicians and about their ability to influence public affairs. Events of the 1960s and 1970s deepened the cynicism and distrust that were already present, and expression of negative attitudes toward the government became commonplace.[17] A major consequence was a tendency to see government in terms of its burdens rather than its largesse. Certainly this is one conclusion drawn from a national survey taken in the early 1970s to determine people's attitudes toward all levels of government. A summary statement expresses it clearly: "The fact that taxes are viewed as either the major or, at least, a major manifestation of how government affects the lives of people personally bespeaks a basic problem. . . . With a large number of Americans, government means tax payments going out and only tangential returns on their investment coming back."[18] Most people saw government as a burden rather than a blessing. It took more from them in taxes than it returned in benefits.

Political Information and Voting

American privatism has important consequences both for levels of information and for the way people see the act of voting. Given the attitudes we have found—the high value placed on personal advancement and the burdensome image of government—people lack strong motivation to acquire political information. Not surprisingly, then, many people lack information about the political system itself and about leading political issues and personalities. Robert Lane and David Sears present a good summary that has a general application over the years:

> A review of this information picture tends to dishearten some students of government and partisans of the democratic system. A little over a third of the people know the names of their Congressmen. . . and a little less than half know which party controls Congress and thus which party is "responsible" for the legislative record. A large proportion do not know the centrally important issues at any one time, most people are unaware of the nature and meaning of the Bill of Rights, the central features of the electoral system, the names of the three branches of government.

They add that from other studies it is clear that "more people are willing to report on what the government ought to be doing than are able to say what it is doing." They also suggest that this information gap means that many people must make political choices via slogans and catchwords, not on the basis of informed, reasoned judgments.[19] At any rate, limited levels of political knowledge fit in with what we know about the inactive public's personal priorities.

As to the way people perceive the vote, Lester Milbrath and M. L. Goel found voting a "separate mode of participation from party and campaign activity." Voting stood apart from other kinds of political activity and could even be questioned as a measure of mass mobilization:

> In the Buffalo Survey (1968), voting clustered with other patriotic acts: "love my country"; "show my patriotism by flying the flag"; "pay all taxes"; "respect the police"; "support my country in wars I don't agree with." This clustering indicates that voting is more an act by which the citizen affirms his loyalty to the system rather than an act by which he makes demands on the political system; in the Buffalo survey persons emphasizing this mode are called "patriots." A person casting a vote rarely believes that it will make an important difference to the political outcome. It is more likely that a person votes out of a sense of civic duty, a sense of a common social norm, and because it is a way of living up to his own definition of himself as a good member of the community. The act of voting does not require as much information and motivation as do most other political activities. Many people vote who are not politically involved. . .[20]

Political theorists typically dwell on the importance of the vote as an instrument of popular control of government. But to many ordinary citizens the vote is simply a duty, like paying taxes. It does have value and is "good" but does not make much difference in a person's life. From the perspective of an individualistic privatism, this attitude makes sense.

The Pattern of Political Participation

This picture of mass participation is in some ways an odd and even depressing one. It necessarily oversimplifies in trying to describe in a fairly brief compass the political activities of tens of millions of people. Yet certain trends and broad patterns stand out. About 25 to 30 percent or so of the population is normally active and attentive, with about 10 percent functioning as complete activists and another 15 percent or so functioning as campaigners. This group is a kind of political elite that presumably interacts with the inner elite at the top of the system, assuming such an elite exists. Certainly the values of the politically active tend to be well represented in the system, more so than the values of the inactive.

On the other hand, about 70 percent of the population is normally inactive politically, but among this percentage are two groups, the 4 percent who are parochialists and the 20 percent who are communalists. Some of the inactives vote but about 20 percent or so of the population does not even bother with this minimum.

In the matter of voter turnout, conflicting trends are at work. Turnout in presidential elections has been falling since 1960. On the one hand, turnout by blacks and women has been rising, and a variety of other developments favor participation. Rising socioeconomic standards plus changes in voter registration should tend to enhance participation. But lowering the voting age to eighteen incorporated a group known to be less active than their elders. In addition, many young people who might have entered the electorate and adhered to a party became alienated from politics during the 1960s. And although voting is an imperfect measure of participation, it is tempting to relate such trends to Nie's study of the negative impact of TV watching on political activism. TV watching *may* account, in part, for the fact that participation has not increased as might be expected with rising standards of living.

Whatever the trends in participation, we find that public attitudes toward politics are quite different from the civics book accounts of the solid citizen who prizes his democratic political rights. Instead we find that most people are most concerned with their economic well being, health, their children's opportunities, and the like. We find a "curious divorcement" of private life and personal concerns from the public affairs, a divorcement summed up as privatism. Furthermore political cynicism and distrust have increased and government itself is seen as a burden. From this perspective political information does not matter much, and much of the public has hazy and incomplete knowledge of the political system and of the leading issues and political personalities. Voting is seen as a duty, like patriotism and paying taxes. For the individual the vote accomplishes little. It is a form of participation, according to Milbrath and Goel, that ranks apart from other forms of political activity and is questionable as an indicator of mass mobilization.

Quite possibly this attempt to characterize the political world of the ordinary citizen oversimplifies and distorts unjustifiably. Yet even the skeptical would surely admit that a plausible case can be made that the bulk of the population sees politics as a peripheral matter and divorces the personal sector from the public sector. People are not irrational but uninterested. But this separation of the public from the private sector should not be taken to mean that Americans reject the political system as a whole. As the previous chapter on political culture indicated, there is plenty of reason to believe that the core values of the system are widely accepted, but that many Americans combine a basic faith in the system with an impressive array of negative attitudes toward politics, government, and citizenship. We pointed out earlier that the United States has generally experienced an unusual combination of political stability and social turmoil. In a sense the turmoil is normal and is not usually a threat to the system. Similarly, we may view the privatism and related negative political attitudes as in large measure normal and not usually threatening to the system.

Such attitudes may be undesirable and could be dangerous if they became intensified. But the system itself makes it easy for people not to be involved. Certainly those who are not involved enjoy the same rights as those who are and in this respect have rights without politics. Indeed, if political involvement drains time and resources from activities aimed at self-advancement, it may be judged counterproductive. This line of thought might even be pushed toward the conclusion that the politically active citizen is, to put it bluntly, some kind of nut. But before dealing with such possibilities we really need further specific information about the conditions and ideas of the mass of the people. As we would expect, studies of the American family offer many useful insights for this search, because the family contributes so heavily to the early socialization of the young and to patterns of thought and action that carry over into adulthood.

NOTES

1. Julian L. Woodward and Elmo Roper, "Political Activity of American Citizens," *American Political Science Review,* 44 (1950), 872–885.
2. Sidney Verba and Norman H. Nie, *Participation in America* (New York: Harper & Row, 1972), pp. 79–80.
3. In practice there is likely to be an overlap and a blurring of the members of these modes of participation. Certainly politicians engage in civic affairs to further their political careers, and it is reasonable to suppose that some communalists from time to time are drawn into political campaigns.
4. In a refinement on the Verba and Nie classification, one authority on participation includes "communicators" and "protesters." See Lester Milbrath and M. L. Goel, *Political Participation,* 2nd ed. (Chicago: Rand McNally, 1977) pp. 14–17.
5. *Gallup Opinion Index,* December, 1972, p. 13.
6. Verba and Nie, *Participation in America,* p. 157.
7. Gerald M. Pomper, *Voter's Choice: Varieties of American Electoral Behavior* (New York: Dodd, Mead, 1975) pp. 69 ff.
8. *Gallup Opinion Index,* June, 1968.
9. Norman H. Nie, Sidney Verba, and John R. Petrocik, *The Changing American Voter* (Cambridge, Mass.: Harvard University Press, 1976) pp. 350–352. The authors remark that "Less than 50 percent of those under twenty-four voted in 1972 compared with a 66 percent turnout among those over thirty." They see the younger group as one "whose allegiance has yet to be captured by any political movement."
10. Norman H. Nie, "Future Developments in Mass Communications and Citizen Participation," in Albert Somit, ed., *Political Science and the Study of the Future* (Hinsdale, Ill.: Dryden Press, 1975), p. 141.

11. Ibid., p. 148.
12. Playboy Interview, "Joseph Heller," *Playboy*, June 1975, p. 65.
13. Anthony Downs, *An Economic Theory of Democracy* (New York: Harper & Row, 1957), p. 259.
14. Samuel Stouffer, *Communism, Conformity, and Civil Liberties* (Garden City, N.Y.: Doubleday, 1955), pp. 61 ff.
15. Lloyd A. Free and Hadley Cantril, *The Political Beliefs of Americans* (New Brunswick, N.J.: Rutgers University Press, 1967), p. 97.
16. William Watts and Lloyd A. Free, eds., *The State of the Nation* (New York: Universe Books, Potomac Associates, 1973), p. 21.
17. Warren E. Miller and Teresa E. Levitin, *Leadership and Change* (Cambridge, Mass.: Winthrop, 1976), pp. 226–229. The authors offer a well-taken caution that the "precipitous decline in trust in government" documented by a variety of surveys should not be accepted as "conclusive evidence of the decay of popular support for American political institutions" (p. 227).
18. Senate Subcommittee on Intergovernmental Relations, "Confidence and Concern: Citizens View American Government" (Cleveland, Ohio: Regal Books/King's Court Communications, 1974), p. 27. The data for this monograph came from a survey conducted by Louis Harris and Associates in September 1973.
19. Robert E. Lane and David O. Sears, *Public Opinion* (Englewood Cliffs, N.J.: Prentice-Hall, 1964), p. 61.
20. Lester Milbrath and M.L. Goel, *Political Participation*, 2nd ed. (Chicago: Rand McNally, 1977), p. 12.

SUGGESTIONS FOR FURTHER READINGS

Robert Agronoff. *The Management of Election Campaigns*. Boston: Holbrook, 1976. Chapter 3 reviews political involvement and its stratification into various forms of activity. The book is also of interest for its lengthy analysis of the many ways candidates try to reach voters.

Bernard R. Berelson, Paul F. Lazarsfeld, and William N. McPhee. *Voting: A Study of Opinion Formation in a Presidential Campaign*. Chicago: University of Chicago Press, 1954. This old voting study still repays study and is especially famous for a concluding chapter on democratic theory and practice that defends a less-than-ideal electorate.

Walter Dean Burnham. *Critical Elections and the Mainsprings of American Politics*. New York: W. W. Norton, 1970. Burnham is well known for his analysis of the historical patterns of voter involvement in the political system and their implications for the present.

Angus Campbell, Phillip E. Converse, Warren E. Miller, and Donald E. Stokes. *The American Voter: An Abridgement*. New York: John Wiley, 1964. This book was long considered the basic study of voting behavior. This abridgement contains the essentials from the original hard-to-read version.

Guiseppe Di Palma. *Apathy and Participation: Mass Politics in Western Societies*. New York: Free Press, 1970. A thoughtful comparative analysis that includes reflections on "apathy and democracy."

William H. Flanigan and Nancy H. Zingale. *Political Behavior of the American Electorate*. 3rd ed. Boston: Allyn and Bacon, 1975. A standard, readable source that covers material on suffrage, turnout, and patterns of voting.

Jane S. Jaquette, ed. *Women in Politics*. New York: John Wiley, 1974. Section 1 focuses on the changing patterns of women's participation.

Louis Maisel and Paul M. Sacks, *The Future of the Political Parties.* Beverly Hills, Calif.: Sage Publications, 1975. Chapter I relates physical changes in the electorate to patterns of voting.

Peter Morris and Martin Rein. *Dilemmas of Social Reform: Poverty and Community Action in the United States.* 2nd ed. Chicago: Aldine, 1973. Regarded as a classic study of the problems and prospects of community action that seeks to mobilize the poor.

Richard G. Niemi and Herbert F. Weisberg, eds. *Controversies in American Voting Behavior.* San Francisco, Calif.: W. H. Freeman, 1976. The opening section contains readings on democratic participation and its rationality.

Nelson W. Polsby and Aaron Wildavsky. *Presidential Elections: Strategies of American Electoral Politics.* New York: Charles Scribner's Sons, 1976. Chapter 1 concentrates on "participants."

Gerald M. Pomper. *Elections in America: Control and Influence in Democratic Politics.* New York: Dodd, Mead, 1968. Good analysis of the role of elections in the political process. Pomper makes a persuasive case that party platforms actually do matter.

Gerald M. Pomper. *Voter's Choice: Varieties of American Electoral Behavior.* New York: Dodd, Mead, 1975. Includes some analysis of participation in defending the concept of the "responsive voter."

H. T. Reynolds. *Politics and the Common Man: An Introduction to Political Behavior.* Homewood, Ill.: Dorsey Press, 1974. Chapter 5 covers conventional political behavior and theories of it. Chapter 8 covers unconventional politics, such as political violence.

5 · The Family: Still Alive and Influential

Our account of political culture and mass participation provides a setting for the exploration of mass opinion through the individual's early years of life. Whether young people grow up to become liberals or conservatives, active protesters or apathetic citizens trying chiefly to advance themselves, depends in some measure on the family. How one young man who was to become a strong Democrat and prominent in national party circles began in his early years can be seen in the following account by Lawrence F. O'Brien:

> My earliest memories are political. In 1924, when I was seven, my father attended the Democratic National Convention, and I can remember him returning home with a souvenir hat shaped like a teapot—a jibe at the Republican Teapot Dome scandals. I remember my father taking me up to shake hands with Al Smith during the 1928 presidential campaign and with Franklin D. Roosevelt four years later. I remember evenings when I would walk with my father through working-class neighborhoods in our home town of Springfield, Massachusetts, as he was getting names on nominating petitions or urging people to register and vote. On one such evening, as we walked along together, my father told me something I never forgot, "The votes are there, Lawrence, if we can only get them out."[1]

O'Brien's family background was exceptional. Most young men and women in America do not have this kind of early background acquired from a highly political father. We can understand why O'Brien would grow up to have a strong identification with the Democrats, the New Deal, and succeeding Democratic administrations. But even if most families are not so strongly political, they generally socialize their children quite effectively in the basic values of the system.

The Family Is Far from Dead

Before looking at what the family does, we should first establish that the family is not dead or dying. Certainly there is much talk about the "dying" American family, and a long list of evidence can be cited. The divorce rate and the number of separations and desertions are among such items. Where there are children, critics see the offspring of broken families as left alone to fend for themselves. Even in unbroken families an increasing number of women work and, again, children are left unattended in the home. And after work, the critics say, parents do not choose to spend time with their children. There are no longer Sunday picnics or large family dinners or outings. For these and other reasons many of today's children are neglected and uncared for. They grow up watching TV or joining destructive gangs. Declining grades, lack of discipline in the schools, the vandalizing of schools on a large scale, and climbing rates of juvenile delinquency and crime may all be blamed on the "dying" American family. This pessimism is aptly expressed by the well-known authority Urie Bronfenbrenner, of Cornell University, who argues:

> The question is, who *is* caring for America's children . . . Increasing numbers of children are coming home to empty houses . . . Sometimes children are alone for hours with nothing but TV. The TV isn't going to care for them . . . The kids find other kids who are coming home to empty houses. They create a peer-group culture, and it's likely to be an ugly culture—a culture of destroy, of break, or act out.[2]

No doubt the family is changing, but reports of its demise are greatly exaggerated. One respected authority, Mary Jo Bane, has examined historical trends in the American family and found some surprises. As a reviewer described her work, "She reaches conclusions diametrically opposite those of such well-known behaviorists as Urie Bronfenbrenner . . ."[3] For one thing, the extended family that included grandparents, as well as parents and children, was never in the majority. In colonial America roughly 6 percent of families were three-generational, and they were about 6 percent of families in 1970. For another, Bane found more two-parent families in contemporary America than in colonial America (84.3 percent as against 70 percent). In the past, high death rates often disrupted families, as divorce does in modern times. She admitted that divorce rates were high but thought they might be nearing a peak. In any event, she noted that most divorced people remarry. Furthermore, according to Bane's analysis, it is doubtful that mothers in past times, who worked long and hard without benefit of labor-saving devices, could give much more time to their children than many of today's working mothers.

Certainly Bane's careful analysis serves as a healthy corrective for those who think the American family has almost destroyed itself, for she assembles a large body of data from the census, from polls, and from family related studies, to chart long-term trends. The result pretty well demolishes the myth of the happy extended family as the typical pattern of the past and shows, instead, that there is much continuity, with the nuclear family pattern persisting throughout. Bane also reminds us that some trends, such as the divorce rate, are not all bad: a divorce may be a means by which a modern woman liberates herself from an intolerable marriage, a marriage situation that her grandmother would probably have accepted regardless of its bad effects on the whole family. All in all, Bane presents a persuasive case that the nuclear family is still quite strong and important, in spite of the strains upon it and the modifications that are occurring.

That conclusion is reinforced by another major study of the quality of American life. Using a carefully drawn 1971 sample survey, the authors review what they call "happiness reports," in which people comment on their state of happiness or lack of it, and they cite as one major finding: "Usually the strongest single correlate of these happiness reports involves the individual's marital status. Persons who are divorced or separated, or males who remain single after the customary period for marriage, are especially distinctive in their willingness to confess limitations on their happiness."[4] As to divorce specifically, the authors point out that "in any given year, the proportion of married couples who complete a divorce is barely more than 1 percent."[5] A table describing the marital status of men and women shows over half of both groups, 51 percent of women and 64 percent of men, to be still in their first marriage. Only 10 percent of women and 6 percent of men were divorced or separated. The other categories were those either remarried, always single, or widowed and not remarried.[6] These figures certainly give us a different perspective from the usual one. And since these authors sought in a variety of ways to explore people's happiness and sense of satisfaction, their summary of the "costs" of single life is revealing indeed: "Whatever the psychological costs of marriage, the costs of being single are greater." And they repeat that "single people, never married, divorced, or widowed do not find their lives as pleasant or satisfying as people who have married or have remained married."[7]

These studies alert us to beware of popular assumptions about the dying American family. There *are* changes taking place, to be sure. Large families are in decline and population growth has been falling toward the replacement rate. Single-parent homes are on the increase, and this brings worries about child care and family stress. Sexual mores have loosened some, although we must be wary of generalizing the more spectacular forms of sexual permissiveness to the whole population. The status of women is indubitably changing, and half or more are working, including those with children. Many women are no longer willing to adopt conventional life styles and roles, and resulting tensions are sometimes hard to live with. Teenage pregnancies are cause for anxiety, and certainly too many young people get into trouble, in school and elsewhere. But the family does persist; and unless it continues to survive, the country will be in serious trouble. Unlike more highly collectivized societies, the United States, with its pervasive individualism and privatism, has little to take its place.

The Making of "Good Americans"

Now that we can speak with some assurance of the persistence of the nuclear family, changing though it is, we can go on to examine its influence on political socialization. Through this influence young people become, or are supposed to become, good Americans and good democrats who accept and admire the nation's political system. Studies show that the attachment to the political community or nation develops early and is powerful. According to two scholars of the socialization process, Richard Dawson and Kenneth Prewitt:

> The earliest and, under normal conditions, most durable political orientation a child acquires is his identification with his political community. Very young children the world over know to what nation they belong. This identification is often accompanied by a strong sense of loyalty. The five-year-old French child says, "I am French and France is the best country in the world. The tricolor is my flag and I feel excited when I see it." Neither the national goals nor the political institutions of France will be at all clear to this five-year-old. His intense attachment is independent of any detailed knowledge about France. He is likely to be completely ignorant of his country's history and will have, at best, only a vague knowledge of national boundaries and even of who else belongs to the political community.[8]

We obviously have here a fundamental influence that occurs very early in life but tends to persist throughout life. Small wonder that nationalism is often described as the most powerful of modern mass emotions. And while America and its families turn out good little Americans it is interesting to note a similar kind of nationalistic emphasis in the official doctrine of the Soviet Union:

> It is the parents' sacred duty to instill in their children from an early age such precious qualities as conscious love of the socialist homeland, devotion to the cause of Communism, honesty, diligence and the desire to serve the people loyally and to defend the gains of the Revolution. This calls for constant and concerned penetration into the spiritual world of children and patient and comprehensive upbringing work.[9]

Societies the world over seek to create loyal citizens. But unlike most Soviet training of the young, what occurs in the United States includes a mixture strong in religious overtones. Another American study gives data on the mingling of nationalism and religion. David Easton and Robert Hess found that when asked about the pledge of allegiance, second- and third-grade children spoke of God along with flag and country: "Not only do we find the explicit statement that God is the object of the pledge, but when probed with regard to its functions, many children interpreted the pledge as a prayer. They saw it as a request either to God or to some unidentified but infinite power for aid and protection."[10] The authors add, "Religion's affect, it appears, is being displaced upon political objects, less by design than by the natural assimilation of political with religious piety and ritual." Nor do they assume that the sorting out of the political and the religious as the child grows older necessarily weakens this bond: "The initial and early intermingling of potent religious sentiment with the political community has by that time probably created a tie difficult to dissolve." Here we see the basis for the American civil religion, a subject that will come up again when we analyze religious influences. In America the bonds to the nation have potent religious elements that interact and are likely to reinforce each other. The good American is *not* an atheist.

The Making of "Good Citizens"

A second group of basic values to which the family contributes is those associated with the regime, the values of constitutional democracy. Easton and Hess write:

> Our pre-testing suggests that, as with regard to the political community, in a relatively stable system such as the United States firm bonds are welded to the structure of the regime quite early in childhood. By the time children reach the seventh and eighth grades, most of them have developed highly favorable

opinions about such aspects of the political structure as the Presidency, Congress, or our government in general. The Constitution has become something of the order of a taboo that ought not be tampered with in its basic prescriptions. Yet children know very little about the formal aspects of the regime and much less, if anything, about its informal components.[11]

Easton and Hess suppose that much of the acquisition of regime values is mediated by the president of the United States, a towering figure who is seen as good. He "makes the laws," "runs the country," and "helps the country most . . ." In fact, "For most children at this stage, the President *is* the country." Other lesser authority figures such as the policeman contribute to acceptance of regime authority. But it is also likely that family practices contribute. A major study comparing a variety of influences in the political cultures of five countries asked questions about patterns of family decision making—what influence the respondents could recall on family decisions, their freedom to protest family decisions, and their actual protests of family decisions. Large percentages of the Americans said they recalled such participation and protests. In general, older respondents remembered less influence on family decisions than younger ones.[12] This pattern of responses fits our historical experience, since earlier families were more likely to be father dominated. Certainly it is plausible to suppose that a relatively democratic pattern of family decision making would contribute to democratic adult attitudes. In such a setting children could learn that there are diverse points of view which should be tolerated, that everyone has a right to put in his own two cents' worth, that some protest is acceptable.

The concept of "rule by the people" may be recognized long before there is much knowledge of what it means. According to Dean Jaros, "The third or fourth grade child considers the role of citizen to involve neatness, orderliness, obedience, and avoidance of any kind of antisocial behavior. This conception of the citizen . . . gives way by seventh or eighth grade to a conception with some participatory emphases."[13] This last may include little more than voting, but an element of participation has become associated with "rule by the people." In politically active families like Lawrence O'Brien's, a powerful awareness of "rule by the people" as including political activity would arise at an early age.

In addition to the basic values of the national community, the family may contribute to preferences associated with such institutions as the political party. Jaros writes that "party identification . . . proves to be extremely widespread in American children." Although parties do not mean much to a child, "even as early as fourth grade, as many as 60 percent of the children themselves claim allegiance to one or the other of the major parties . . . Indeed, even in *second* grade, only a third of the children are unable to attach meaning to the names of the parties."[14] Jaros adds that this finding fits in with the two major parties' long history encompassing successive generations of Americans, and he notes persuasively that "the most partisan youth are found in Great Britain and the United States, exactly those countries that have the greatest proportion of partisan adults *and* the oldest and most stable party systems."

Party affiliations may develop early, but what of attitudes toward candidates and issues? Jaros, in his summary, reports that youngsters tend to have a favorable evaluation of all candidates. They display "reluctance to perceive any public figure unfavorably." In line with this attitude, children up to perhaps eighth grade dislike conflict and disagreement and believe everyone should "work for the common good." There is not much awareness of issues until at least the eighth grade, and even then "only 6 percent are able to make distinctions between parties."[15] For this small group the awareness of party issues is still pretty much limited to such vague ideas as seeing the Republicans as the party of the rich.

One of the important changes in recent times has been the decline of party identification, which is especially pronounced among young people. After describing the impact of the events of the 1960s and early 1970s—the Vietnam war, racial unrest, and Watergate—one study shows that "about half of the entering voters since the late 1960s have joined the electorate as Independents. . . . By 1974, 14 percent of the electorate were voters who came of voting age after the 1964 election and had no party affiliation."[16] As to the related tendency of some young people to turn away from politics altogether, this voting study finds nonvoting on the increase: "Less than 50 percent of those under twenty-four voted in 1972 compared with 66 percent turnout among those over thirty." This tendency to reject both parties and to become independent voters is a debatable loss. But that the younger generation should turn from national politics altogether is hardly a development we can relish.

Family Focus on Self-Advancement

One aspect of family influence in early years is often neglected because it is primarily nonpolitical and is not dealt with in the social and political surveys we have been using. But the powerful motivation most Americans have to "get ahead" is inculcated early and is a strong, if often negative, factor in political attitudes. Americans are strivers. We have already seen that most people are nonpolitical and are primarily oriented toward personal concerns, including living standards and the desire to improve material well-being. Most Americans devote their energies to this quest much more than to politics. The family shapes these priorities and fosters what becomes in most American adults a strong though flexible achievement aspiration. We have confirmation of this get-ahead drive in a comparison of the economic aspirations of Americans and citizens of several West European countries. As it summarizes the American findings:

> The continuous extension of work and educational efforts as well as the rising level of innovative consumer demand by Americans stand out sharply in cross-cultural comparisons. The American, confident of his own power to advance his well-being, steps up his wants at an equal pace with, or even faster than, his accomplishments. Impatience goes along with optimism and thus is conducive to dynamic adaptation and the reinforcement of wants and efforts. This pattern was not found to be common to other affluent societies.[17]

Not much later the authors add that "American society in 1970 still stands out from European nations . . . in that differences in social status, real as they may be, appear to place lesser limitations on aspirations in the former than in the latter."

As we interpret these remarks they mean that Americans are strivers of a distinctive sort. Americans value success. They are willing to work for it and will invest in education to advance themselves. Their wants also advance at least as fast as their accomplishments. Hence there is "innovative consumer demand." People want "more" and will try new things to satisfy their needs. Other passages in this profile of American economic aspirations tend to reinforce its individualistic and private nature. Americans were found to spend much more on cars than others and to use them heavily rather than mass transportation.[18] Americans were more critical than Europeans of welfare policies and the welfare state.[19] Naturally, then, "Many more Americans than West Europeans attribute their progress to their own efforts rather than to any outside forces."[20] Individualism also surfaced in the comparison of spending on leisure-time pursuits. Americans tended to prefer puttering around their own homes, in the yard or working at hobbies inside. Otherwise they mentioned trips to visit relatives and recreation out-of-doors.[21] These pursuits all contrasted with the European's traditionally more city-oriented amusements. Most Europeans, in contrast to Americans, did not own their own homes. They lived in apartments and tended to visit in neighborhood coffee houses and beer halls.

Another intriguing aspect of this study illuminates the tendency of American consumer wants to be flexible and to expand with income. The authors write:

While shortly after World War II only a few basic products were mentioned by substantial proportions of respondents—a house, a car, a refrigerator, etc.—in the 1960s sizable proportions were found to desire a greater variety of items, especially those concerned with leisure-time pursuits. As a result, the average number of wishes expressed increased substantially in the 1950s and also in the 1960s. Thus, over twenty years, there has been no indication of any increased feeling of saturation on the part of the American people.[22]

This economic portrait shows us that American individualism and self-reliance, though often exaggerated in the telling, are not unreal. Americans strive hard to succeed and tend to keep savings low and to consume heavily. The continuous extension of work and educational efforts, the low savings, the optimism, and the "innovative consumer demand" are all of a piece with these rising aspirations. Nor does this pattern seem to be one we could attribute to an elite manipulating consumer wants. Rather it is a pattern that pervades our society and that families transmit quite willingly to their young. An elite might use such attitudes to serve its own purposes, but it is hard to see that an elite could eliminate or seriously check such popular consumer pressures.[23]

This American motivation for economic success and the consumerism that accompanies it is illuminating. Much American striving is oriented not toward politics but toward economic betterment perceived in rather private terms as advancement for oneself and one's family, and most American families do a good deal more to prepare their children for success economically than for success in the political arena. We can see now why Americans tend to stress personal concerns, including the economic, and divorce the private from the public sector.

Variations in Family Influence

One possibly important difference among families is social class. Do poor or lower status families tend to bring up their children in ways that differ much from those of middle-class families? Jaros, who has also studied the Appalachian poor, thinks the difference "not especially great" but does mention orientations toward compliance with the law:

Lower-class children are more inflexible about the law, more unquestioning about obedience, and more convinced of legal fairness. This greater degree of lower-class support for the established order has been noted among adults and is visible in many ways today—not the least of which is the level of working class support for the Vietnam war. Since the child-rearing practices with regard to response to rules and regulations are known to vary by social class it is reasonable to attribute these childhood class effects on compliance to the laws as stemming from differential treatment by parents.[24]

The point is that the poor tend to be more willing to comply with authority.

Robert Hess and Judith Torney also believe that social status differences are not great in the political area, even in expressed interest in political affairs. But there are some differences in actual political activity, with the middle-status people more active as a rule. Hess and Torney speculate that this difference probably derives from the fact that, in practice, middling families do more to reinforce participation and involvement than lower-status families.[25] Compliance and passivity are more likely to be the rule among the poor.

One other significant variation was long neglected but began to receive considerable attention in the 1960s, with studies of the socialization of blacks. Milton D. Morris provides a useful summary of these studies, reporting that they vary considerably in method, scope, and depth, yet virtually all of them arrive at similar conclusions. The consistency of findings and the "absence of significant conflicting results" make these studies especially convincing. Morris lists the following characteristics: "(1) blacks are less trusting (or more cynical) toward the political system, (2) blacks feel less efficacious or confident about their capacity to influence governmental performance, and (3) blacks tend to be more authoritarian (or deferential toward authority) than are whites."[26] Thus cynicism, lack of confidence, and authoritarianism are well-confirmed aspects of black socialization. In contrast, however, as we shall see in examining ethnic differences, blacks tend to be a good deal more willing than whites to engage in active protest. Willingness to defer to authority does not mean unwillingness to buck the system. And we have already found in our examination of mass participation that blacks have become more active than we would expect given their socioeconomic characteristics, a fact attributed to black consciousness. It is the poor whites who seem to be distinctively compliant and passive.

Another variation that received much attention in the 1960s is youthful rebellion. Campus turbulence during the 1960s provoked heated discussion about its causes, but according to Jaros, youthful rebellion was *not* directed against the parents. The rebel leaders really seemed to be acting in accord with their parents' principles and ideals. Samuel Lubell, the pollster, who interviewed hundreds of students on campuses around the country, came to a similar conclusion. Among the students in the New Left he found that "the most important stream" was made up of sons and daughters of one-time socialists, communists, and other leftists.[27] These young people could recall having been "exposed to intense political activity while young and having been members of high school radical groups." One young man said, "My father brought me up to be a radical." Another remarked "I was only five when my parents—they were communists—took me to my first demonstration." This did not apply to everyone in the New Left, of course. One student said, "I have a taste for radicalism; my father does not." But in the main, the leaders of the youthful rebels of the 1960s were not in revolt against their own parents' values, whatever else they opposed.

The Socialization and Politics of Women

Black parents and radical parents make a difference in political orientations. What of the socialization of girls as compared with boys, and do women differ much in their opinions from men? Jaros spells out differences between the sexes that go back to the early years: "Even as early as the fourth grade, boys are better informed about politics, more attuned to the possibility of political change, and more willing to evaluate political figures." His explanation for this difference is a combination of family influence in father-dominant families and "general socialization." As he sums it up, "From the beginning, boys are encouraged to be aggressive and outgoing, while girls are taught to be domestic and concerned with personal relations."[28]

Kirsten Amundsen, in examining the plight of women, analyzed the "idology of sexism" and vividly describes some of these early differences in sex role orientations. One woman who examined children's literature in stores and libraries reported a "conspiracy of conditioning." First there was the omission: "In the world of picture books, females appear in only about 20 to 30 percent of the illustrations." Second, there was the portrayal of girls as passive, although also manipulative at times, next to active boys. Amundsen quotes this woman as exclaiming, "When I came across a picture of a little girl sailing paper boats, I was overwhelmed with gratefulness."[29]

Another telling example comes from a study of a questionnaire distributed to parents of children in a private nursery school. The qualities approved divided along sex lines. Amundsen writes, "Parents of girls stressed their malleability, cooperativeness, and willingness to take direction . . . Disapproval was given to assertiveness and affinity to quarrel. Boys, on the other hand, were praised for being independent, assertive, and inquisitive, and severely put down for being timid and fearful." Such standards, Amundsen argues, are "subtle and pervasive." They are

learned through "the family, first of all, and through the education process, the media, church, and . . . peer groups."[30] The family is likely to in-
itiate the process, which is then reinforced by other agencies of socialization.

The political impact of these early experiences is probably obscured
somewhat by the size and variety of the female population. As we have
already noticed, sex differences in voter turnout which once were quite
significant have declined, especially among better educated women outside the South. As to party identification, in the 1950s women tilted in
the direction of Republicans. Some years later, in 1968, women were
marginally Democratic and they were somewhat more so in 1972. According to Gerald Pomper, women under thirty were notably Democratic by a margin of 39 percent as compared to 24 percent Democratic
among young males.[31] In voting as distinct from party identification
there was little difference until 1972, when males were 7 percent stronger
for Richard Nixon. In 1976 men and women split their votes for the two
major candidates in the same percentages.

On issues men and women vote much alike much of the time but there
are differences. The major difference centers on issues relating to war,
the use of force, and punishment. Women tend to be more pacific than
men. Pomper cites sources that found women more opposed than men to
the two world wars, the Korean war, and the Vietnam war. Women
more than men approved the Congressional War Powers Resolution of
1973 designed to curb presidential discretion in the use of military force
abroad. In domestic affairs Pomper found data revealing that women
differ little from men on race and welfare issues but do differ some in
their preference for less forceful and more "social" methods of dealing
with urban unrest. Women are also less willing than men to use force in
coping with campus unrest, although no more favorable to student rebels
than men. It is not surprising, then, to find that women tend to be more
in favor of strict gun control. Consistently, according to Pomper, wom-
en tend to favor the less forceful response, even though they tend to divide much like men on other issues relating to the unrest under discussion. This consistency is striking, since, as we saw in analyzing American
violence, male attitudes toward violence tended to relate strongly to its
objectives. We should not, of course, oversimplify and conclude
sweepingly that all women are always pacifists. In general, however,
men and women differ importantly in their attitudes toward the use of
force and violence.

Some other variations may be seen in data that Dennis Ippolito and his
coauthors cite from 1974 Gallup surveys on nine different issues. As expected, women were less favorable than men to capital punishment, were

slightly more in favor of amnesty for Vietnam war resisters, and were much more in favor of gun registration. They did not differ appreciably from men on Defense Department spending reductions but were slightly more opposed to reductions in spending by the Department of Health, Education, and Welfare. More surprisingly, women opposed legalized abortion appreciably more than men. Perhaps even more surprisingly, 83 percent of men favored the Equal Rights Amendment as compared to 73 percent of women.[32]

In 1976 Gallup released data that shows other differences between men's and women's opinions.[33] On a question about voting for a woman president, 73 percent approved nationally, with 75 percent of men and 71 percent of women approving. There was no real difference about voting for a woman for Congress, but the ERA again brought disagreement. That year only 57 percent expressed approval, a considerable drop from two years earlier. Men again approved by a higher margin, 59 percent, than women, 55 percent. (See Table 5–1.)

One of the most interesting questions in this 1976 survey asked women about the "ideal life style" for women. There were a number of choices, with a small 6 percent of the women polled undecided. First at 44 percent was the choice including "Married, children, no full-time job." Second with 32 percent was, "Married, children, full-time job." Third at 9 percent was "Single, full-time job." The leading choice was a married life with children and no full-time job, the more conventional style. But second was the preference for marriage, children, *and* a job. That so many women are willing to combine the demands of a home with children and

Table 5–1   Comparison of Male and Female Responses on Selected Issues

Issue	Percent Giving Positive Response		
	National	Male	Female
Woman for President[1]	73	75	71
Woman for Congress[1]	88	88	89
Equal Rights Amendment[1]	57	59	55
Anti-Abortion Amendment[1]	45	42	48
Abortion illegal in all circumstances[2]	19	17	20
Register all firearms[3]	67	61	72
Decriminalize marijuana[4]	53	56	50
Prohibition[4]	19	15	23
Belief in God[5]	94	92	96
Belief in life after death[5]	69	65	73

Sources: 1 *Gallup Opinion Index* (March 1976), p. 6
2 *Gallup Opinion Index* (April 1978), p. 26
3 *Gallup Opinion Index* (September 1975), p. 9
4 *Gallup Opinion Index* (April 1977), pp. 6–7
5 *Gallup Opinion Index* "Religion in America 1976," Report #130, based on surveys conducted in 1975, pp. 14, 19.

a job and to call this way of life "ideal"—indicates significant changes in women's thinking. Apart from the one-sided preference for married life, these choices represent considerable diversity and help us understand why women's opinions on such issues as ERA are divided.

Women as a group have diverse opinions, whether about life styles or politics. This diversity and the conventionality of some of these opinions at times frustrate women's liberation activists and has contributed to splits in the movement. But when we think about the great size of the female population, the range of age groups, and the variety of childhood experiences American women have had, this diversity should not surprise us.

Variations Due to Aging

In the course of examining variations in family and early socialization experiences we have discussed lower-status people, blacks, radical youth, and women. One other major variation is caused by age. Does family influence diminish and perhaps disappear in time? This area is awkward to study because it is hard to isolate the changes due to aging alone over the long time involved and there is the problem of accurate recall. Perhaps for this reason it is not studied as often by political scientists as by politicians, who are careful to include age breakdowns in their voter surveys.

We have already seen one political effect of age: older people vote more heavily than the young. Milbrath notes it used to be thought that participation increased with age, peaked in middle years, and declined with old age. But close analysis of the older age group with an eye to sex and education differences has changed this generalization somewhat. With these differences taken into account, the decline among the elderly, Milbrath found, occurred mainly among those of lesser educational attainments. There was not a generalized withdrawal.[34]

The contrast in participation rates of young and old age groups has enhanced the impact of the aged on the political system. It is surely no accident that the Social Security system, a centerpiece of the welfare state, was enacted quite early in the welfare state's growth. Since that time the system has grown enormously, to become the largest single item of spending in the federal budget. Medicare, a form of socialized medicine, was enacted to benefit the aged, but national health care for all age groups has proven much more difficult to legislate. In 1969 a reporter tried to estimate from government figures the benefits distributed to the aged in comparison with those to the young and concluded, "For the fiscal year starting this July it is expected that the outlay per person 65 and over will be $1,750, while that for the American under 21 will be a mere

$190."[35] These figures are rough estimates and we do not argue that all the difference is due simply to the political activism of the aged. But the rough correspondence between activism and the allocation of government benefits is suggestive.

Are the aged more conservative than the young, as is often supposed? On the face of it they are. Ippolito's study of Gallup polls shows that younger people were more likely to support busing, amnesty, abortion, and the ERA, and to oppose capital punishment and reductions in social spending. He concluded that there were clear differences, with the aged more conservative than the young.[36] The voting study by Nie, Verba, and Petrocik, which investigated both partisanship and ideological differences, supports this belief. It found that "partisanship does appear to be a long-term, habitual commitment of individuals." But changes have occurred. Those who formed their partisan ties before the 1960s tend to maintain firm ties with their party. But those entering the electorate in the 1960s were less likely to form such ties, and the events of that decade contributed to a weakening of party ties even among older voters.[37]

As for ideological differences, Nie, Verba, and Petrocik found evidence for the conventional thesis that people become conservative as they age:

> In summary, the young have played a part in the opinion changes of these groups of voters. In almost every instance, they have made the group more liberal than it would otherwise be compared to the fifties. . . . However, it would be incorrect to say simply that the young are generally more liberal than the old. Some groups of young voters are much more conservative than other groups of old voters. What does seem to be generally the case is that the young in each group tend to be less conservative than their elders—for example, young southerners are less conservative than older southerners. . . But the young differ among themselves in the same way that older citizens do.[38]

Some older people are more liberal than some younger ones, and young ones differ among themselves, but the older members of each group are generally the more conservative members.

There is support for the conservatism and aging thesis, but it may not be the last word. Possibly, as Jaros suggests, people do not so much change as become fixed in the opinions they formed when young.[39] This tendency toward fixed opinions means that older people change less in response to events than young people. In a period when change itself seems to be the only constant, such relatively fixed opinions would be a conserving and conservative influence, regardless of their original ideological content.

Whatever the precise dynamics of conservatism and aging, we may need to give the subject more attention in the future. In the 1960s many people felt that the young were the wave of the future. But times changed. Birth rates dropped and the population began aging rather than "greening."[40] The mood in which youthful protest flourished gave way to more cautious and ambivalent times. Perhaps these changes, including the aging of the population, will be no more lasting than those of the 1960s.[41] But if they prove to be of some permanence the country will have to give more attention to the needs of those in their middle and late years. Changes in the economy, the political system, life styles, and forms of entertainment and recreation could occur. If the aging of America has indeed replaced the "greening," the concerns of older citizens will become increasingly prominent.

The Family in Perspective

We began our quest for family influences in politics and public opinion by showing that the family is strong, though changing, and that it contributes importantly to basic values of the system. Party identification is less strongly transmitted than it used to be, but the family does a pretty good job in turning out good citizens as well as consumers. Most of the citizenry include a privately oriented individualism among their basic values. There are significant differences in socialization for blacks and radical youth but not much for lower-status families, although the latter tended to be more compliant and passive.

As for women, their early experience in the family and elsewhere tends to encourage a more malleable, less aggressive, and more home oriented outlook. As adults they vote almost as much as men. Their partisanship and voting usually but not always parallel those of men. On issues women stand out as more pacific than men. They have also been less supportive than men of ERA and even of a female candidate for president. Their life style preferences are overwhelmingly for married life and a plurality favored a home with children and no job. As for the aged, they participate more than the young and have benefited disproportionately in the allocation of government spending. There is support for the thesis that aging brings conservatism but there are old leftists and young conservatives. There is a strong possibility that, with aging, opinions become more fixed and resistant to change.

We cannot attribute all of these influences solely to the family. Much of the time family influences are hard to sort out, and debate rages over the impact of family versus school. Nonetheless, the family influences fundamental values that we carry through life but that are not always obvious in reactions to events of the day. Most of the time we take our patriotism for granted and talk about the weather, the latest scandal, or the cost of living. But in doing so we need not forget that the family has influenced our reactions to these and grander matters.

NOTES

1. Lawrence F. O'Brien, *No Final Victories* (New York: Ballantine Books, 1975), p. 5.
2. "Nobody Home: The Erosion of the American Family," *Psychology Today*, May 1977, p. 40. This article reports an interview with Bronfenbrenner. A more extended treatment of the theme of family instability is Bronfenbrenner's "Who Cares for America's Children?" in Victor C. Vaughan III and T. Berry Brazelton, ed., *The Family—Can It Be Saved?* (Chicago: Year Book Medical Publication, 1976), Chapter 1.
3. August Gribbin, "The Family is Not Dying," *National Observer*, March 5, 1977, p. 1. Bane's book is *Here To Stay: American Families in the Twentieth Century* (New York: Basic Books, 1976). Much of Bane's perspective is summed up by her own comment in the Introduction: "Yet, as I delved further into the data that describe what Americans do and how they live, I become less sure that the family was in trouble" (p. xiv).
4. Angus Campbell, Philip E. Converse, and Willard L. Rodgers, *The Quality of American Life* (New York: Russell Sage Foundation, 1976), p. 25.
5. Ibid., p. 101.
6. Ibid., p. 323.
7 Ibid., p. 438.
8. Richard E. Dawson and Kenneth Prewitt, *Political Socialization* (Boston: Little, Brown, 1969), pp. 20–21.
9 The statement cited in the text is quoted in Anne E. Freedman and P.E. Freedman, *The Psychology of Political Control* (New York: St. Martin's, 1975), p. 98. The statement is identified as from *Pravda* in 1969.
10. David Easton and Robert D. Hess, "The Child's Political World," in Norman Adler and Charles Harrington, eds., *The Learning of Political Behavior* (Glenview, Ill.: Scott, Foresman, 1970), pp. 43–44.
11. Ibid., p. 44.
12. Gabriel A. Almond and Sidney Verba, *The Civic Culture* (Princeton, N.J.: Princeton University Press, 1963), pp. 331, 339.
13. Dean Jaros, *Socialization to Politics* (New York: Praeger, 1973), p. 43.
14. Ibid., p. 49.
15. Ibid., p. 48.
16. Norman H. Nie, Sidney Verba, and John R. Petrocik, *The Changing American Voter* (Cambridge, Mass.: Harvard University Press, 1976), pp. 351–352.
17. George Katona, Burkhard Strumpel, and Ernest Zahn, *Aspirations and Affluence* (New York: McGraw-Hill, 1971), pp. 171–172.
18. Ibid., p. 171.
19. Ibid., p. 199.
20. Ibid., p. 42.
21. Ibid., pp. 110–111.
22. Ibid., p. 73
23. The authors refer to John Kenneth Galbraith's argument for producer sovereignty replacing consumer sovereignty and suggest that "interaction" rather than consumer or producer sovereignty may occur. See p. 116n. Galbraith expresses his ideas in his *The New Industrial State*, 2nd rev. ed. (New York: Houghton Mifflin, 1971). His theory that consumer wants are manipulated is widely shared in one form or another by critics of American society.
24. Jaros, *Socialization to Politics*, p. 83.

25. Robert D. Hess and Judith V. Torney, *The Development of Political Attitudes in Children* (Chicago: Aldine, 1967), pp. 224–225.
26. Milton D. Morris, *The Politics of Black America* (New York: Harper & Row, 1975), p. 142.
27. Samuel Lubell, *The Hidden Crisis in American Politics* (New York: W. W. Norton, 1970), pp. 186–188. Richard Flacks, who also researched the student activism of the 1960s and was quite sympathetic to it, has written, "Research on the social origins of the early student activists strongly supports our view that, overwhelmingly, they were sons and daughters of 'intellectual' and liberal parents who saw the activity of their offspring as fulfilling, rather than rebelling against, their families' tradition of social concern." See Flacks, *Youth and Social Change* (Chicago: Markham, 1971), p. 79.
28. Jaros, *Socialization to Politics*, p. 82.
29. Kirsten Amundsen, *The Silenced Majority* (Englewood Cliffs, N.J.: Prentice-Hall, 1971), p. 112.
30. Ibid., p. 116.
31. Gerald Pomper, *Voter's Choice* (N.Y.: Dodd, Mead, 1975), pp. 76 ff.
32. Dennis S. Ippolito, Thomas G. Walker, and Kenneth L. Kolson, *Public Opinion and Responsible Democracy* (Englewood Cliffs, N.J.: Prentice-Hall, 1976), p. 92.
33. *Gallup Opinion Index*, March 1976, pp. 6 ff.
34. Lester W. Milbrath and M.L. Goel, *Political Participation* (Chicago: Rand McNally, 1977), pp. 114–115.
35. Bruce Biossat in his syndicated column of April 27, 1969. See also Harold Watts and Felicity Skidmore, "An Update of the Poverty Picture Plus a New Look at Relative Tax Burdens," *Focus*, Institute for Research on Poverty Newsletter, 2 (Fall 1977), 5 ff. The institute is at the University of Wisconsin, Madison.
36. Ippolito et al., *Public Opinion and Responsible Democracy*, pp. 95–96.
37. Nie et al., *The Changing American Voter*, p. 73.
38. Ibid., pp. 266–227.
39. Jaros, *Socialization to Politics*, p. 74. Jaros uses the term "nonsubstantive conservatism."
40. The reference is to Charles Reich's *The Greening of America* (New York: Bantam Books, 1971). The book was widely hailed as a rationale for the youth revolt and a projection of the peaceful revolution, the "greening" that was to come with Consciousness III.
41. According to Mary Jo Bane's analysis of trends in family size there is not likely to be much growth in childless families but there will be fewer large families with many children. See her *Here To Stay: American Families in the Twentieth Century* (New York: Basic Books, 1976), Chapter 1.

SUGGESTIONS FOR FURTHER READINGS

Norman Adler and Charles Harrington. *The Learning of Political Behavior.* Glenview, Ill.: Scott, Foresman, 1970. A book of readings that samples many of the important contributions to the subject.

Richard E. Dawson, Kenneth Prewitt, and Karen Dawson. *Political Socialization.* 2nd ed. Boston: Little, Brown, 1977. A revised and updated version.

David Easton and Jack Dennis. *Children in the Political System.* New York: McGraw-Hill, 1969. An important contribution by two political scientists well known for their work on socialization.

Edward Greenberg. "Children and Government: A Comparison Across Racial Lines." *Midwest Journal of Political Science*, 4 (May 1970), 249–275.

Fred I. Greenstein. *Children and Politics.* New Haven, Conn.: Yale University Press, 1965. A well-known study by a political scientist.

Dean Jaros, Herbert Hirsch, and Frederick J. Fleron. "The Malevolent Leader: Political Socialization in an American Subculture." *American Political Science Review,* 62 (June 1968), 564–575. An interesting study of political attitudes among poor whites in Appalachia.

Christopher Jencks and others. *Inequality: A Reassessment of the Effect of Family and Schooling in America.* New York: Basic Books, 1972. An advocate of equality reaches controversial conclusions about the capacity of education to overcome the inequalities that arise from family differences.

Rita Mae Kelly and Mary A. Boutilier. *The Making of Political Women: A Study of Socialization and Role Conflict.* Chicago: Nelson-Hall, 1978. A cross-national study of women who have been or are in political positions and such aspects of their lives as their families.

Kenneth Keniston. *Youth and Dissent: The Rise of a New Opposition.* New York: Harcourt Brace Jovanovich, 1972.

Kenneth Keniston and the Carnegie Council on Children. *All Our Children: The American Family Under Pressure.* New York: Harcourt Brace Jovanovich, 1977. A well-known social psychologist studies the family with a particular eye for the disadvantaged.

Kenneth Langton. *Political Socialization.* New York: Oxford University Press, 1969.

Richard Merelman. "The Development of Policy Thinking in Adolescents." *American Political Science Review,* 65 (December 1971), 1033–1047.

Alan D. Monroe. *Public Opinion in America.* New York; Dodd, Mead, 1975. There is a useful discussion of the various aspects of early socialization in Part II, Opinion Formation: Micro-Politics.

Richard Niemi, Roman Hedges, and M. Kent Jennings. "The Similarity of Husbands' and Wives' Political Views." *American Political Quarterly,* 5 (April 1977), 133–148.

Diane Ravitch. *The Revisionists Revisited: A Critique of the Radical Attack on the Schools.* New York: Basic Books, 1978. A counterattack on criticism of the school system during the 1960s and early 1970s.

Roberta Sigel, ed. *Learning About Politics.* New York: Random House, 1970.

"Special Report: Saving the Family," *Newsweek,* May 15, 1978, pp. 63–78. A readable and up-to-date commentary on some of the problems and potential of the family.

Charles Herbert Stember. *Sexual Racism: The Emotional Barrier to an Integrated Society.* New York: Harper Torchbooks, 1978.

June L. Tapp and Lawrence Kohlberg. "Developing Senses of Law and Legal Justice." *Journal of Social issues,* 27: 2 (1971), 65–91. The concept of moral development is applied to early stages of growth.

6 · Education: Mass Enlightenment and Its Many Dimensions

Like the family, education helps prepare young Americans for adult lives in the system. And there is much of it. Mass education is education for the masses, indeed, in America. The United States pioneered in the democratizing of education, and as of the early 1970s it still led the world in the proportion of its population enrolled in schools, especially at the higher education level. Education is often invoked as a remedy for almost every conceivable problem, individual and social. Yet even if we ignore such rhetorical excesses, education does, and is expected to do, a great deal.

In a nation of strivers worshiping at the shrine of success, education is a vital step in the unceasing American quest for better occupations, incomes, and styles of living. Politically, education helps develop motives and skills which contribute to citizenship, such as an interest in political information and the use of it to form political opinions. Education also contributes to social divisions that shape the nation's parties and coalitions, in that the better educated tend to have somewhat different opinions from those of lesser schooling. Education probably accomplishes less than either its critics or its defenders believe, but it is unquestionably of far-reaching importance.

Mass Scale of the Educational Process

Education in the United States is a massive enterprise that involves enormous numbers of students. One confirmation of its size comes from a set of 1972 figures presenting gross enrollment ratios for the age groups representing both high-school and college-level education in eight leading industrialized nations. At both age levels United States enrollment ratios exceeded those of the nearest competitors, Sweden and the Soviet Union, by a good margin and especially so at the higher education level.[1] Any country that educates so many people must obviously spend heavily on education, and figures cited by Ben Wattenberg dramatize the point:

> Since 1960, *consumer* spending for education has gone up faster than for housing, clothing, medical care, food, beverages and tobacco—faster in fact than for any other tabulated grouping. In terms of actual dollars, expenditures for education—mostly coming from *self-imposed* taxes levied by elected local and state governments close to the people—have soared from $9 billion in 1950 to $25 billion in 1960 to, incredibly, $107 billion in 1974, the largest major *governmental* dollar increase, absolute or relative, of any category of public expenditure.[2]

Per pupil spending rose accordingly, as Wattenberg's figures also demonstrate: "In 1950, the per pupil expenditure in America was $378; by 1960, it had risen to $546; in 1968, it was $828; and by 1972, had gone to $1,026—in constant, adjusted-for-inflation dollars." By 1972, spending on education amounted to 7.5 percent of the Gross National Product. In the same year spending on national defense, including veterans' outlays, amounted to just 7 percent of GNP. By 1976 education was again an estimated 7.5 percent of GNP while defense had fallen to 5.8 percent.[3]

Official figures on school enrollments and degrees conferred are another index of mass education. In 1974 there was a total of nearly 59 million students enrolled. More than 32 million were in grade school. Nearly 15.5 million were in high school and at least 8.5 million were in higher education.[4] The percentage of people eighteen or older who had completed high school rose from 60.0 percent in 1950 to 73.7 percent in 1974—a slight dip from the high in 1972 of 75.1 percent. Median school years completed rose from 9.3 in 1950 to 12.3 in 1974. Thus in 1950 the median was a little over a year past grade school, and by 1974 the median included completion of high school. In 1974, 954,376 bachelor's degrees were granted. In addition there were 278,259 master's degrees and a surprising number of doctorates, 33,826. The grand scale of these figures obviously means that education is highly valued.

A striking feature of mass education in the United States is its relatively decentralized functioning. This aspect is clearly important to an assessment of the effects of education on socialization. As the late V. O. Key, Jr., a well-known and widely respected political scientist, observed:

In many regimes the educational system is far more intimately articulated administratively with the governing apparatus than is the American practice. No central ministry of education in Washington controls the content of instruction. Even within the states a considerable degree of decentralization to local authorities characterizes the elementary and secondary schools, while institutions of higher education, both public and private, enjoy a high degree of independence from the general governmental structure.[5]

But Key added that this did not mean each school was free to go its own way. School boards have never been notorious for their willingness to encourage deviants and dissenters, and both formal and informal controls exist to maintain boundaries: "The administrative position of the educational system is essentially a mixture of autonomy and of intermittent and piecemeal control at the margins of that area of autonomy." Thus the United States has a system of mass education that functions on an impressive scale but is also thoroughly decentralized. But what does activity undertaken in the name of education do to people politically?

The Making of Patriots

At the most basic level, education functions like the family to indoctrinate the young in the basic values of the system. Key wrote, "All national educational systems indoctrinate the oncoming generation with the basic outlooks and values of the political order."[6] As Key said, this role has been of special importance in the United States because of the waves of immigration that entailed the need to create new loyalties. The Soviet Union, also a somewhat diverse nation, indoctrinates its citizens too. We are told that Russian educators do not believe that children can absorb "complicated ideological information," so they tend to stress "character molding" and to personalize governmental authority in representations of their great leader, V. I. Lenin. Writing of the "omnipresent" Lenin, Ann and P. E. Freedman quote an authority as stating, "There are pictures of Lenin in every classroom, busts sit on felt tablecloths in 'Lenin corners,' and the preschoolers are told stories about 'our Lenin' or 'Uncle Lenin.' 'Learn to live as Lenin lived,' they are told. Soviet children are taught to love Lenin as Christian children are taught to love Christ."[7] In the same tradition, when North Vietnam gained control of all of Vietnam, the government set about reeducating the population with such books as *Study and Follow Uncle Ho's Teachings.*[8] The reference, of course, is to Ho Chi Minh, Vietnam's national hero. We may safely assume that every country has its George Washingtons and Abraham Lincolns whom the young are trained to see as larger-than-life heroes.

Dawson and Prewitt describe this process of indoctrination: "The myths and legends from the past, the policies and programs of the present, and the goals and aspirations of the future are taught selectively. Consciously or not, textbooks and other teaching materials justify and rationalize political practices."[9] And V. O. Key summarized in felicitous words what this indoctrination entails in the United States:

> The characteristic national values and outlooks permeate the entire school curriculum from the kinds of problems posed in arithmetic to the formal instruction in civics. School children acquire some knowledge of American literature, a matter by no means lacking in political significance. Instruction in American history acquaints the child with the great episodes in our past, with our traditional national heroes, and with many of the ideals of the society. History tends to be a sensitive subject; instruction is somewhat selective. The greats of the past are elevated into paragons who would scarcely be recognized by their contemporaries; those episodes that redound most to our national glory receive emphasis; and the picture of the past is deficient in cracks and crevices.[10]

The young are given an idealized and myth-laden version of the nation's past and present, with emphasis on the ideals the country is supposed to embody.

David Easton and Robert Hess write that authority and the often sordid world of politics are especially idealized. They believe that adults have a "strong tendency" to shelter the young from the political facts of life, and they draw an interesting parallel:

> In many ways it is comparable perhaps to the prudery of a Victorian era that sought to protect the child from what were thought to be the sordid facts of sex and parental conflict. In our society politics remains at the Victorian stage as far as children are concerned. Some adults—and there is reason to believe they are numerous—feel it is inappropriate to let the child know about what is often felt to be the seamy and contentious side of politics. He is too young, he will not understand, it will disillusion him too soon, awareness of conflict among adults will be disturbing—are some of the arguments raised against telling the whole truth. . . . Adults tend to paint politics for the child in rosier hues. And the younger the child the more pronounced is this protective tendency.[11]

Classroom practices as well as teaching content can contribute to an understanding of democracy, but an authoritarian classroom run by a stern disciplinarian who brooks no questioning does little to foster an awareness of democratic participation. A five-nation survey by Gabriel Almond and Sidney Verba inquired, among other things, about what opportunities to take part in class decisions, and even to protest, adults could remember. (These questions were similar to those we cited earlier in our examination of the kinds of democratic practices people had in their family life.) In this survey 45 percent of the United States respondents recalled that they felt free to discuss unfair treatment in school or disagree with the teacher; this was the highest percentage for any of the five nations. Forty-six percent said they could recall actual discussions of that nature with their teacher. To a question about freedom to participate in school discussions and debates, 40 percent said they did participate; this percentage too was far above that for any of the other nations.[12]

Perhaps the respondents idealized their early school experiences. But if we are to give these responses much credit, then sizable percentages of Americans had relatively democratic school experiences. And whatever the limitations of this brand of schooling, it is surely preferable to an authoritarian and nonparticipant brand. Those inclined to scoff might notice the change that took place in West Germany after World War II. Dawson and Prewitt describe both the occupying powers and the German government as wishing to remake the country into a democracy. Education was seen as central, and there was to be a change not only in the curriculum but also in the classroom. Student participation was to be fostered. Dawson and Prewitt admit that it may be "too early" to evaluate the success of this program in changing national attitudes, but they offer a revealing bit of information. Only 6 percent of those who were twelve between 1941 and 1945, the last years the Nazis were in power, reported participation in classroom discussion and debate. On the other hand, 38 percent of those who were twelve between 1946 and 1953, the early period of the new regime, could remember such participation.[13] Surely this difference is not insignificant.

That education functions in part to indoctrinate young people may be offensive to some but is a fact of life we should recognize. To judge from the consensus that prevails among American adults, it is successful. We may prefer George Washington to Lenin, but we still, in our own way, indoctrinate our young.

Individualism and Self-Advancement

A second function of education is to foster skills that will enable individuals to advance themselves and, in so doing, advance society. A highly developed economy requires a population skilled in an infinite variety of tasks. Key observed: "The rise of compulsory universal education coincided with the rise of modern nationalism and the industrialization of society. The operation of an industrial system requires wide dissemination of at least rudimentary skills in reading, writing, and mathematics."[14]

What education means to the individual is apparent in figures that relate income to education. In 1972 males who were in the age bracket eighteen to sixty-four, the normal working years, and who had completed less than eight years of school, had an annual mean income in constant 1972 dollars of $6,200. (See Table 6-1.) For those with eight years of school the figure was $7,700. Those who had completed high school earned an annual mean income of $9,400. For those who had completed four years or more of college, the figure was $15,500. For a population of strivers, these differences are dramatic.[15]

Table 6-1   Relationship Between Education and 1972 Income for Males 18–64

Education	Annual Mean Income in Constant 1972 Dollars
Less than 8 years	6,200
8 Years	7,700
Completed high school	9,400
Completed 4 years college	15,500

Source: U.S. Bureau of the Census, *Statistical Abstract of the United States, 1976* (97th ed.), Washington, D.C., 1976, p. 128.

Still, there are those who argue that the dollar value of education is on a downhill grade, especially with college expenses rising. A study by Leonard A. Lecht, director of a business research organization, found, however, that important differences persist. On the basis of census data Lecht concluded that in 1974 college trained men earned 36 percent more than their high-school counterparts, usually had better fringe benefits, and were less susceptible to unemployment.[16] Albert Shanker, president of the United Federation of Teachers, has reviewed similar studies and believes that in addition to increased earnings and steadier employment, college graduates tend to advance faster, maintain higher levels of earnings for a longer time, have better fringe benefits, and, above all, are more satisfied with their work and their lives than noncollege people.[17] Shanker's list is impressive testimony to the economic advantages of college education and education in general. Most Americans could not cite such figures but almost everyone does recognize that education helps people to advance themselves, economically and in other ways.

Wattenberg argues that the expansion of education has had a "deeliting" effect, especially at the college level. He explains the great expansion in education from the 1950s on as due in part to the new middle class emulating the old. He traces this expansion, with figures, from the early years with Head Start through high school and the decline in dropouts up through college. Higher education itself expanded beyond the traditional colleges into junior and community colleges. In 1960 only 32 percent of young Americans entered college, but by 1971 the figure was 46 percent, although in 1972 and 1973 there was a slight drop to 43 percent. In an italicized statement Wattenberg wrote, "Today, about 60 percent of college students are from families where the head of the household had not even completed a single year of college. And today, 21 percent of young people from homes with family incomes of from $3–5,000 are enrolled in college, a larger rate than the TOTAL figure for either France or Germany or England or Italy."[18] Wattenberg's figures leave us a rosy picture of mass education expanding the middle class.

That this process has its limits is apparent from another set of figures. These were assembled by Albert Shanker from Census Bureau information in support of his concern about the effect that budget cuts in education in New York City might have on opportunities for people from poor families to rise in the world. According to Shanker's figures, in 1969 families with less than $3,000 annual income in constant 1973 dollars had 16.4 percent of their dependents enrolled in college. At the other end, families with incomes of $15,000 and above had 58.5 percent of their dependents enrolled. In 1973 the percentages were 12.7 percent and 53.7 percent respectively.[19] Two points stand out immediately. One is the low percentage of dependents from poor families enrolled in college as compared with families in the top income bracket. A second point is that both percentages dropped in the 1970s. Wattenberg may be right about the expansion of the middle class, with new middles emulating the old. But if Shanker's figures are correct, this process, at least at the college level, was halted or even reversed in the 1970s.

That Americans invest in education to advance themselves undoubtedly goes far in accounting for the nation's impressive expenditures. Yet it would be false to stress this motive exclusively. The mixture of practicality and the desire to learn that often occurs may be seen in some responses of freshmen entering college in the academic year 1976–1977. A survey of men and women entering 393 representative colleges and universities asked them to give the reasons considered "very important in deciding to go to college." The highest percentage, 72.9, were in the category "Learn more about things." But almost as high a percentage, 71.0, cited "Able to get better job." Next was "Gain general education," at 64.0 percent. But after that, with 53.8 percent, came "Able to make more money." A total of 43.9 percent listed "Prepare for graduate school."[20] Of course the latter reply may be taken either way—graduate education may be intended in part to gain the better jobs and incomes associated with advances in education— and it symbolizes the fact that Americans pursue education because of the expectation of economic benefits to come plus the desire for learning and general self-improvement. Education is not sought solely for economic reasons but it would be folly to overlook their importance.

Training for Citizenship

So far we have stressed the effects of education in providing support for the system and in helping individuals advance themselves. There is also the need to train citizens, people with some interest in public affairs, in acquiring information and forming opinions, and in acting upon them politically.

The Political Character of Adolescence, by Kent Jennings and Richard Niemi, is a major study of education and political development. The authors studied a representative sample of high-school seniors and their teachers and parents in 1965. Then, as now, a high-school education was the terminal point in the academic training of the majority of Americans. To analyze "political development over the life cycle," Jennings and Niemi first described the typical pattern shown in earlier socialization studies, a pattern in which political orientations began early, grew "rapidly although with varying speed," and reached "stable, nearly adult levels by the end of elementary school."[21] In their own study Jennings and Niemi focused on seven aspects of political learning: political interest; mass media usage; party identification; perception of party differences; the good citizen; political trust; and political efficacy. Those who ranked high on these aspects of political learning would be active and interested citizens. They would feel that politics mattered, that they could influence the system and that politicians were not all bad; they would acquire information, form opinions, and relate their political knowledge to the parties and their positions.

One of the most interesting set of findings pertained to the qualities of the "good citizen." Jennings and Niemi described the conception of this role in the early years of elementary school as including much "in the way of social, neighborly, and religious behavior." By the eighth grade this conception usually became more political, "with a general interest in public affairs, participation in the electoral process, and obedience to the laws—in that order—constituting the bulk of the good citizen's attributes."[22] Jennings and Niemi found that much of this political content persisted among their high-school seniors. There were two broad clusters of responses. One of these clusters encompassed active, participatory orientations. Thirty-nine percent of the replies were in this cluster. On the other hand, 31 percent fell into the loyalty, obedience, and passivity cluster. Ten percent indicated community activism and concern. Jennings and Niemi do not say so, but this last group seems to be the same as Verba and Nie's "communalists."[23] Other attributes associated with the good citizen in Jennings and Niemi's research included "Good interpersonal relationships and proper social behavior" and, in addition, "Moral, ethical, and religious attributes." In sum, nearly 40 percent cited qualities that were active and participatory, 10 percent cited community activism, and the others cited more passive qualities.

Jennings and Niemi compared student orientations with those of their parents and concluded that some "attrition has set in." Overall, the parents' conception of citizenship tended to be less active than the students', and this was especially true among parents with less education. The authors suggested two reasons for the generational difference. One is the tendency for students to "reproduce classroom rhetoric about good citizenship," a rhetoric they tend to take more seriously than their parents. A second reason is the actual experience of the parents: "Since the conduct of everyday life usually does not involve explicit political acts such as voting, and for many people involves only the most cursory efforts to absorb and interpret political information, there is perhaps a substitution process at work whereby activities that most people *do* engage in become attributes of the good citizen."[24] Most people lead nonpolitical lives but also hold to the ideal of citizenship. To avoid conflict between the ideal and reality they reinterpret citizenship to mean much of what they do in their everyday affairs. The good citizen then becomes simply a person who leads a normal, decent life. Jennings and Niemi concluded that overall there is change in political attitudes and it is not confined to the high-school years. In early years the good citizen is seen as chiefly nonpolitical. By high school political content has intruded, and about 40 percent have an active and participatory conception. Adults later on revert to a more varied and less active concept that tends to perceive the good citizen in terms of the workaday world with not much political content.

The previous pattern of early and rapid political development, with a plateau reached by high school and not much development thereafter, seems inadequate to Jennings and Niemi. Instead, they argue for a more varied and complex pattern in which the various orientations related to political development change in different ways.[25] Changes during high school seemed to occur most in areas of cognitive capacities, especially in perceptions of the political parties. Political conceptions and politically related activities also showed signs of increasing. Political trust changed too; the idealism of early years tended to give way to cynicism. Jennings and Niemi also challenged the "permanent plateau" concept of development by arguing that change took place *after* high school, much of it probably in the first decade or so of adult life. There were changes in political interest, political trust, and views of political parties, as well as in citizenship norms. Overall, then, the high-school years are an important and varied period in political development.

It has long been assumed that a major influence in these years is the high-school civics curriculum, whose courses are widely given on the basis that they instill the qualities of the good citizen. Jennings and Niemi looked at eight qualities which a civics course might be expected to add to students' lives. These included attitudes of interest, efficacy, and trust, as well as "civic tolerance," and of course included political knowledge and sophistication and the willingness to talk politics. The conclusions would delight the cynical. Jennings and Niemi make no bones about it: "Our findings certainly do not support the thinking of those who look to the civics curriculum in American high schools as a major source of political socialization. When we investigated the student sample as a whole we found not one single case out of the ten examined in which the civics curriculum was significantly associated with students' political orientations."[26]

The "overall findings are unambiguous," Jennings and Niemi say, but they make one notable exception: the courses did affect black students from less-educated families. These black students tended to become more civic minded, like their white counterparts. For black students from educationally deprived homes the civics course provided what the home did not. But for those from the better-educated families the civics course did little. Oddly enough, on some "quasi-participative measures" the civics course actually "served to depress black performance" for those blacks from the better-educated families. Thus civics courses influenced blacks in both positive and negative ways, but whites changed little.

Jennings and Niemi end this part of their study with gloomy speculation on the role of the civics curriculum and the need for a "radical restructuring" if it is to be continued as an important feature of high-school education.

In concluding their study, Jennings and Niemi analyze in some detail the many difficulties of sorting out the relative influence of home and school. These comments remind us of the context, the system as a whole, and the role of home and education in it:

> In the nature of things the family and schools are unlikely candidates as major *sources* of change in the political culture, at least in the American case. Usually, what modest political teaching the family does in the area of system norms is positively supported by, and seldom contradicted by, other primary agents. In fact one reason the United States elementary and secondary schools so often look bland is that they are generally not proponents of change. They do not, by and large, seek to alter the developmental path of politics along which the children are bound, but rather support the movement thereon by supplying appropriate tools such as literacy and by reinforcing widespread values of the political order.[27]

This passage reinforces our own view that family and education both indoctrinate and contribute heavily to the attitudes and skills needed for self-advancement within the system. Most Americans want to get ahead, not to challenge the system. As Jennings and Niemi agree, events may impinge upon this socialization process as they did for a time during the 1960s. The system "bent" to accommodate the protest but in retrospect appears not to have changed much. Certainly it is doubtful that conceptions of the good citizen developed appreciably. Indeed, the tendency of some young people to become either independents or nonparticipants suggests that if there was any change, it was in the direction of a more passive conception of citizenship.

The five-nation study by Almond and Verba offers another important contribution to the analysis of the impact of education on political learning. The authors found some ways in which education, including college education, had a like effect in all five nations. This cross-national uniformity was summed up in nine distinct points.[28] In general, the more highly educated people felt more trust and confidence in their environment; they felt they could make a difference; they were more aware of the impact of government, more likely to follow politics and to acquire information; they formed opinions on a wider range of subjects; they were more willing to discuss politics with a variety of people; and they were more likely to be active members of organizations.

Almond and Verba help us to summarize the influence of education on political thought and action through their broad cross-national perspective. Education fosters an enlarged interest in the world and what is happening politically and enhances the feeling that a person can make a difference. With these feelings the more highly educated people tend to acquire information, form opinions, and then carry these opinions into discussions and organizational activities.

The Making of Liberals and Conservatives

At the same time it fosters support for the system, education sharpens differences. It contributes to the formation of party differences and those of political ideologies. These are the kinds of differences V. O. Key analyzed under the heading "direction of opinion." They relate to forms of liberalism and conservatism, which in turn relate to political coalitions such as the New Deal and its alternatives.

In analyzing data from the 1950s on a set of questions about domestic economic issues, Key presented evidence that the college educated took a more conservative position than those with a grade-school education. The college educated tended to be less enthusiastic about governmental activities on behalf of medical care, job guarantees, aid to education, and government-sponsored housing than those at other education levels. In exploring differences of opinion on foreign policy issues, Key found the college educated more willing to sanction involvement abroad with the problems of other nations than were those with less education. On this dimension, the college educated were more liberal than the less educated.[29] Already, then, we have a serious complication: the college educated were economic conservatives and foreign policy liberals, whereas the less educated were just the opposite.

Key singled out these differences but treated them with restraint. Dye and Zeigler develop the contrasts much more sharply as a fundamental feature of their elitist theory. One statement summarizes their perception of the relationship between education and ideology:

> We are accustomed to associating conservatism with the upper classes, but the facts are not that simple. While the poorly educated public may be more "liberal" with respect to *economic* matters—they favor more welfare measures and more government intervention into economic life than do the upper strata of the society—they are in fact more "conservative" than elites when conservatism is defined as an emphasis on tradition, order, status hierarchy, duty, obligation, obedience, and authority. Commitment to order and authority is much more a characteristic of poorly educated people.[30]

The contrast between educated elites and the great unwashed masses is developed at some length by Dye and Zeigler in their chapter on mass attitudes. The masses are those who receive a limited education, up through high school at most. The elite are those with college education and especially those who combine college with high incomes. In earlier days, in the prime of the New Deal, the masses were the have-nots who rallied behind the New Deal philosophy of using the government to provide jobs and other benefits to the mass of people. The elite of college-educated people tended to oppose the New Deal, and were usually seen, as Dye and Zeigler point out, as supporting the Republicans and conservative economic policies. But in a whole range of other issue areas the better educated have tended to be liberal. In contrast to the elite's enlightened perspectives, the masses are portrayed as intolerant in matters of First Amendment freedoms of expression, as racially bigoted, as nationalistic, warlike, authoritarian, and inclined to follow demagogues who preach strong measures in dealing with foreigners abroad and unrest at home. The masses become synonymous with the "hard hat" blue collar workers who attacked disruptive college students. The perspective of Dye and Zeigler is at one with those who have seen Archie Bunker as the embodiment of mass attitudes. The people become the "dark masses" who are a threat to democracy.

Dye and Zeigler cite studies that lend support to this contrast and in addition carry their argument into an analysis of the background of the masses. For they argue that the socialization of the masses in home, school, and in the kinds of jobs they hold all tend to create closed, narrow minds. The mass man and woman grows up typically in an authoritarian home environment. They learn early to obey and to expect punishment, perhaps violence, for disobedience. In school they are taught patriotism, loyalty, the evils of communism, and the value of adhering to the status quo. Controversial social subjects, such as race, are neglected. A passive conception of citizenship is taught rather than a politically realistic and participatory activism. As adults they gravitate into routine work that may pay adequately but allows little opportunity for independence, responsibility, and creativity. Dull, routine jobs further dull and narrow the minds of those who occupy them. The concept of "working-class authoritarianism" elaborated by the well-known sociologist Seymour Martin Lipset is brought to bear. The masses are prejudiced authoritarians because their training and education have made them that way. Once formed by these powerful influences, they are unlikely to change.

Education and Ideology: New Research

Education makes a difference, but to see the masses as little more than a teeming population of Archie Bunkers venting their bigotry on those about them appears to be an exaggeration, to say the least. Certainly there is conflicting evidence that merits a hearing. Perhaps the best place to start is with the contrast on economic issues. True, we have found that

college-educated people normally tend to be more Republican and conservative on economic issues than those with less education. But Everett
Ladd and Charles Hadley present evidence of a change in recent years
toward what they call an "inversion" of the New Deal class order:

> Over the last ten years . . . a shift of considerable magnitude has occurred. It
> has been as rapid a break from the past as it has been extensive. In most policy
> areas, whites in the higher socioeconomic status categories have become
> decisively more liberal than the middle to lower cohorts. There are exceptions
> in economic policy, but even these are being reduced.[31]

Ladd and Hadley explore this shift at some length. They note that in the
past those of high socioeconomic status tended to be more internationalist and civil libertarian than those less well off but were still predomin-
antly conservative and especially on economic issues. Recently, however, changes in the composition of this group and changes in the nature
of the issues have altered this outlook. Once primarily a business-
oriented group, it has since grown to include some of the middle class
and intelligentsia. Social issues related to culture, racial equality, and life
styles have created a brand of new liberalism with which it can sympathize.

Even the traditional economic conservatism of the high socioeconomic
group has declined. Thus, according to Ladd and Hadley, the "old
ideological objections to intervention by the state have been . . . greatly
weakened." In summarizing this inversion of the New Deal class order,
Ladd and Hadley state flatly: "The high social strata now consistently
provide a greater measure of support for liberal programs and can-
didacies than do the lower strata. This is no temporary phenomenon. No
return to the New Deal pattern should be expected." Gerald Pomper's
analysis of the unique qualities of the Jimmy Carter Democratic coalition
of 1976, which we discussed earlier, seems to confirm Ladd and Hadley's
thesis.[32]

The contrast between college-educated elites and the masses on
economic issues has evidently blurred. But what of other issue areas?
One example well worth studying is Watergate. Dye and Zeigler have to
account for that scandal, but there is no way it can be attributed to the
masses directly. The president and the members of his staff have to be
ascribed elite status. Dye and Zeigler resolve the problem with an analysis of elite repression in response to a perceived threat. They argue that
during the 1960s the masses were disturbed by a whole series of troublesome events, and that this set the stage for elite reaction in the form of
harsh and repressive measures. But even with this ingenious theory, Dye
and Zeigler acknowledge that the elite behaved badly, not in accord with
the values elites are supposed to uphold.

Furthermore, they acknowledge that elite misconduct has precedents: "Repressive behavior is typical of elites who feel threatened in crises, as events in American history show." They list historical precedents as far back as the Alien and Sedition Acts and as recent as the jailing of thousands of Japanese-Americans during World War II, as well as many questionable and illegal practices of earlier administrations than Nixon's. In this perspective Watergate becomes simply a "more spectacular illustration" of elite repression when threatened. Dye and Zeigler admit that the Nixon Administration was "especially blameworthy" but warn that those who contend "Watergate is unique or unprecedented are either partisan or naive. Elite repression is a continuing threat to democratic values."[33] This way of accounting for Watergate by authors committed to an elite value system is particularly valuable in helping us question the sharp contrast often drawn between elites and masses.

Perhaps the most careful and systematic attempt to challenge the thesis that the working class is authoritarian is a lengthy study by the social scientist Richard F. Hamilton. For one thing, Hamilton took note of the reputation of workers for taking a tough, aggressive stance on foreign affairs and refuted it: "In summary, the evidence here does not support the image of jingoistic and warlike masses. It indicates just the opposite: that the tough hard line is a proclivity of established, educated, upper-middle-class white Protestants."[34]

Hamilton then reviewed the literature purporting to establish mass authoritarianism and bigotry and questioned aspects of the methodology involved in the studies. He questioned as well the tendency for social scientists to develop among themselves a "response set" which accepted the evidence for working-class authoritarianism as "clear and consistent," so that the expectation became a self-fulfilling prophecy. By contrast Hamilton claimed that "the evidence is not 'clear and consistent.' Basically this review of the previous evidence indicates that the research to date does not show the manual workers to be *consistently* more prejudiced than the nonmanuals . . . widespread acceptance of the working class authoritarianism claim is based on a selective appreciation of the available evidence."

As for intolerance, Hamilton concluded, "The evidence with respect to attitude toward Negroes indicates that outside the South there is essentially no difference between manuals and nonmanuals. Outside the South and with the farm-reared excluded, there is essentially no difference between manuals and nonmanuals in their support for the rights of the 'accused man.' "[35] There did seem to be less working-class tolerance for admitted communists, socialists, and atheists, but Hamilton does not believe this should be blamed on an ingrained authoritarianism due to home, school, and job. Some of it he attributes to small-town people and southerners, groups he perceives as inclined to be intolerant. He also argues that elites themselves foster threats, such as "red scares," that play upon people's fears. If Hamilton is right, the evidence for mass authoritarianism and bigotry is *not* "clear and consistent" and the theory of authoritarian early socialization of the masses is questionable.

Andrew Levison is another writer who has challenged those who label workers as bigoted and aggressively patriotic. After reviewing evidence from surveys and local voting on issues related to race, he found that the workers were not the "worst racists." One study he cited is especially to the point: "The highest incidence of antagonism to open housing is among white collar low income workers, not the [white] working class . . . [their] *support for the laws in the referenda somewhat exceed that of their bosses and social superiors, the business proprietors and executives.*" After further research in this area Levison concluded, "Thus, 'real life' votes on open housing, or segregationist referenda and elections between liberals and conservatives, show that workers have been, if anything, slightly more progressive than the middle class." He believed that white workers genuinely accepted black workers' demands for simple justice, and he saw white workers' resentments as largely directed against affluent liberal elites who ignored workers' problems and considered them a disorganized and prejudiced mass.

Levison also challenged the propensity to see hard-hat workers as nationalistic supporters of foreign wars. Like Hamilton he found evidence that the workers were not the strongest supporters of the Vietnam war. Outbursts of worker anger directed against peace demonstrators arose, Levison believes, from class resentment rather than prejudice and nationalism. The workers' own children were drafted or had to go to work in factories while the children of those who were well off got into college, where they used their freedom to disrupt campuses and their own education. What the workers resented was elitism and snobbery, not opposition to the war itself.[37] Levison finished his analysis with a broad claim: "While racism and militarism do exist, workers are no worse and perhaps even better than the middle class on many issues, and none of the problems which pitted them against blacks or students results from any 'inevitable' conservatism." Levison does not try to portray workers as paragons, but his evidence casts additional doubt on the supposedly clear contrast between the authoritarian masses and their enlightened betters.

The public opinion study by Ippolito, Walker, and Kolson reinforces such doubts. The Gallup surveys these writers used included nine separate issues that ranged across a variety of subjects, with the respondents subdivided into three major educational groupings: college, high school, and grade school. Some of the differences were as expected but some were not. The college educated opposed reductions in social welfare

spending by quite a margin over the grade-school group, but they opposed busing by a huge 74 percent, whereas the grade-school group opposed
it by 51 percent. The college and grade-school groups differed hardly at
all on the subject of Vietnam amnesty. The greatest difference emerged
on the abortion issue, on which they were virtually mirror opposites,
with the college educated favoring it by about 71 percent and the grade-
school group opposing by 70 percent.[38] Thus we find a mixture in which
the college educated appear, in some measure, as economic liberals and
racial conservatives. Again we are surely warranted in seconding the
warnings of Hamilton and Levison that the evidence for working-class
authoritarianism is not "clear and consistent," that it varies according to
issues and circumstances.

Nor should we forget that in our examination of political culture in
Chapter 3 we found a study of tolerance from the 1970s that sounded a
fairly optimistic note. The people were not so bad after all. We also
found that what people see as legitimate and permissible is influenced by
the goals of those being judged, and that the application of the broad
principles of the system is not a simple matter. These considerations add
weight to the cautions of Hamilton and others about contrasting the
"dark masses" with a supposedly enlightened elite.

The Masses, Their Education, and the System

We began this analysis of education by describing its sheer scale as one of
the nation's major enterprises, perhaps its largest. As for education's influence, during the early years of life it supplements the family in indoc-
trinating the values of the system, contributing to the consensus that has
made the nation's political culture so durable. At the next level education
provides skills and training for self-advancement. Citizenship training
accompanies education, although its effects are mixed. Nearly 40 percent
of high school students studied professed an active conception of the
good citizen, but in adult years this conception gave way to a more
passive one related to private rather than public concerns. Traditional
civics courses had little effect on anyone except black students from less-
educated homes. In general, the better educated and especially the college educated tended to have an enhanced interest in politics and the
world, to pick up information, to form opinions and act on them. The
cynic might argue that the nation's vast system of mass education is more
successful in preparing people for an active life of self-advancement
economically than in fostering a willingness to participate regularly in
public affairs.

Finally, education contributes to differences of opinion. It helps form liberals and conservatives. The better educated, it has been argued by many, tend to be economically conservative but liberal on other issues relating to individual rights, race, foreign policy, the use of force, and the like. The masses were seen as economic liberals but as authoritarian bigots with conservative responses to noneconomic issues. Home, school, and job were seen as reinforcing the narrow, closed minds of the masses. But in reviewing the evidence we found many reasons to question these assessments. There is some evidence of an inversion of the classes even on economic issues, a development that reflects a blurring of traditional class lines and ideologies. Watergate has to be seen as elite misconduct and the elite-oriented authors, Dye and Zeigler, see it as part of a pattern of elite repression in face of threats. The reanalysis of the studies of worker attitudes on issues of foreign policy, race, and the like by authors such as Hamilton and Levison casts doubt on the "clear and consistent" evidence of working-class authoritarianism. The workers do not always emerge as jingoes or racists and the well educated at times do.

Education makes a difference in these opinions but not as sharp a difference as it did in the past. Education has expanded, the middle class has grown, even the college educated have become a large and diverse group. Many of today's issues cut across the national political scene, and people react to them in different ways. There is good reason now to put aside stereotypes of the less educated as authoritarians ranged against the enlightened college-educated elites. At any rate, we must now turn to the subject of religion.

NOTES

1. Richard L. Seigel and Leonard B. Weinberg, *Comparing Public Policies: United States, Soviet Union, and Europe* (Homewood, Ill.: Dorsey Press, 1977), p. 258.
2. Ben J. Wattenberg, *The Real America*, rev. ed. (New York: G. P. Putnam Capricorn Books, 1976), p. 70.
3. U. S. Bureau of the Census, *Statistical Abstract of the United States, 1976* (97th ed.), Washington, D. C., 1976, pp. 115, 326.
4. Ibid., Section 4, Education, pp. 112–150. These figures should be treated as approximations, especially in higher education; the numerous kinds of adult education present some problems for any overall head count.
5. V. O. Key, Jr., *Public Opinion and American Democracy* (New York: Alfred A. Knopf, 1961), pp. 321–322.
6. Ibid., p. 316.
7. Anne E. Freedman and P. E. Freedman, *The Psychology of Political Control* (New York: St. Martin's, 1975), p. 108.
8. Associated Press dispatch, *Norman* (Okla.) *Transcript*, June 17, 1975, p. 3.
9. Richard E. Dawson and Kenneth Prewitt, *Political Socialization* (Boston: Little, Brown, 1969), p. 152.
10. Key, *Public Opinion*, pp. 316–317.

11. David Easton and Robert D. Hess, "The Child's Political World," in Norman Adler and Charles Harrington, eds., *The Learning of Political Behavior* (Glenview, Ill.: Scott, Foresman, 1970), p. 46.
12. Gabriel A. Almond and Sidney Verba, *The Civic Culture* (Princeton, N.J.: Princeton University Press, 1963), pp. 332–333.
13. Dawson and Prewitt, *Political Socialization*, p. 166.
14. Key, *Public Opinion*, p. 316.
15. Readers can easily check education and income data in a source such as *The World Almanac and Book of Facts, 1978* (New York: Newspaper Enterprise Association, 1977), p. 181.
16. *National Observer*, June 20, 1977, p. 9.
17. Albert Shanker, "Where We Stand," *New York Times Week in Review*, December 12, 1976, p. 7. Paid advertisement. As readers of the *Times* will recognize, these advertisements expressing Shanker's opinions on events of the day appear weekly.
18. Wattenberg, *The Real America*, p. 81.
19. Shanker, "Where We Stand," *New York Times Week in Review*, July 18, 1976, p. 9. Paid advertisement.
20. *The Chronicle of Higher Education*, Jan. 10, 1977, pp. 12–13.
21. M. Kent Jennings and Richard G. Niemi, *The Political Character of Adolescence: The Influence of Families and Schools* (Princeton, N.J.: Princeton University Press, 1974), pp. 152–153.
22. Ibid., pp. 271–272.
23. Sidney Verba and Norman H. Nie, *Participation in America* (New York: Harper & Row, 1972), p. 91.
24. Jennings and Niemi, *The Political Character of Adolescence*, p. 274.
25. Ibid., p. 282.
26. Ibid., p. 205.
27. Ibid., pp. 334–335.
28. Almond and Verba, *The Civic Culture*, pp. 380–381.
29. Key, *Public Opinion*, pp. 336 ff.
30. Thomas R. Dye and L. Harmon Zeigler, *The Irony of Democracy: An Uncommon Introduction to American Politics*, 4th ed. (North Scituate, Mass.: Duxbury Press, 1978), p. 131.
31. Everett Carll Ladd, Jr., with Charles D. Hadley, *Transformations of the American Party System*, 2nd ed. (New York: W. W. Norton, 1978), pp. 213 ff.
32. Gerald Pomper, Chapter 3, The Presidential Election, in Gerald Pomper, Ross K. Baker, Charles E. Jacob, Wilson Carey McWilliams, and Henry Plotkin, *The Election of 1976* (New York: David McKay, 1977); see especially pp. 60 ff.
33. Dye and Zeigler, *The Irony of Democracy*, pp. 17–21.
34. Hamilton, *Class and Politics in the United States* (New York: John Wiley, 1972), pp. 452–454.
35. Ibid., pp. 459–460.
36. Levison, *The Working-Class Majority* (New York: Penguin Books, 1975), p. 148.
37. Ibid., pp. 160–162.
38. Dennis S. Ippolito, Thomas G. Walker, and Kenneth L. Kolson, *Public Opinion and American Democracy* (Englewood Cliffs, N.J.: Prentice-Hall, 1976), pp. 94–95.

SUGGESTIONS FOR FURTHER READINGS

Philip G. Altbach. *Student Politics in America: A Historical Analysis.* New York: McGraw-Hill, 1974.
Nelson F. Ashline, Thomas R. Pelluzzo, and Charles I. Norris, eds. *Education, Inequality, and National Policy.* Lexington, Mass.: D.C. Heath, 1976. Readings that delve into one of the major controversies in education.

Caroline Bird. *The Case Against College.* New York: Bantam Books, 1975.

Howard R. Bowen. *Investment in Learning: The Individual and the Social Value of American Higher Education.* San Francisco: Jossey-Bass, 1977.

Phillip Converse and Howard Schuman. "Silent Majorities and the Vietnam War," *Scientific American,* 222 (June 1970), 70–75. A study of attitudes of the college educated toward the Vietnam war when it was still highly controversial.

David Easton and Jack Dennis. *Children in the Political System.* New York: McGraw-Hill, 1969. Political scientists explore early political socialization.

Robert D. Hess and Judith V. Torney. *The Development of Political Attitudes in Children.* Chicago: Aldine, 1967. Looks at schooling as well as the early years.

Christopher Jencks and Others. *Inequality: A Reassessment of the Effects of Family and Schooling in America.* New York: Basic Books, 1972. Jencks is an advocate of equality but this well known and controversial study casts doubt on education's contribution to mobility.

Charles Kadushin. *The American Intellectual Elite.* Boston: Little, Brown, 1974. A carefully drawn study of the American intelligentsia.

Seymour Martin Lipset. *Political Man: Where, How and Why Democracy Works in the Modern World.* Garden City, N.Y.: Doubleday, 1959.

Joel Seligman. *The High Citadel: The Influence of Harvard Law School.* Boston: Houghton Mifflin, 1978. A critical look at Harvard law training.

June L. Tapp and Lawrence Kohlberg. "Developing Senses of Law and Legal Justice," *Journal of Social Issues,* 27:2 (1971), 65–92. Applies a theory of moral development to socialization.

Norman C. Thomas. *Education in National Politics.* New York: David McKay, 1975. An examination of federal education policy and its formation during the 1960s.

Judith V. Torney, A. N. Oppenheim, and Russel F. Farnen. *Civic Education in Ten Countries.* Stockholm: Almquist and Wicksell, 1976. A carefully executed comparative study that includes the United States.

7 · Religion: A Nation of Believers

Like the family and the educational system, religion matters a good deal to the mass of Americans—more than many commentators acknowledge. In the United States the framework of religious belief goes beyond individuals and their faith to become in effect a civil religion. Officially church and state are separate. Unofficially religion permeates the system and contributes to support of it. At times religion has fueled an impulse for reform, an impulse that was readily apparent in the politics of the 1960s; but believers more often prefer a religion that comforts rather than challenges. Religion also relates importantly to the political parties and the coalitions that run through them. Catholics were long a mainstay of the Democrats. Protestants and especially the Protestant Establishment favored the Republicans. Southern Protestant Democrats were for decades a regional anomaly handed down from the past. Jews, a small but influential group, have long favored Democrats.

As important as these religious differences have been to the parties in the past, there are some indications that their influence on partisan attitudes is on the wane. On the other hand, the election in 1976 of Jimmy Carter, a "born again" Christian, is a strong reminder that religion reaches into American politics in many ways. As George Gallup suggested on the basis of a 1976 international survey, the United States may be in the first stages of a "spiritual renewal."[1] Certainly religion appeared to be thriving as the nation headed into the last quarter of the twentieth century.

The Religious Tradition and Major Faiths

Religion has long been important in the United States but the national religious tradition is distinctive. The church was separated from the state rather early in the nation's experience, when the First Amendment enjoined a separation at the national level. Over the years the states joined the trend to reinforce the separation at all levels. This early separation probably eased the national adjustment to the waves of immigration during the latter part of the nineteenth century and the early years of the twentieth. Certainly this influx, itself a unique experience among nations, added enormously to our ethnic and religious diversity.

These constitutional and population developments contributed to a religious pattern characterized by both voluntarism and diversity. There has never been a state religion, and there has not even been a truly unified and dominant religion. Protestant domination was always constrained to some degree both by differences within the large Protestant group and by the presence of considerable numbers of non-Protestant believers. In the words of S. M. Lipset, "American churches had to compete in the marketplace for support. And, conversely, membership in a given religious denomination was a voluntary act."[2] On balance, this voluntarism and the religious heterogeneity that went with it probably contributed to strengthening religion in America.

The nation's religious variety may be seen in the faiths and denominations listed in response to pollsters' questions about people's preferences in such matters. Among the major pollsters Gallup in particular has often included questions on religion; we have therefore relied heavily upon his surveys. The Gallup religious survey published in 1976 found that 61 percent of Americans were Protestant, 27 percent were Roman Catholic, and about 2 percent were Jews.[3] A remainder of 4 percent included "All others." Six percent specified "No religious preference." Among the Protestants 20 percent were Baptists, 11 percent were Methodists, Lutherans accounted for 7 percent, and 5 percent were Presbyterians. In a further survey from the early 1970s Gallup reported Episcopalians to be 3 percent of the total. At that time Protestants were about two-thirds of the total, a bit above their 61 percent in Gallup's 1976 report.[4] The Protestant group is obviously a large and diversified group that ranges from fundamentalists to others, such as Unitarians, whose Christian credentials may be questioned by some of the devout. Baptists are the largest Protestant group, but Catholics, at more than one quarter of the national total, are the largest single religious group.[5] Perhaps the success of that famous Baptist Jimmy Carter will give added impetus to Baptist growth. Several small denominations, such as the Episcopalians and Presbyterians, do not attract large numbers. But these groups tend to attract the well educated and affluent who are influential out of proportion to their numbers. Among the cynical it has even been said that aspiring officeholders may begin as humble and umpretentious Baptists and end up as wealthy Episcopalians.[6]

Believers and Their Beliefs

That Americans are a nation of believers may not shock readers, but the extent and depth of this professed faith may be surprising. As we have already noticed in examining early socialization in home and family, children often blend patriotism and religion. Certainly the typical adult American is a believer. The evidence is quite one-sided. For instance, in response to the question "Do you believe in a God or a universal spirit?" 94 percent of Americans answered in the affirmative in Gallup's 1976 survey. In 1968, when they were asked simply "Do you believe in a God?" 98 percent of Americans responded with a "Yes."[7] Obviously people may mean many different things when they refer to a deity or a "universal spirit," yet the fact that so few profess disbelief is surely significant.

Other responses show the same willingness to profess a religious faith of some nature. In the 1968 survey 85 percent claimed to believe in heaven,[8] 65 percent believed in hell, and fully 60 percent believed in the devil. Nearly three-fourths claimed to believe in life after death. In the 1976 survey, nearly 70 percent professed a belief in immortality. Reincarnation may or may not be seen as a form of life after death, but one-fifth of those answering in 1968 professed to believe in it. If these survey results are to be trusted, Americans are overwhelmingly believers and most believers retain rather traditional forms of faith.

In addition, Americans *say* that religion matters to them. In the 1976 survey 86 percent reported that their religious beliefs were either "Very important" or "Fairly important," with over half in the first category. And although more than half of those polled in a 1975 survey thought religion was losing its influence on American life, individuals found support in it. Three-fifths said they believed that "Religion can answer all or most of today's problems."[9] Only one-fifth thought it "Old-fashioned." Another set of questions from the 1975 survey asked about confidence in institutions. The "church or organized religion" came out far ahead of the public schools, the Supreme Court, Congress, newspapers, labor unions, and big business. On another question, one-fourth described themselves as "Very religious" and three-fifths as "Fairly religious." Only 11 percent said "Not at all religious."

Another interesting question in the 1975 survey was: "How often do you feel that you follow your religious beliefs and take concrete action on behalf of others. . .?" In answer, 58 percent of the churchgoers said "Almost always" and 22 percent said "Often," for a total of 80 percent. Only 17 percent of churchgoers responded with "Occasionally" and the percentages for "Seldom," "Hardly ever," and "Can't say" were minute. Among nonchurchgoers one-third said "Almost always" and 18 percent replied "Often," a total of 50 percent. About one-fifth responded with "Occasionally." Only 28 percent of the nonchurchgoers responded with "Seldom," "Hardly ever," or "Can't say." Thus among churchgoers and nonchurchgoers large percentages claimed to follow their religious beliefs and to "take concrete action on behalf of others" either "Almost always," "Often," or "Occasionally." Only about a quarter of the nonchurchgoers fell into categories designating a separation of faith from action on behalf of others. These figures are intriguing. Respondents are judging themselves and are free to interpret what is meant by "concrete action" in accord with their faith. Still, it is apparent that large percentages *think* they relate religious precept and action with some frequency.

Apart from what people say they do, there is the matter of action. In the 1976 survey 71 percent claimed to be a member of a church or synagogue. As for attending church during "an average week" 40 percent had done so in 1975. Surveys for previous years found this same 40 percent attending church from 1971 on. Over the years Gallup has been measuring church attendance he has found that Protestants have changed little since 1964. There was also little change in the limited number of Jews, nearly 20 percent, reporting attendance at a synagogue. The main change nationally has been a drop in Catholic attendance, with a drop at all age levels but especially so among the younger Catholics. Most of this drop occurred during the latter part of the 1960s. The overall stability in reported church attendance since 1971 seems to indicate that the Catholic decline has been halted. Indeed, Catholics have consistently exceeded Protestants in their church attendance by 54 percent to 38 percent.

Another religious activity is Bible reading, a subject on which Gallup reported in the 1975 survey. Respondents were asked if they had read "any part of the Bible at home within the last year." This wording would naturally rule out travelers who might pick up the Bible to read in motels and hotels when the usual home entertainments were not available. Nationally, 63 percent responded affirmatively. Among Protestants, 75 percent claimed to have read the Bible during the past year. Catholics' church attendance tends to run ahead of Protestants' but Protestants are more likely than Catholics to read the Bible.

Industrialization and the Faithful

Comparisons across nations and over time confirm the importance of religion to Americans. Gallup, in summarizing his findings from the 1976 survey, found the United States to be in an odd position, standing "at the top of the industrial societies in the importance religion plays in the lives of its citizens." Religion was also quite important in parts of the globe characterized by low levels of education, such as sub-Sahara Africa, the Far East, and Latin America. There were signs of a collapse of faith in Europe and industrial nations elsewhere, but not in the United States. Repeated surveys in the United States have found the belief in a supreme being in some form persistently high—about 90 percent—whereas similar surveys have found declines in many nations of Western Europe and in Australia. (See Table 7-1.)

Table 7-1   Belief in God or a Universal Spirit in Selected Democratic Nations and Regions, 1975

Nation or Region	Percent Affirming Belief
United States	94
Canada	89
Italy	88
Australia	80
Benelux	78
United Kingdom	76
France	72
West Germany	72
Scandinavia	65
Japan*	38

Source: Gallup Opinion Index, Report #130, "Religion in America" 1976.
*Japan is the only nation listed that is not in the Judaeo-Christian tradition.

As for the future, Gallup wrote, "Looking at religious trends for the nation as a whole, little evidence can be found of any widespread growth in disenchantment with religion in the last decade and a half." He cited a special survey conducted among young people in Dayton, Ohio, a setting selected as a "weathervane" area for the nation. Gallup found attitudes such that the "church might have surprising success in trying to reach young people." As he described it young people were "remarkably religious," "pro-church in certain respects," and "hungry for the mystical and transcendant." He did find criticism and in some respects "organized religion came under heavy fire" from the young. Yet this criticism did not entail a wholesale rejection of all religion. The potential was there if church leadership could reach it.

What these figures add up to is a distinctive religious tradition characterized by voluntarism, diversity, and high levels of faith. And in this last especially the United States is unique among the industrialized nations. Most Americans say their religious beliefs are important to them and are used in their daily lives; half of the nonchurchgoers make such a claim for their faith. Even if we take some of this information on American religious belief and practice with a grain of salt, we are surely warranted in concluding that the United States is a nation of believers. Some of this faith may well be hypocritical and worse, but it is hard to deny that in one form or another religion retains a pervasive hold on Americans.

The Unofficial Civil Religion

The American tradition of voluntarism and diversity, combined with official separation of church and state, has produced a "civil religion" that unofficially melds a secular state and a highly religious people. This idea has been slow in gaining recognition and has remained somewhat elusive and controversial. Martin E. Marty, writing about it in the 1970s, cited one explanation of civil religion expressed in the 1950s by Will Herberg. Herberg summarized this civil religion as

> an organic structure of ideas, values, and beliefs that constitutes a faith common to Americans as Americans, and is genuinely operative in their lives. . . Sociologically, anthropologically, it is the American religion, undergirding American national life and overarching American society. . . And it is a civil religion in the strictest sense of the term, for in it, national life is apotheosized, national values are religionized, national heroes are divinized, national history is experienced . . . as a redemptive history.[10]

But it was Robert N. Bellah who in 1967 brought the subject to the fore. His well-known article dwelt heavily on the use of religious symbolism and principles in national life. In the early days of the republic, Bellah argued, there was an early form of the civil religion: "What we have, then, from the earliest years of the republic is a collection of beliefs, symbols, and rituals with respect to sacred things and institutionalized in a collectivity. This religion—there seems no other word for it—while not antithetical to and indeed sharing much in common with Christianity, was neither sectarian nor in any specific sense Christian."[11] Even then there was a pervasive religious feeling that applied in the public sector but which was not associated specifically with any particular faith.

Bellah carried this analysis into the present with an exploration of the meaning of references to God in John F. Kennedy's inaugural address in 1961. After all, in view of the separation of church and state it could be said that the president should leave religion aside. But Kennedy, like other presidents, did not. As Bellah explained:

> Although matters of personal religious belief, worship, and association are considered to be strictly private affairs, there are, at the same time, certain common elements of religious orientation that the great majority of Ameri-

cans share. These have played a crucial role in the development of American institutions and still provide a religious dimension for the whole fabric of American life, including the political sphere. This public religion is expressed in a set of beliefs, symbols, and rituals.[12]

But it was more than "beliefs, symbols, and rituals." It also provided a "grounding for the rights of man which makes any form of political absolutism illegitimate" and a "transcendant goal for the political process." Religion, then, helps legitimate political rights and the purposes or goals of the nation. Insofar as these rights and goals are prescribed by an authority above and beyond the government, the government is held to a high standard, a standard independent of it. Religion thus helps to reinforce the democratic idea that government serves the people and should be held accountable to their moral and religious ideals.

Civil religion remains an elusive idea capable of varied meanings, not all of them benign. High ideals may be perverted to serve destructive ends. The civil religion did not prevent Americans from holding slaves well into the 1860s. Nor is the record of American violence, at home and abroad, easy to fit into a scheme of human ideals rooted in the people's religious feelings. But even most critics would probably concede that the nation has been better off with a civil religion and without one altogether.

An older Gallup survey lends significant support to the concept of a civil religion. In 1958 Gallup tested people's reactions to a variety of characteristics of candidates for president. This was of course two years before the country elected its first Catholic president. The survey asked people if they would vote for a "generally well qualified candidate" who also happened to have one or another characteristic that might influence voter judgment. These characteristics included being a Catholic, a Baptist, a Jew, a Negro, a woman, and an atheist. Only 3 percent said they would vote against the Baptist candidate, but 25 percent opposed the Catholic and 28 percent opposed the Jew. Forty-three percent opposed the woman, 53 percent opposed the Negro, and a full 75 percent opposed the atheist.[13] The candidate described as nonreligious, even antireligious, was much less acceptable than the candidate who was either female or black. The good American, including the officeholder, should be a believer of *some* sort.

A study conducted by a number of sociologists and published in 1976 acknowledges the sparse research on the subject of civil religion and also confesses to some problems of definition. For their purposes they relied on Bellah's ideas plus "related literature, consultation, and imagination," and they took as their sample a group of people who had attended a Protestant religious crusade in May of 1970 and had agreed to cooperate in further research. Thus the research had serious limitations. Nevertheless, the authors stated quite plainly in conclusion, "Despite the lack of previous evidence, the anticipated civil religion dimension is found to exist empirically. As anticipated, it exists somewhat apart from three other church religion dimensions . . . The separate existence of civil religion is in accord with the Hammond, Yinger, and Bellah thesis."[14] Certainly this evidence is in accord with what we know of the public's religious beliefs and the tendency for religion to pervade public life.

This civil religion is important but is a set of beliefs and practices not easily specified. Certainly it does color citizenship, and elected officials are expected to acknowledge some faith, whatever it may be. In addition, the nation and political system are supposed to have a religious basis that reinforces, legitimizes, and provides ideals for what is officially a secular system. Divine Providence is threaded through things American and has long been an aspect of the political culture. In the eyes of most people God is on America's side, and there is not much concern about the niceties of separating church and state.

Religion, Reform, and Quiescence

Religion pervades the system's rituals. But does it, whether as a civil religion or in some other form, address the controversies of the day directly? Does it challenge as well as comfort? Rodney Stark and Charles Glock explain the difference: "The comforting function is to provide persons with inner peace, with the ability to cope with their various existential anxieties. The challenging function, on the other hand, refers to efforts of the churches to exert moral leadership, to arouse members' interest in matters larger than themselves."[15]

That the church has entered the political arena to challenge aspects of the existing order and to provide a reformist impulse was evident in the activism of the 1960s. Perhaps the best example occurred in conjunction with the passage of the Civil Rights Act of 1964. This major piece of legislation wound through Congress for months and was finally signed by President Johnson in the summer of 1964. In the spring, religious leaders from all three major faiths, Protestant, Catholic, and Jewish, announced a national interreligious convocation. Religious officials described it as the "largest gathering of ministers, priests, and rabbis ever before assembled in a witness to racial justice." Church historians of the three faiths were also quoted as claiming that this large gathering would be "the first time in the history of Christendom that the church has spoken with one voice, if at all, on an issue of such contemporary social and political concern."[16] This unprecedented gathering of religious leadership was functioning effectively in a "challenging" role, exerting their moral force to arouse members' interests in an issue of major social and political significance.

But when religion functions to challenge rather than to comfort, those who prefer the latter may react unhappily, and the evidence available suggests that most of the faithful do prefer the latter. A Gallup survey of 1968, asked, "Should the churches keep out of political and social matters—or should they express their views on day-to-day social and political questions?" In response 53 percent said "Keep out," 40 percent opted for "Express views," and 7 percent had "No opinion." Gallup pointed out that this marked a change from 1975, when 44 percent favored the "Keep out" alternative and a slight plurality of 47 percent favored the expression of church views. In the 1968 survey three main reasons were given by those who opposed having the church speak out.[17] The most important reason was the feeling that the church's first duty is "to comfort the individual." Second was the view that religious leaders lacked the expertise to cope with social and political problems. Third was the desire to have the churches "concentrate on raising the levels of religious belief and practice."

Stark and Glock confirm this characteristic preference. They note that not only do much of the laity prefer comfort to challenge but that the *"comfort-seekers constitute the bulk of the most active Christian laity: it is their money and participation upon which contemporary Christian organizations rest. Thus, there is built-in resistance to the challenge function in the churches.* Efforts to confront these people with challenges lead to conflict and often to rebellion."[18] The very activists who are of central importance to the voluntary activities of the church are mostly "comfort-seekers." Stark and Glock recognize that the potential for lay rebellion varies from church to church but nonetheless conclude, "In this sense, the contemporary churches are held captive by a comfort-seeking laity who want their pastor to devote all his time to private religious needs."

We may add to this the warning of Albert J. Menendez, who states succinctly that "most Americans, including even many churchgoers, tend to compartmentalize private beliefs and public decisions."[19] Here we have another dimension of privatism, in which religion perceived as primarily to comfort rather than to challenge becomes largely an extension of personal concerns. This widespread attitude of course acts as a constraint on those who would prefer a church that challenges, and is especially hard on activist religious leaders.

The impact of such built-in resistance could be seen as the 1960s wore on and church activism fell off. Increasingly the answer among the laity to the question "To march or not to march" was negative.[20] By the early 1970s a survey of religious leaders found many of them frustrated and willing to leave the church. Nearly 40 percent of young Protestant and Roman Catholic clergymen in the survey reported such thoughts and among young Jewish clergymen the proportion was six in ten. They were, Gallup reported, "disillusioned and bewildered over their role in church and society." A Methodist minister in Virginia said, "The laity has grown complacent. They have become a hindrance to the true aims of the church. They want a social club rather than an active and challenging organization."[21]

At times American religious beliefs provide a challenging and reformist impulse, and they did so significantly during the 1960s. Yet overall, most Americans tend to see their religion as an extension of the personal sector rather than a call to public action.

Religion and the New Deal Coalition

American religious beliefs gave rise to a civil religion that helps sustain and unify, but the relationships of religious groups to political parties contribute to divisions. According to Ladd and Hadley, the Catholic-Protestant division as it relates to the parties has roots in American history that long antedate the New Deal:

> For more than a century, stretching from well before the Civil War until years after World War II, the *Protestant-Catholic* division served as the great organizer of American ethnic struggles. In the sense intended by this depiction, *Protestant* and *Catholic* represent not so much religious as more general ethnocultural traditions . . . And the Democratic party functioned as the partisan home of large majorities of Catholic Americans as it did battle with largely Protestant, and at times anti-Catholic, opponents—the Whigs and subsequently the Republicans.[22]

Protestant and Catholic represented somewhat different world views rooted in religion and projected onto party divisions. Ladd and Hadley examine these differences, noting, incidentally, that southern Protestants were somewhat apart within the regional differences that set off the South. The Jewish vote has long been one-sidedly Democratic,[23] although in 1976 it was below the Democratic norm.

Ladd and Hadley argue that the major division between Protestants and Catholics persisted up through the election of 1960, when "with the emergence of a new ethnocultural frontier, the historic Protestant-Catholic divide began to lose its grip on American life."[24] The changes that took place in the United States during the 1960s and afterward worked to mute religious differences and corresponding partisan differences. The Catholic bloc began to shift away from the New Deal Democratic coalition. Ladd and Hadley diagram this shift dramatically by singling out the trend in the vote of Catholics who were also non-southern big city whites. From 1936 up through 1972 the trend in their vote was, with some variations, less and less Democratic. There has been a "decline in the relative margin of Democratic support among such overlapping groups as big city, working-class whites outside the South, and urban Catholic voters."[25]

Projection of these trends over several decades is particularly persuasive. On this basis there is good reason to believe that Catholic voters, and Protestant voters too, have been loosening their ties to the party coalitions that long shaped the political scene. Ladd and Hadley see the major reasons for the loosening of Catholic ties to the Democrats as a combination of rising affluence and the intrusion of new, noneconomic issues associated with the 1960s. Catholic workers were becoming increasingly middle class. And although not necessarily increasingly conservative on economic and welfare-state issues, they were not comfortable with the rising demands for social and cultural change by blacks, women, and other groups. In these remarks there are overtones, although muted, of Kevin Phillips' argument for an emerging conservative majority based largely on a growing white middle class.

The Narrowing Gap

Evidence for shifting Catholic attitudes and a muting of Catholic-Protestant differences may be seen in a series of Gallup polls from the late 1960s. The issues included economic matters, integration and other racial problems, crime, and even "jail for drinking drivers." On some issues, such as those having to do with crime and looters, there was no real difference. On such matters as the guaranteed income Catholics were appreciably less opposed, by a margin of 53 percent to the Protestants' 61 percent.[26] Catholics were also less likely to see integration as proceeding "too fast" and were more receptive than Protestants to open-housing laws. Here the Catholics were a bit more liberal than Protestants but not by much. There was a more marked difference on "jail for drinking drivers." Less than a third of Catholics favored such punishment but nearly 45 percent of Protestants endorsed it. The difference probably relates to the willingness of some Protestants to oppose any consumption of alcohol and to support Prohibition.

But the most telling responses were those about divorce and birth control. On a question pertaining to the easing of divorce laws, Protestants and Catholics differed not at all. A series of questions related to "artificial methods of birth control" actually included reference to Pope Paul VI's encyclical banning such methods. This introduces an element that one might think would give Catholics pause and tend to differentiate their responses quite sharply. But on a question that referred explicitly to the pope's position on birth control, Catholics divided 54 percent in favor of birth control and only 28 percent against. Protestants split not much differently, with 62 percent in favor, only 8 percent more than the Catholics, and 13 percent opposed. These American Catholic respondents were evidently not greatly influenced by the reference to their church leader's position. Certainly they expressed preferences surprisingly close to those of non-Catholics.

A further question asked if a person could practice birth control and "still be a good Catholic." Protestants and Catholics split unexpectedly here: 65 percent of the Catholics felt they could be good Catholics and practice birth control but only 49 percent of the Protestants thought so. In this case, and perhaps in others as well, some Protestants were evidently out of touch with their Catholic brethren. Further questions relating to government release of birth control information revealed little difference between Catholics and Protestants. The one issue in this series on which a sharp difference emerged was one that pertained to celibacy for priests. Protestants were quite willing to permit priests to marry, by a majority of 75 percent. Catholics split with 42 percent in favor and 49 percent opposed. (Presumably, however, this issue is not likely to become of major concern to the political parties.)

In the main, then, we can see that Catholic-Protestant differences had narrowed by the late 1960s. Catholics still tilted a bit more to the left on economic and racial issues than the Protestants but not by much. If Protestant-Catholic views on divorce and birth control had by this time become quite similar then there is good reason to conclude that by the late 1960s religion mattered much less to partisan conflict than it once did.

Further evidence of declining religious differences and waning church influence on officeholders is available in Menendez' analysis of religion and politics. One bit of evidence is a study cited by Menendez in which the author determined that in the Senate there were thirty-one members who could be counted on "consistently to defend Catholic values and support fair treatment of Catholic citizens and their institutions." This group would amount to about one-third of the Senate, an impressive bloc. The author found, however, that 90 percent of Baptist senators were in this select group but only 54 percent of Catholic senators.[27] It seems odd to think of Baptist senators "consistently" defending Catholic values, but a proposal in 1976 to provide federal aid to parochial and private schools split Catholic senators, with six opposed and seven in favor.

This narrowing of religious differences reached a culmination of sorts in the election of 1972. Of course in carrying the country by a landslide vote of just over 60 percent, Richard Nixon tilted all groups in a Republican direction. Still, it is significant that the Catholic vote split for the first time in a direction that favored the Republican by a slight margin of 52 percent.[28] Momentarily, at least, Republicans gained a majority of a group that was a major bloc in the old New Deal coalition.

Yet there is still the election of 1976 to account for. Although Gerald Pomper concluded that the Jimmy Carter coalition did differ significantly from the classic New deal coalition,[29] Menendez subjected the religious vote to particularly close scrutiny.[30] Carter did carry the Catholic vote, Menendez found, with about 55 percent. But "Catholics were the soft underbelly of the Carter-Mondale strategy for reconstructing the Roosevelt coalition. The Democrats were somewhat more successful among other segments of the coalition." Democrats had to have this Catholic vote to win but were just barely successful. Jews also voted for Carter but, Menendez thought, below their Democratic norm. On the other hand, Carter did better than usual, for a Democrat, among Protestants. Baptists in particular, according to Menendez, "gave him a majority of their votes," the first Baptist majority given a Democrat since 1948, when Harry Truman—also a Baptist—won the presidency. "Even in 1972 George McGovern ran 18 percent better among Catholics than Protestants. The gap narrowed to 9 percent or less in 1976 and may continue to do so." And in analyzing the Catholic vote around the country Menendez inclined to the view that "suburban Catholics gave a majority for Ford."

Menendez' view is that "The relative decline in Catholic Democratic vote support in 1976 was probably due to a combination of many factors: distrust that a small town Southerner could really understand the needs of urban dwellers; traditional Catholic reserve about candidates who emphasize public morality." But this analysis lends itself to the interpretation that the Catholic vote was, in part at least, candidate and issue oriented rather than party oriented. By the mid-1970s the Democrats could no longer count on the Catholics' loyalty. Their vote was up for grabs. This change did not come about overnight, but Catholics have changed, as the nation has. They may vote Democratic in a given election, but they may also *not* vote Democratic. And unless some particularly potent issue or candidate appears to arouse Catholics as John Kennedy did in 1960, it is likely that their vote will not differ greatly from the Protestant vote.

The Pattern of Religious Belief

American history fostered a national religious experience of diversity and voluntarism. Americans continued to be believers; secularism did not set in. Most Americans believe in a supreme being and accept the traditional religious world view of heaven, hell, the devil, and immortality. They think religion important in their lives, retain confidence in it above other institutions, and claim to follow religious precepts in dealings with others. By 1976 there were even signs of a religious renewal. Religious feeling has carried over into an unofficial civil religion that undergirds and legitimates the system, yet also provides ideals by which to judge the nation and its government. In any case, the good American should be a believer. Religion is seen as a normal and natural part of the system, alongside an officially secular state. People's religion may serve either to comfort or to challenge. Religious activism was readily apparent during the 1960s, especially on racial issues and the war, but the preference of most believers for a religion that comforts constrained this activism. The "renewal" cited by observers in 1976 would seem to fit comfortably with the American tendency to privatize religion.

But apart from the generalized religious acceptance of most Americans, the different denominations and faiths have long been related to political party divisions. For many decades Catholics were a bastion of support for Democrats while Protestants outside the South supported Republicans. The New Deal coalition drew heavily upon the Catholic vote and also the small but strategic Jewish vote. This pattern persisted through 1960, when the old religious world view went into decline. By the late 1960s Protestants and Catholics were not far apart on the issues, even some issues of special sensitivity for Catholics. This trend continued into the 1970s, and by 1976 the Carter coalition had majority Catholic support but also much Protestant support. The differences between the religious groups were smaller than ever.

Divisive issues persisted. Some Catholics felt strongly about such issues as abortion and aid to parochial schools. Jews felt strongly about Israel. And there were some fundamentalists on hand who regarded all the others as sinners bound for the flames of hell. Yet in the main religious differences did seem to be waning even as, rather paradoxically, the country verged on a spiritual renewal. With a Sunday School-teaching Baptist in the White House the nation's religious tendencies, both public and private, were presumably well assured for a time. Unfortunately, it is not possible to be as optimistic about the nation's ethnic affairs, the next topic in our analysis of mass influence.

NOTES

1. *Gallup Opinion Index*, "Religion in America, 1976," Report No. 130, p. 5. This report was a portion of a global survey on religion conducted by the Gallup organization for the Charles F. Kettering Foundation.
2. S. M. Lipset, *The First New Nation* (New York: Basic Books, 1963), p. 160.
3. *Gallup Opinion Index*, "Religion in America, 1976," pp. 34–35.
4. *Gallup Opinion Index*, April 1971, p. 71.
5. Albert J. Menendez, *Religion at the Polls* (Philadelphia, Pa.: Westminster Press, 1977), pp. 16–17. Menendez lists Baptists as totaling 29 million and Catholics 48 million.
6. There is a hint of support for this perhaps overworked political maxim in the finding that "a higher percentage of Episcopalians are converts from other churches, than in any other major denomination." See Menendez, *Religion at the Polls*, p. 131.
7. *Gallup Opinion Index*, February 1969, p. 5. Gallup has asked this question a number of times over the years and the response is always on the order of nine to one in the affirmative.
8. *Gallup Opinion Index*, February 1969, pp. 16 ff.
9. *Gallup Opinion Index*, "Religion in America, 1975," Report No. 114. This report is based on surveys conducted in 1973 and 1974. See pp. 14 ff.
10. Quoted in Martin E. Marty, *A Nation of Behavers* (Chicago: University of Chicago Press, 1976), p. 186.
11. Robert N. Bellah, "Civil Religion in America," *Daedalus*, 96 (Winter 1967), 8.
12. Ibid., 3, 4.
13. George H. Gallup, *The Gallup Poll: Public Opinion 1935–1971*, vol. 2 (New York: Random House, 1972), pp. 1574–1576.
14. Ronald C. Wimberly, Donald C. Clelland, Thomas C. Hood, and C.M. Lipsey, "The Civil Religious Demension: Is It There?" *Social Forces*, 54 (June 1976), 898.
15. Rodney Stark and Charles Y. Glock, "Prejudice and the Churches," in Glock, ed., *Religion in Sociological Perspective* (Belmont Calif.: Wadsworth, 1973), p. 99.
16. New York Times Service dispatch, *Daily Oklahoman*, April 10, 1964, p. 16.
17. *New York Times*, April 12, 1968, p. 10.
18. Stark and Glock, "Prejudice and the Churches," *Religion in Sociological Perspective*, p. 100.
19. Menendez, *Religion at the Polls*, p. 168.
20. One analysis of these trends is Francine du Plessix Gray's "To March or Not to March," *New York Times*, June 27, 1976, p. 6.
21. *Gallup Opinion Index*, April 1971, p. 1.
22. Everett Carll Ladd, Jr., with Charles D. Hadley, *Transformations of the American Party System*, 2nd ed. (New York: W.W. Norton, 1978), pp. 46–47.
23. Ibid., p. 63.
24. Ibid., p. 121.
25. Ibid., p. 234.
26. *Gallup Opinion Index*, "Views of Protestants and Catholics on Issues," February 1969, pp. 35 ff. The surveys reported here were conducted in 1968.
27. Menendez, *Religion at the Polls*, pp. 203–204. For more discussion of the Catholic population, politically and in other respects, see Andrew Greeley, *The American Cath-*

olic (New York: Basic Books, 1977). Greeley sees a weakening of the hold of the institutional church on Catholics, although not a rejection of Catholicism itself, and is critical of church leadership.

28. Menendez has an analysis of this election and of reasons for Nixon's appeal to Catholics. See *Religion at the Polls*, pp. 89 ff.
29. Gerald M. Pomper, Ross K. Baker, Charles E. Jacob, Wilson Carey McWilliams, and Henry A. Plotkin, *The Election of 1976* (New York: David McKay, 1977), Chapter 3.
30. Menendez, *Religion at the Polls*, pp. 188 ff.

SUGGESTIONS FOR FURTHER READINGS

E. Digby Baltzell. *The Protestant Establishment: Aristocracy and Caste in America.* New York: Random House Vintage Books, 1964. Class, Protestantism, and anti-Semitism in America.

Robert N. Bellah. *The Broken Covenant: American Civil Religion in a Time of Trial.* New York: Seabury Press, 1975. Bellah is the chief proponent of the civil religion thesis.

Charles Y. Glock, ed. *Religion in Sociological Perspective.* Belmont, Calif. Wadsworth, 1973. Readings collected by two well-known scholars of this subject.

Charles Y. Glock and Rodney Stark. *Christian Beliefs and Anti-Semitism.* New York: Harper Torchbooks, 1969. Two sociologists of religion present their perspective.

Andrew M. Greeley. *The American Catholic.* New York: Basic Books, 1977. Greeley, a forceful writer with a point of view, explains and defends modern American Catholicism.

Will Herberg. *Protestant, Catholic, and Jew.* New York: Doubleday, 1955. Well written and provocative even if now a bit dated.

Robert Jewett. *The Captain America Complex.* Philadelphia, Pa.: Westminster Press, 1973. An examination of the consequences for foreign policy of a national religious heritage linked to a zealous nationalism.

Everett Carll Ladd, Jr. with Charles D. Hadley. *Transformations of the American Party System.* 2nd ed. New York: W. W. Norton, 1978. A good analysis of religion and politics, past and present.

Stephen D. Isaacs. *Jews and American Politics.* New York: Doubleday, 1974.

Gerhard Lenski. *The Religious Factor: A Sociologist's Study of Religion's Impact on Politics, Economics, and Family Life.* Garden City, N.Y.: Doubleday Anchor Books, 1963. A well-written and interesting study based heavily upon a Detroit area survey.

Gary Marx. "Religion: Opiate or Inspiration of Civil Rights Militancy Among Negroes?" *American Sociological Review*, 32 (February 1967), 64–72. Marx questions the extent to which black churches contribute to civil rights militancy.

Milton Rokeach. "Part I. Value Systems in Religion. Part II. Religious Values and Social Compassion." *Review of Religious Research*, II (Fall 1969), 3–39. Rokeach examines forms of religious expression and their relationship to values such as compassion.

Leo Rosten, ed. *Religions of America: Ferment and Faith in an Age of Crisis, A New Guide and Almanac.* New York: Simon and Schuster, 1975.

Rodney Stark, Bruce Foster, Charles Y. Glock, and Harold Quinley. *Wayward Shepherds: Prejudice and the Protestant Clergy*. New York: Harper & Row, 1971. A continuation of Glock and Stark's study of religion and anti-Semitism that also tests in a California setting the relationship between religion and social activism.

M. C. Thomas and C. C. Flippen. "American Civil Religion: An Empirical Study." *Social Forces*, 51 (December 1972), 218–225. The study tests Bellah's civil religion thesis on a limited scale and fails to find strong support for it.

8 · Ethnic Differences: Assimilation and the Quest for Equality with Diversity

Many of the influences we have discussed so far tend to reinforce the system. This is notably true of the family and of education. Religion also contributes, in spite of doctrinal differences, via the civil religion sustained on a voluntaristic basis. But the nation's unusually complex population mix seems to operate in the other direction, toward diversity and differences. Frequently the "differences" have taken the form of prejudice, hostility, and violence. To see the nation as made up of undifferentiated "masses" does no justice to the country's ethnic and racial diversity. When President Franklin Roosevelt addressed the Daughters of the American Revolution as "my fellow immigrants" he punctured their pretensions but also reminded them of an important truth.

Perhaps the Indians should not have allowed that first boatload of settlers to land. But they did, and new Americans have been arriving since. At times they came in great numbers. According to one authority, Milton Gordon, "The 41 million immigrants who have come to America since the founding of the nation constitute the largest population transfer of its kind in the history of the world . . ."[1] Most newcomers joined the system voluntarily but some entered involuntarily as slaves under conditions that were brutal and demeaning.[2] The Mexican-Americans living in territory seized by United States forces in the nation's expansion south did not enter voluntarily. Many Asians came as menial laborers and suffered their share of discrimination and lynchings. For that matter, the native Americans, the Indians, joined the system—insofar as their anomalous position can be called joining—on terms that were anything but free and uncoerced.

Restrictive legislation passed during the 1920s sharply reduced the flood of new Americans from Europe and Asia, but immigration continues at the rate of a few hundred thousand per year. In addition others have entered illegally, mostly from Mexico and more recently from the Caribbean. The number of Mexicans who join their Chicano brothers illegally is hard to determine with any accuracy but probably totaled well over 5 million by the mid-1970s. The United States is unique among modern nations—with Israel a partial exception—in the extent to which it has drawn its population from diverse groups of people.

The formation of a strong and durable nation in spite of this diversity is a feat that requires us to give special attention to ethnic groups and the varied ways in which they have been perceived and related to the American polity. The meaning of "ethnic group" varies but, following the usage of one noted authority, we may briefly sum it up as a feeling that a group shares a common sense of "peoplehood."[3] And, of course, we have already seen something of how related kinds of diversity have influenced the political system. We need first to examine concepts of assimilation and their implications; then we shall focus on black-white relationships, the area that most dramatically illustrates the challenge America faces in dealing with ethnic diversity. Blacks, the most loyal of the Democratic coalition's supporters, are a large and highly visible minority whose presence tests the coalition and the society at large. The importance of this group may be recognized in *Statistical Abstract* figures listing black population for 1976 as nearly 25 million, which was 12 percent of the total of about 215 million.

Concepts of Assimilation

The struggle to pull together in one nation a highly diversified population is reflected in all the concepts of assimilation that relate minorities and the core culture. The major concepts that Milton Gordon presents include Anglo-conformity, the melting pot, and pluralism. Assimilation has not meant any one single thing.

According to Gordon, Anglo-conformity theory "demanded the complete renunciation of the immigrants' ancestral culture in favor of the behavior and values of the Anglo-Saxon core . . ." Anglo-conformity had its variations but all had as a "central assumption the desirability of maintaining English institutions (as modified by the American Revolution), the English language, the English-oriented cultural patterns as dominant and standard in American life."[4] It could be racist but was not necessarily so. In racist form it saw the Aryan or Nordic races as superior and led to policies such as a chauvinistic stress on American antecedents, antagonism to foreigners, and opposition to immigration. But the early American leaders who fought against an established religion and saw America as a haven for the persecuted obviously differed from the angry exclusionists. To some advocates of Anglo-conformity the issue was culture more than race. Today it is difficult not to notice racial overtones in all forms of Anglo-conformity, and on this ground it is easy to criticize and reject. As Gordon states, it has probably been "the most prevalent ideology of assimilation in America throughout the nation's history."[5] Militant blacks who attack America as essentially a racist society also perceive the Anglo-conformity model as still dominant.

A contrasting model is the melting pot, a theory that achieved much currency at the turn of the century and thereafter. In the melting pot no one ethnic strain would be dominant. Indeed, no identifiable strains would persist indefinitely. All would melt or fuse together to create a new type. As expressed by Gordon the melting pot concept would think of American society "not simply as a slightly modified England but rather as a totally new blend, culturally and biologically, in which the stocks and folkways of Europe were, figuratively speaking, indiscriminately mixed in the political pot of the emerging nation and melted together by the fires of American influence and interaction into a distinctly new type . . ."[6] In this concept all ethnic groups are treated as equal, but it is also true that groups disappear in the fusing of identities that is to become the new American type. For this reason Gordon views this process of acculturation as "hardly distinguishable in nature from that of Anglo-conformity."[7] Irish, Poles, Jews, and others are to disappear as identifiable groups sustaining a "sense of peoplehood." The melting pot would be tough on those who did not melt easily.

Yet as Gordon adds, some ethnic merging has occurred on a religious basis. Nationalities that have a common religion have tended to intermarry and to break down nationality lines. Protestant nationality groups like the English and Germans have tended to intermarry. So have the Irish, the Italians, and the Poles within their common bond of Catholicism. The third major religious group, Jews, have largely married other Jews, often of different national origins. A single national melting pot to fuse all groups never existed. Instead there evolved what some have called a "triple melting pot" formed from the three major faiths, Protestant, Catholic, and Jewish.[8] In addition there are racial groups, especially the blacks, which were not permitted to assimilate with the others. Given these and other variations on the assimilation process, Gordon eventually projects a complex society in which some groups have assimilated or melted almost completely while others persist as distinctive groups because of religious, racial, and national differences.

For all its variations the melting pot concept has an appealing egalitarian ring and is akin to the ideal of racial integration in a free, equal, and harmonious society. In this vein the late Martin Luther King wrote of integration as necessary to liberation. He saw a liberated society as one freed of racism and he took liberals to task for not accepting interracial marriage. As King expressed it, "The question of intermarriage is never raised in a society freed of the disease of racism."[9] King's ideal of a liberated, nonracist society accords reasonably well with the melting pot idea.

Whatever the attractions of the melting pot, many reject it in favor of a third concept of assimilation, pluralism. Pluralism, which Gordon refers to as "cultural pluralism," is complex. For it is a compromise which recognizes that a common culture in some things is desirable but also insists on the desirability of preserving some ethnic distinctiveness. Subsocieties with their own folkways should persist within the larger society. A basic distinction is drawn between primary and secondary relationships. Primary relationships pertain to the home, family, intermarriage, and to the close personal bonds that may extend into the neighborhood and community associations. These the pluralist would preserve as ethnically distinct. Secondary relationships are connections between people that are usually not highly personal but are characteristic of the economic and political sector and the system's culture as a whole. In these matters people should be treated as equal and ethnic identifications should be disregarded. As Gordon sums up this combination, cultural pluralism means "keeping primary group relations across ethnic lines sufficiently minimal to prevent a significant amount of intermarriage, while cooperating with other groups and individuals in secondary relations of political action, economic life, and civil responsibility."[10] Thus the pluralist accepts the political culture and other public sector relationships as the same for all but demands that close personal relationships be governed by distinctive ethnic bonds.

An eloquent statement by a Mexican-American in south Texas, John Salazar, vividly expresses much of the sense of the pluralist position:

> We want equal opportunities for jobs and equal pay for equal work. We want to share the material benefits of American technology. We also want the right to be different from the Anglos. We want to maintain the Mexican family, the dignity of the individual, and the beauty of the Spanish language. I would never trade Latin dignity for Anglo boisterousness. I don't want to be like my Anglo neighbors. I want to be John Salazar, a Mexican-American. This coun-

try should be big enough to allow us the freedom to be different without being oppressed.[11]

Salazar's statement speaks for itself. But there is a catch in the pluralist position: it fosters discrimination in the personal or primary group sector, while the pluralist insists upon full equality in secondary or public sector relations. As Gordon puts it:

> There are built-in tensions between the simultaneously desired goals of ethnic communality and full civic equality, and these tensions create for the cultural pluralists a poignant dilemma. The dilemma is particularly acute for the two large minority religious groups—the Jews and the Catholics—who do not wish to see their young people "lost" to the numerically and culturally dominant Protestant subsociety . . .[12]

Nor does Gordon see any course of action which completely resolves the dilemma. Thus John Salazar wants his distinctive home and family life, and to maintain this group identity he would normally prefer that his sons and daughters marry Mexican-Americans, not Anglos. Discrimination in this personal sector is seen as benign. Yet he also wants all the economic opportunities available to any other American without a hint of discrimination. He wants equal pay for equal work and of course he also wants all the political rights any Anglo enjoys. Discrimination in this, the public sector, is seen as an evil to be combated. But whatever the tensions of the pluralist position, it does recognize a desirable diversity, and it has in practice been the position adopted by many groups in adjusting to American society.

In addition to these chiefly sociological concepts of assimilation, the political scientist Robert A. Dahl has proposed the theory that ethnic groups pass through three stages of political assimilation. This perspective directly relates ethnic group behavior to the political system. Dahl's views have not gone unchallenged but, nonetheless, his theory probably ranks as the major concept of political assimilation.[13] In the first stage an ethnic group is largely proletarian, with the worst kinds of jobs and with meager incomes and low status. Their condition also tends to foster a good deal of solidarity. As first- and second-generation immigrants they share common circumstances and similar kinds of problems in coping with discrimination and economic hardship. Ethnic ties further reinforce the bonds that arise from these socioeconomic conditions. The result is that "the group ordinarily has a high degree of political homogeneity." At this stage they may still look to leaders outside, but some members of the ethnic group are able to win lesser political offices and thereby acquire some experience and influence.

The second stage is one in which the group has moved up economically and becomes more heterogeneous. Its members acquire better jobs, become more self-confident, and improve their status. This heterogeneity tends to reduce political homogeneity although much sensitivity to ethnic origins persists. Ethnic leaders are able to challenge successfully some of the established political figures and may begin to win prominent offices. Ethnic ties, even if less strong than before, still provide a bloc of votes not available to the nonethnic candidate.

The third stage is one in which much assimilation has occured. The ethnic group has moved further up into the middling and upper strata of society. A middle-class type of life diversified into a variety of occupations, interests, and associations tends to erode ethnic ties and render them almost meaningless. Their place is taken by other interests largely centered on socioeconomic matters, not ethnic bonds. Candidates for political office need to gauge their appeals accordingly, so that ethnic appeals tend to fade. With some exceptions the day of the ethnic bloc vote has pretty well passed into history.

Dahl's conception of the stages of political assimilation obviously has application to our political activities locally and nationally . Certainly ethnic ties have long been influential in American politics and were further evident in the political behavior of groups that came to putlic attention during the 1960s, such as blacks, Puerto Ricans, Mexican-Americans, and Indians. Indeed, the civil rights activities of the 1960s which frayed the New Deal coalition also served to intensify ethnic consciousness in groups in which it had been waning. Dahl's theory has had its critics, including those who challenge his basic assumption that ethnic groups eventually assimilate politically.[14] Yet his idea of relating political activity to changing ethnic socioeconomic conditions and status has merit and is useful in understanding our complex political system.

Unquestionably there has been much assimilation and many Americans no longer feel an effective "sense of peoplehood" aside from their "Americanism." But there are still many Americans who take pride in their distinctiveness, whether ethnic, racial, or religious. And to such groups, ethnic politics somewhere along the "stages of assimilation" is likely to matter.

Black Segregation and Inequality

Among the many groups that contribute to the nation's diversity, blacks stand out as the group who are most severely testing the system's capacity for assimilation, socially, politically, and in other ways. If America is able to assimilate this old, sizable and highly visible minority of about 25 million people in a manner that is largely satisfactory to all, it will have accomplished much indeed. Black segregation and inequality persist on such a scale as to be incompatible with the benign pluralism advocated by John Salazar. And these conditions provide the basis for a pattern of ethnic politics that falls far short of assimilation, whether blacks are assumed to be involved in the first or second stage, or, more likely, a combination of them.

As to segregation, a famous document of the late 1960s summed up the trend as follows: "Our nation is moving toward two societies, one black, one white—separate and unequal."[15] Blacks were concentrated in central city ghettos burdened with a multitude of problems while the white population streamed to the affluent suburbs. Not much later, in 1971, a report based on special censuses in fifteen cities concluded that the percent of blacks living in segregated neighborhoods had *increased* since 1960.[16] This trend appeared to continue well into the 1970s and was particularly evident in the nation's cities and their school systems. Concern with "white flight" intensified as observers noted "growing black enrollments and diminishing white enrollments in many major cities. Nine of the largest twelve cities in the country and fourteen of the largest twenty now have majority black enrollments in their public school systems."[17] This analysis from late 1975, just before the election year, also noted that "no one disagrees that white flight from urban schools has been large or that this trend has made school integration far more difficult." Oddly enough, the South, once the bastion of segregation, had changed. For, this analysis reported, "The South's public schools are now the most desegregated in the country, mainly because of extensive court-ordered busing." Experts could disagree about the causes but it was difficult to deny a widespread pattern of black inner cities and white suburbs.[18]

Still, this pattern is not absolute. Some mixing has occurred. Campbell, Converse, and Rodgers, in their carefully designed cross-sectional sample of the population, found that in 1971 "65 percent of the respondents reported living in neighborhoods of their own race."[19] Neighborhood in this case was rather narrowly defined but nonetheless the figure suggests that about two-thirds of the population was living in a racially segregated locality, whether all white or all black. However, this figure also meant that about one-third lived in mixed neighborhoods. There was evidence for the movement of blacks into the suburbs and this movement has probably contributed much to whatever neighborhood mixing occurs.[20] Yet in the main the persisting pattern has been one of considerable racial separation. Thus as legal segregation in its many forms was progressively dismantled in the South and elsewhere, a pattern of de facto segregation based upon housing patterns has taken its place throughout the country. It would be hard to justify this pattern as a desirable form of pluralism.

Second, and in addition to this de facto segregation, there is the matter of continuing economic disparities between whites and blacks. Salazar's concept of pluralism obviously entailed a desire to enjoy the fruits of the nation's material abundance on a par with others. One basic measure of economic well-being is a group's median family income. According to Lucius Barker and Jesse McCorry, black median income was 51 percent of white median family income in 1945, just after World War II.[21] In the mid-1950s it rose to become about 55 percent of white income. After dropping off it rose again during the 1960s, and by 1968 black median family income was 60 percent of whites'. Yet by 1973 it had fallen off slightly to less than 60 percent.

Figures supplied by *Newsweek* enable us to carry the comparison through the mid-1970s. By 1975 median black family income stood at close to $8,800,[22] about 60 percent of the income of the typical white family. After adjustments for inflation they were actually "slightly worse off" than six years earlier. Overall, then, it appears that black family income did gain on that of whites during the 1960s, but since that time the ratio has remained fairly constant. Black incomes rose but so did that of whites. Thus a basic inequality persisted.

Other trends were mixed, according to *Newsweek*. The typical black teenager, once a dropout, "now graduates from high school." Blacks were "20 percent of all college students, double the percentage in 1965 . . ." Increasingly, also, blacks were gaining white-collar jobs and union cards. And young, black, intact families living outside the South had "apparently achieved economic parity with whites." On the other hand, there were signs of some problems that tended to accentuate disparities. There was a slight rise in the substantial percentage of blacks in poverty from 30.3 percent in 1974 to 31.3 percent. There was a growth in the percentage of black households headed by a woman with no husband: "35 percent vs. 28.3 percent five years earlier." And there was unemployment. In August of 1976 black unemployment stood at 13.6 percent; among whites it was 7.1 percent. An Urban League analysis that probed for evidence of "hidden unemployment" concluded that the black level of unemployment might have gone over 25 percent during the year. Unemployment among black teenagers was particularly acute. The official figure was 40 percent but the Urban League analysis projected a rate of 64 percent.

Overall, the prevalence of persisting and substantial economic inequalities for much of the black population is clear enough. One might argue, as Wattenberg and Scammon once did in a famous and controversial article, that blacks have made progress.[23] But as of the mid-1970s a gap between blacks and whites remained and was not narrowing markedly, if at all.

Overall, then, it is apparent that substantial segregation and inequality persist in the relations between blacks and whites. These are the conditions that make for ethnic politics, a politics of mobilization rather than assimilation. Broadly similar conditions of discrimination and deprivation apply to other ethnic groups as well, such as Puerto Ricans, Chicanos, and Indians. Thus we might expect that ethnic politics, albeit in varied forms, will appear more desirable than assimilation to them as well.

Black Attitudes and the System

We recall from our analysis of early socialization in the family that black socialization tends to differ from that of whites. One authority found from his review of the literature on the black subculture that blacks tend to be more cynical, less trusting, and more "authoritarian (or deferential toward authority)" than whites.[24] These attitudes suggest that blacks would tend to regard any program, whether it be a modernized New Deal or whatever, with some suspicion. At the same time we found blacks to be more politically active than their socioeconomic characteristics would indicate. Group consciousness buoyed by an emergent black pride has enhanced black activism. These characteristics suggest a potential for participation that the system has not yet dealt with satisfactorily.

The civil rights movement of the 1950s and 1960s raised many questions about how blacks might participate in the system. A survey made in 1970 supplies part of the answer. On the basic question "How will blacks make real progress?" black respondents endorsed, by margins of more than 90 percent, such measures as becoming "better educated," "starting black-owned businesses," and "electing more blacks to public office."[25] More than 80 percent approved of working more closely with whites who wanted to help blacks. Less conventional methods also won some support. Thus 68 percent supported organizing boycotts against discrimination, and more than 40 percent backed street protests and support of militant leaders and organizations. Slightly more than 30 percent agreed that violence might be necessary to win their rights. The pattern is striking. Huge majorities here endorsed traditional measures of self-advancement focused on education, business, and elections, yet quite substantial percentages supported less conventional activities.

Part of the 1970 survey centered on leadership and organizations. When blacks were asked about the leaders and organizations that they respected, either a "great deal," "some," or "hardly at all," traditional leaders and groups headed the list. Most favorably regarded were the National Association for the Advancement of Colored People; the

Southern Christian Leadership Conference, founded by Martin Luther King; Cleveland Mayor Carl Stokes; Ralph Abernathy; and Charles Evers of Mississippi. At the bottom of the list were organizations such as the Black Panthers and Black Muslims and well-known militants of that period such as Eldridge Cleaver, Stokely Carmichael, and Bobby Seale. Percentages in their favor ranged only from 30 to 23 percent. This lower order of favorable responses for militants was nonetheless significant. Even at the lowest end of the positive ratings it included nearly a quarter of the respondents.

The willingness to endorse unconventional methods of political expression is confirmed by Gerald Pomper's analysis. Pomper presented tables arranged by race and racial subgroups to display attitudes toward such forms of action as protest marches, civil disobedience, and demonstrations. Blacks were consistently more supportive. As Pomper explained it, "In 1972, some two-thirds of blacks accept efforts to halt government through sit-ins and mass demonstrations, but only three of eight whites are even neutral toward such behavior. In both races, younger and more educated respondents are more permissive but black tolerance is greater than that of whites in all groups."[26]

A related group of issues pertains to integration and the recognition of blacks as a pluralistic element in the system. John Salazar wanted the "right to be different" and so do blacks. Perhaps for this reason, their attitudes toward integration may be changing. Blacks have characteristically favored integration. For instance, in a survey of black opinion published in *Newsweek* in 1969, fully 78 percent of blacks expressed a preference for an integrated school.[27] Seventy-four percent said they preferred an integrated neighborhood. Nearly four out of five disagreed when asked if blacks could make more progress "running their own schools, businesses and living in their own neighborhoods rather than by integrating." About one-fifth thought that blacks should have a separate nation but nearly 70 percent disagreed. Here we have one-sided majorities expressing a preference for integration, including that of neighborhoods.

Yet this same survey also found many blacks sympathetic to the recognition of "soul." "Soul," admittedly, was hard to define but the responses suggested group identity and pride. When asked if most blacks believe that "black is beautiful," 74 percent agreed. More than 50 percent agreed that blacks have a "special soul that most whites have not experienced." And 50 percent agreed that blacks make "better soldiers in combat than whites." As for attitudes toward violence, 64 percent thought there would be more riots, 31 percent though riots were justified, 11 percent said they would join a riot, and 21 percent thought that blacks could not win rights without violence. Thus in the late 1960s large majorities favored integration, but, on the other hand, substantial percentages were in favor of "soul," and substantial minorities were willing to accept some violence, and a fifth wanted a separate nation.

During the late 1960s and early 1970s, Charles Bullock and Harrell Rodgers found evidence of growing black alienation, distrust, and disaffection. A Detroit survey concluded that by 1971 "distrust of the government was the norm for Detroit's black population." Blacks were also "increasingly critical in their evaluation of whites . . ." In 1971 a majority of a national sample of blacks agreed with nine of ten negative statements about whites, with "81 percent stating that most whites consider blacks inferior." For that matter, "68 percent of black respondents said that whites have a mean and selfish streak . . . 79 percent said that whites will give blacks a break only when forced."[28]

Similar reactions came to light in an opinion survey by Daniel Yankelovich that was the basis for editorial comment by *Ebony*.[29] Several themes emerged. The strongest was the "fixation on black identification. Blacks neither think of themselves as, nor aspire to be, 'just Americans.' Instead, they emphasize at least equally the word 'black' and pride in being black." A second theme was a sense of "deep despair, frustration, and impatience about the inequities of American society . . . Four out of ten blacks believe the American system is no longer viable and that radical alternatives are necessary." A third theme was that "fewer than half (47 percent) support the traditional concept that integration is the best method for overcoming racial inequities." Preferred solutions varied. None had a majority and 16 percent preferred separation. Some 36 percent favored a modified integration that would first end present inequities and then encourage integration among equals. Black opinion was evidently turning away from an ideal of integration. Black pride and self-awareness were on the rise, along with feelings of frustration, anger, and despair.

But even as black opinion swung away from generalized approval of integration to become increasingly frustrated and angry, pro-integration sentiment persisted on two seemingly unrelated issues. One is the explosive issue of busing for school children for purposes of racial integration. Whites in general oppose it one-sidedly, but in 1974 a Gallup survey found three-fourths of the black respondents in favor.[30] A survey of 1976 asked respondents to choose among five means of integrating schools.[31] Oddly enough, only 6 percent of nonwhites approved busing in this context. It appears that most blacks do not want their children bused any more than urban whites do, but they support busing, in part at least, as a way to avoid the inferior schools often found in black ghettos.

The other topic reflecting some persistence of pro-integration attitudes is interracial marriage. The subject is not a prominent national issue like busing but may be important as a possible barometer of racial feeling. A 1972 Gallup survey found that 58 percent of blacks expressed approval, with 21 percent disapproving and 21 percent in the "no opinion" category.[32] No doubt many blacks saw this sensitive and highly personal issue as did Martin Luther King. To him it was a measure of a free and open society of equals. It did not mean large numbers of blacks wanted to marry whites.

So far we have found generalized black attitudes to be a mixture, but it would appear that black opinion has in recent years moved away from the integration advocated by Martin Luther King toward a pluralism similar to that of John Salazar.

Blacks, Economic Issues, and the Democratic Coalition

Since economic matters are often at the heart of what may be called the "quality of life," it is appropriate to begin this section with some findings from Campbell, Converse, and Rodgers' major study. The authors found, not surprisingly, that blacks were less happy than whites, less satisfied with their lives in general.[33] Blacks did not differ from whites in their readiness to "express feelings of stress" but they were "considerably less self-confident" than whites. Additionally, blacks were "very much less willing to express trust in their fellow man." This relationship held up in comparisons between subgroups of blacks and whites. It was not a matter of lesser income and education among blacks. As the authors noted, "The experience of being black appears to exert a unique influence . . ." Examining reactions to specific domains of life, the survey showed that "black discontent exceeds white most clearly in standard of living, level of savings, housing, amount of schooling, and neighborhood, in that order." The authors fittingly added that blacks "express more dissatisfaction than white people with those domains, because they fall far short of the societal norms in these domains, and they are aware of it." Blacks faced bad conditions, knew it, and were unhappy about it. This awareness has much potential for mobilization on behalf of liberal activist governmental policies.

This potential is realized to some extent, as the pattern of black voting has shown us. For years blacks have supported Democratic candidates more one-sidedly than any other group. And 1976 was true to form. The exact percentage split is disputed but was at least 85 percent for Carter.[34] The reasons Morris suggests are persuasive and supplement the "quality of life" findings.[35] As a deprived group, blacks, especially in the North, have identified strongly with the New Dealish economic policies normally espoused in one form or another by the Democrats since the time of

FDR. Black spokesmen who characteristically express support for activist, liberal economic policies are certainly being responsive to their constituency. In addition, the Democratic party's image is that of a "champion of civil rights." During the Kennedy-Johnson era, 72 percent of blacks responded affirmatively to a question asking if "the federal government could be depended upon to help blacks a great deal." Yet "by 1971 positive responses . . . plummeted to 3 percent."[36] The latter date was of course during the era of a Republican president, Richard Nixon. As a third factor in accounting for black partisanship, Morris suggests the strength of group cohesion. Thus multiple motivations converge to intensify black partisanship and thereby produce heavily Democratic margins.

We may trace these generalities in the pattern of black responses to surveys pertaining to the 1976 election. Traditionally Democrats tend to stress the problem of unemployment over inflation. Among blacks, more than half selected unemployment as the "most important problem," with inflation trailing at 32 percent and the other problems all at less than 10 percent.[37] Another question asked people which party could do a "better job" of handling the problem "just mentioned." Blacks picked the Democrats by a margin of 60 percent, with only 9 percent favoring the Republicans. The remainder, about 30 percent, felt there was "no difference" between the parties or had no opinion. When respondents were asked whether Ford or Carter could do a better job of handling a whole range of national problems, foreign and domestic, blacks invariably preferred Carter to Ford. After the election Gallup asked people if they had split their ticket or voted a straight party ticket. Among blacks 70 percent said they had voted a straight ticket and only 24 percent said they had split theirs (6 percent did not remember). Black support of the Democratic coalition was almost complete.

The Ambivalent Whites

White opinion in regard to the Democratic coalition is much less easy to define, and attitudes toward racial matters contribute heavily to its ambivalence. Racial attitudes have changed, unquestionably, especially since the 1960s, but segregation and inequality persist.

One fundamental issue is the opening of society at large to black participation. In a survey of the status of civil rights as of 1975, Hazel Erskine and Richard Siegel wrote, "Integration of most public accommodations and the right to vote are rarely questioned today even in the South." And as to employment, "At present 95 percent tell pollsters that blacks should have the same chance at any job as whites."[38] Surveys reported by the respected Institute for Social Research, spanning a ten-year period up to 1974, found strong evidence for positive changes in white attitudes. The basic conclusion was that "members of both races reported increasing cross-racial contact in their neighborhoods, workplaces, schools, and among friends. White attitudes toward racial issues grew considerably more favorable over this period . . ."[39] Black attitudes were less clear and less positive, but white attitudes favoring racial equality showed "promise of continuing into the future."

A good measure of willingness to open society to blacks is a willingness to vote for black candidates. According to figures assembled by Milton D. Morris, in 1974 there were nearly 3,000 black officeholders, up from a meager 103 ten years before. This total of elected officials included one United states senator, sixteen members of the House of Representatives, 239 members of state legislatures, and 108 mayors.[40] Related change could be seen in Gallup surveys asking about the public's willingness to vote for a Negro for president. In 1958 less than 40 percent would have done so, but by 1971, 70 percent were willing to vote for a black.[41] In 1976 and 1977 national changes were symbolized by Barbara Jordan, whom Texas sent to the House of Representatives, and Andrew Young, U.S. ambassador to the United Nations. But some of the most noteworthy political gains took place at the level of city mayors. As of 1976 there were 152 black mayors, up from 129 in 1968.[42] Most won office as leaders of small southern cities but the total included black mayors of such large cities as Washington, D.C., Detroit, Newark, Gary, Los Angeles, and Atlanta. More than forty of the black mayors won in cities with white majorities. This black electoral success, which often required elements of the white vote, was a conspicuous development in the evolving pattern of ethnic politics.

School desegregation has long been a thorny issue. In polls conducted over the years Gallup found that by 1975 school integration was widely accepted in North and South as long as white students were either a majority or no less than half.[43] As for the schools "more than half" black, less than a majority of northern parents objected. Nearly 61 percent of southern parents objected, but only 38 percent of southern white parents objected to schools half black! A comparison of poll results with 1963, when 61 percent of southern parents objected to a *minority* of black students in the school indicates considerable change. Busing is another matter, but at least the principle of integrated schools was widely accepted in all regions by the 1970s.

Housing integration is also a divisive issue, in part because it impinges upon primary group bonds and personal relationships. If housing patterns were genuinely integrated, many of the nation's racial problems would be lessened if not resolved. One interesting survey suggests that the problem may be economic or class based rather than racial. In this survey whites were asked their reactions to the possible addition to their neighborhood of three different groups: lower-status blacks, lower-status whites, and "similar status blacks."[44] As for the addition of lower-status blacks, 44 percent of the whites said they would be unhappy and 47 percent responded with "not much difference." In reaction to lower-status *whites* these percentages were 37 and 53 percent, respectively. There was a difference but not much. As for the similar status blacks, 24 percent reported they would be unhappy but 60 percent said it did not make much difference. Ten percent even said they would be "happy." A *New York Times*/CBS News poll of early 1978 found evidence for a further relaxation of attitudes about housing.[45] Among whites nine out of ten said blacks should be able to "live where they can afford to." A total of 66 percent said they would mind "not at all" if a black family moved in next door. These answers imply that there is more objection to poor whites next door than to similar status blacks. They bode well for middle-class blacks who want to move into white suburbs. They bode ill for the poor, and especially for the poor *and* black who try to move in. (See Table 8-1.)

Table 8-1 Reaction of Whites to New Neighbors of Different Race or Socioeconomic Status

	Type of New Neighbors	
	White of Lower Income and Education	Black of Similar Income and Education
Happy	6%	11%
Unhappy	37	24
Wouldn't make much difference	53	60
Don't know	4	5

Source: William Watts and Lloyd A. Free, *State of the Nation* (New York: Potomac Associates, Universe Books, 1973), p. 285.

All these investigations suggest that whites increasingly accept blacks on an equal footing. But some reactions are far from favorable to blacks. For example, negative racial stereotypes persist. These attitudes too tended to diminish somewhat during the 1960s, but impressive percentages still accept aspects of such stereotypes. Even in 1971, 52 percent of whites thought that blacks have "less ambition" and 48 percent thought they "laugh a lot" and "smell different." Forty percent thought blacks have lower moral standards than whites and 39 percent agreed that they want to "live off the handout."[46] Twenty-two percent said flatly that blacks were "inferior to whites." Attitudes reminiscent of some of the worst of Anglo-conformity racism evidently persisted in a measure even beyond the great civil rights protest of the 1960s. Such attitudes presumably diminish with time but remind us of the dark side of the nation's ethnic diversity, even as it changes.

In addition to negative racial attitudes, there was also a reaction to the civil rights movement. Many observers felt that a white backlash had forced the "social issue" into the public arena. This aspect is difficult to treat with any objectivity. Critics felt the term "social issue" was a disguised reference to racism. But those who used it claimed that there was a genuine issue present. To them the term referred to disorder in the streets, crime, violence, and a spirit of permissiveness that tolerated gross violations of conventional standards. Certainly the surveys suggested that something was happening. In 1969 *Newsweek* conducted a special survey and reported at some length on the troubled mood of the country, focusing specifically on the white middle-class majority. There was growing pessimism about the future and large majorities favored "law and order." They wanted the power of the police increased, and believed both blacks and student demonstrators had been treated too leniently. There was also a strong feeling that blacks were "trying to win too much, too fast."[47] Pluralities actually felt that blacks were favored in seeking jobs, education for their children, financial help, and good housing at reasonable cost. These feelings may be seen close up in some of Samuel Lubell's accounts of his polling for the 1972 election. He found the "conflict between blacks and Italo-Americans . . . particularly sharp in cities like Newark, Cleveland, New York, and Philadelphia." The Italians were especially intent on resisting black residential expansion, but in addition many competed with blacks for city jobs and other employment. Lubell also thought that it would make no difference whether a black or white mayor was elected, as far as the "agonies of these cities" were concerned.[48] That these feelings would undercut the Democratic coalition and provide fertile ground for candidates like George Wallace is readily apparent.

Some of this ethnic conflict has boiled over in antagonism against the "liberal establishment." One spokesman for such sentiments, Michael Novak, vigorously attacks the "Protestant and Jewish liberals who dominate the media" and are "ignorant of the Catholic working class."[49] In Novak's eyes, the "institutions of the Establishment betray a neighborhood, drive people out, destroy their dreams and rob their savings. This is a scandal that cries out to heaven." Again the potential for damage to the coalition is obvious. Thus it is not surprising that an NBC poll reported early in 1976 that fully 43 percent of their respondents agreed that blacks "are receiving more than their fair share of government attention and aid."[50] And well into the election year Gallup found that people still listed crime as among the important problems facing the country, even though far below the percentages that listed inflation and unemployment.[51] These reactions to black protest and to white liberals, who are seen as forcing unwanted change upon other whites, suggest that racial change in American has led to some hostility, including hostility toward the "liberal establishment" of the Democratic coalition.

Some of this reaction against the liberal establishment relates to the busing issue. A Gallup survey made in 1974 found 72 percent of whites in opposition.[52] This was at a time when school integration was widely accepted in the North and the South, except when whites became the minority. The 1976 Gallup survey that asked people to choose among five ways of achieving school integration showed only 3 percent of whites in favor of busing as the preferred way.[53] (Nineteen percent of the whites opposed integration altogether.) It is clear that whites have pretty consistently opposed busing by large margins.

Another sensitive subject is marriage across racial lines. A Gallup survey on this question in 1972 found 65 percent of whites opposed and one quarter approving.[54] Curiously enough, the percentage disapproving interracial marriages, as large as it is, is not quite as high as the proportion opposed to busing. In any case this represents some change since 1958, when only about 4 percent approved such marriages. In the 1972 survey disapproval was the highest among the oldest and least among the youngest, although 44 percent of the latter voiced disapproval. If willingness to marry across racial lines were taken as the ultimate test of racial equality, then nearly two-thirds of American whites would fall short of this ideal.

All these figures indicate that, in general, white racial attitudes are a mixture and are changing, although how much and in what ways is far from clear. Information about directions of change often conflicts, and nowhere more than in the vital area of economic issues and the Democratic coalition. Here we face again the question whether whites have become conservatives, moderates, or are perhaps still "really" liberal. The conservative Kevin Phillips has argued that black pressures for change have been a major factor in the evolution of a conservative majority. Moderates like Scammon and Wattenberg argue that the real majority is in the middle, not the right or left. We shall return to this point in Chapter 14, where we offer a final summation and assessment. For now we will try to give specifics of recent changes in opinion.

Lyndon Johnson's Great Society programs of the mid-1960s were clearly identifiable as a continuation of the New Deal heritage, but even then other issues had begun to intrude. The return of a Democrat to the White House in 1976, with large Democratic majorities in both houses of Congress, was not a rerun of 1936 or even 1964. The coalition was different; Carter won narrowly; and the public mood was ambivalent, even somewhat antigovernment. Among whites polled by Gallup 49 percent cited the high cost of living as the "most important problem" and 28 percent cited unemployment.[55] A plurality of 40 percent of whites thought Democrats could best handle the problem mentioned but 26 percent preferred the Republicans and a substantial 24 percent saw no difference (10 percent had no opinion). When asked their choice of candidates, Ford or Carter, in handling a broad range of domestic and foreign problems, white opinion split. Whites preferred Ford for some problems and Carter for others, and in some cases opinion divided evenly. According to Gallup, only 38 percent of whites voted a straight ticket. Whites voted 52 percent for Ford and 48 percent for Carter (1 percent for McCarthy). Whatever its other meanings, this white vote was certainly not an overwhelming mandate for liberals or conservatives, as traditionally exemplified by the two major parties.

Stresses on the Coalition

Where do these profiles of racial opinions leave us—and the Democratic coalition? Generalizations based upon outlines of complex and changing racial attitudes are bound to contain a margin of error but some tentative observations are in order. Seeds of dissension, some of which have already become rather substantial sprouts, are certainly present. Segregation and inequality persist. Black culture, "soul," and other forms of black pride seem to be winning increased support. Politically blacks have become ardent supporters of the coalition. They approve liberal economic and civil rights leadership and group cohesion enhances their partisanship. Their support of the Democrats extends to the party ticket, the organization, and the candidates. Most blacks, we may safely conclude, would endorse the kind of domestic policies that Lyndon Johnson gave the nation in the 1960s.

Whites have responded to black pressures by changing in some respects but also by resistance. A good many whites have felt that blacks pressed for too much too soon. Substantial percentages feel that blacks are actually favored and a kind of reverse discrimination applied to whites. Some of this feeling was vented against what was seen as a liberal establishment that forced change on workers who normally formed the backbone of the coalition. And alongside the lopsided black support for Carter and for a liberal, activist government, whites actually preferred Ford to Carter and were generally more conservative—and more divided—in their party and policy preferences.

This last could be an especially sore point. For blacks are apt to see strong government action as vital to the solution of their problems—or at least the beginning of the solution. But if whites in the main are not willing to support such government activism, their wishes as much the largest group are likely to prevail. The welfare state would not be dismantled, but it would not expand as blacks believe it must if it is to overcome segregation and inequality. A government dominated by the Democratic coalition that failed to respond to the needs of the black community would provide fertile ground for more suspicion and cynicism. Republican efforts to improve their standing with black voters would add to the stresses within the coalition.[56] Some black disenchantment might take a violent form; some could well lead to despair and passivity. Either would strain the coalition and, to whatever extent, the system. Of course the future is never certain, but it looks as though the "new Democratic coalition" of the 1970s and beyond will be under considerable tension in trying to accommodate black pressures for change with white reluctance to move very far or very fast.[57]

The American Dilemma Persists

The masses in America, we have found, are a diverse lot. Immigration from Europe and Asia, the importation of slaves, and expansion at home have contributed to a unique religious and ethnic diversity.

The forging of a united nation from this heterogeneous population made the process of assimilation a major issue. Anglo-conformity prevailed for a long time. The melting pot concept in some measure replaced it, and in more recent times pluralism in various forms has been proposed as an alternative. Political scientists discoursing upon the stages of assimilation—and the forms of political activity that accompany them—have found groups that remain "unmelted" to some degree on the basis of race, religion, or national origin. But the accommodation of blacks, a large and highly visible group with a uniquely oppressive past rooted in slavery, has tested the process of assimilation most of all. Even after the turbulence and change of the 1960s, blacks as a group remained substantially segregated and unequal. The American dilemma, portrayed by Gunnar Myrdal in his classic analysis of the American racial problem, persisted. The gap between the ideal and the reality continued.

Black attitudes were a mixture. Most by far supported conventional goals, methods, and leadership and organization. Yet many were willing to support protests of various kinds and a minority expressed support for violence. Support for integration may be declining, and group identity and pride seem to be increasing. There were also signs of black frustration, anger, and a willingness to believe the worst of whites. In their politics blacks have been firm supporters of the Democratic coalition and of activist economic policies and civil rights programs.

Whites have accepted the opening of the public sector to blacks, and increasing numbers of blacks have won public office, often with crucial help from the white vote. But negative racial stereotypes have persisted among some whites, and large numbers of whites have felt that blacks pushed too hard and too fast. Black willingness to protest and sometimes to resort to violence fed white concern with the "social issue" and support for "law and order." Many whites felt that reverse discrimination had occurred, and their resentment sometimes took the form of antagonism toward the liberal establishment. While white opposition to busing persisted and was one-sided, the willingness of whites to accept black neighbors seemed to be increasing.

These feelings, combined with other issues and events, altered the climate of opinion as the 1960s wore on into the 1970s. It was hard to pin down the mood of whites exactly, but it was clear that the Democratic victory of 1976 was not a rerun of 1964. Whites were more concerned with inflation than unemployment, were divided in their reactions to the candidates, tended to split their tickets, and slightly favored Ford over Carter. There was a potential for strain in the Democratic coalition as it sought to accommodate the somewhat conflicting pressures from blacks and whites.

Whether or not blacks begin to seek alternatives to the Democratic coalition of the 1970s, it seems certain that ethnic politics—of blacks, Mexican-Americans, and many other groups as well—will be around for some time.

But if the persistence of ethnic differences and their manifestation politically seem assured, those of class and economic differentials seem less so. This development bears upon the fate of the Democratic coalition and also upon public response to appeals for radical political and economic change. How the system has accommodated economic differences is the next topic in our examination of mass opinion.

NOTES

1. Milton Gordon, *Assimilation in American Life* (New York: Oxford University Press, 1964), p. 84.
2. The enormous popularity of ABC's TV presentation of Alex Haley's *Roots* in early 1977 seems to have intensified awareness of the country's slave past as nothing else has done. The concluding portion of this TV drama broke all-time audience viewing records, and other portions ranked in the top ten.
3. See Gordon, *Assimilation*, p. 28. Gordon uses the term ethnic group in an inclusive sense: "There is a common social-psychological core to the categories 'race,' 'religion,'

and 'national origin'—the sense of peoplehood—and the term 'ethnic group' is a useful one for designation of this common element."

4. Gordon, *Assimilation*, pp. 85–88.
5. Ibid., p. 89.
6. Ibid., p. 115.
7. Ibid., p. 125. Gordon adds that each group would of course contribute to the blend, the common culture, that finally ensues and to that extent does not disappear entirely.
8. Ibid., pp. 123 ff.
9. Martin Luther King, *Where Do We Go from Here?* (Boston: Beacon Press, 1967), pp. 62, 89.
10. Gordon, *Assimilation*, p. 158.
11. Quoted in William Madsen, *The Mexican-American of South Texas* (New York: Holt, Rinehart and Winston, 1964) p. 110.
12. Gordon, *Assimilation*, p. 254. When Jimmy Carter as a candidate made his controversial reference to "ethnic purity" he may have intended it as reflecting this benign element of discrimination in the pluralist position. At first Carter saw nothing wrong with the statement and stubbornly resisted efforts to persuade him to change. See Martin Schramm, *Running for President* (New York: Simon and Schuster Pocket Books, 1976), pp. 143–146.
13. Robert A. Dahl, *Who Governs?* (New Haven: Yale University Press, 1961), pp. 34–36.
14. Examples include Raymond E. Wolfinger, "The Development and Persistence of Ethnic Voting," *American Political Science Review*, LIX (December 1965), 896–908; Michael Parenti, "Ethnic Politics and the Persistence of Ethnic Identification," *American Political Science Review*, LXI (September 1967), 717–726; Richard A. Gabriel, "A New Theory of Ethnic Voting," *Polity*, IV (Summer 1972), 405–428.
15. *Report of the National Advisory Commission on Civil Disorders* (Kerner Report) (New York: Grossett and Dunlap/Bantam Books, 1968), p. 1.
16. *Black Americans: A Chartbook*, U.S. Department of Labor, Bureau of Labor Statistics, Bulletin 1699, 1971, p. 15.
17. *New York Times Week in Review*, December 21, 1975, p. 3. The author of this thorough, full-page analysis is Diane Ravitch, historian of education at Teachers College, Columbia Univeristy.
18. One scholarly attempt at an explanation is by Harvey Marshall and Robert Jioubou, "Residential Segregation in U.S. Cities: A Causal Analysis," *Social Forces*, 53 (March 1975), 449–460.
19. Angus Campbell, Philip E. Converse, and Willard L. Rodgers, *The Quality of American Life* (New York: Russell Sage Foundation, 1976), p. 242.
20. Harold X. Connally, "Black Movement into the Suburbs: Suburbs Doubling Their Black Populations During the 1960s," *Urban Affairs*, 9 (September 1973), 91–111.
21. Lucius J. Barker and Jesse J. McCorry, Jr., *Black Americans and the Political System* (Cambridge, Mass.: Winthrop, 1976), pp. 34–35.
22. "Blacks—On a New Plateau," *Newsweek*, October 4, 1976, p. 73.
23. Ben J. Wattenberg and Richard M. Scammon, "Black Progress and Liberal Rhetoric," *Commentary*, 55 (April 1973), 35–44. A skeptical view of black economic progress for the 1960s is argued by Wayne J. Villemez and Alan R. Rowe, "Black Economic Gains in the Sixties: A Methodological Critique and Reassessment," *Social Forces*, 54 (September 1975), pp. 181–193.
24. Milton D. Morris, *The Politics of Black America* (New York: Harper & Row, 1975), p. 142.
25. *Time*, April, 1970, p. 29.
26. Gerald Pomper, *Voter's Choice* (New York: Dodd, Mead, 1975), p. 127.
27. "Report from Black America," *Newsweek*, June 30, 1969, p. 20.
28. Charles S. Bullock III and Harrell R. Rodgers, Jr., *Racial Equality in America: In Search of an Unfulfilled Goal* (Pacific Palisades, Calif.: Goodyear, 1975), pp. 150–152.
29. *Ebony*, September 1973, p. 122. See also Faustine Childress Jones, *The Changing Mood in America: Eroding Commitment?* (Washington, D.C.: Howard University Press, 1977), Chapter 3. Jones cites some survey data but mostly deals with elite opinions

among blacks and whites and in governmental circles. The analysis is interesting and supports her contention that among whites there is a declining commitment to equality.

30. *Gallup Opinion Index*, November 1974, p. 4.
31. *Gallup Opinion Index*, February 1976, p. 6.
32. *Gallup Opinion Index*, November 1972, pp. 11–12.
33. Campbell, Converse, and Rodgers, *The Quality of American Life*, pp. 448 ff.
34. *Time*, November 22, 1976, p. 16.
35. Morris, *Politics of Black America*, pp. 185 ff.
36. Bullock and Rodgers, *Racial Equality*, pp. 150–151.
37. *Gallup Opinion Index*, December 1976, pp. 21 ff.
38. Hazel Erskine and Richard L. Siegel, "Civil Liberties and the American Public," *Journal of Social Issues*, 31:2 (1975), p. 20.
39. "Cross-Racial Contact Increases in Seventies: Attitude Gap Narrows for Blacks and Whites," *Newsletter*, Institute for Social Research, University of Michigan, Ann Arbor, Mich., Autumn 1975, pp. 4, 7.
40. Morris, *Politics of Black America*, p. 154.
41. *Gallup Opinion Index*, November 1971, p. 13.
42. *New York Times Week in Review*, January 30, 1977, p. 7.
43. *Gallup Opinion Index*, February 1976, pp. 9–10.
44. William Watts and Lloyd A. Free, eds., *State of the Nation* (New York: Potomac Associates, Universe Books, 1973), p. 102.
45. *New York Times*, February 2, 1976, p. 28. This survey has to be treated with some caution. The composition of the sample was such that only 489 whites were interviewed and one-fifth were New Yorkers.
46. Bullock and Rodgers, *Racial Equality*, p. 155.
47. "The Troubled American," *Newsweek*, October 6, 1969, p. 45.
48. Samuel Lubell, *The Future While It Happened* (New York: W. W. Norton, 1973), pp. 55–57.
49. Michael Novak, "Black and White in Catholic Eyes," *New York Times Magazine*, November 16, 1975, pp. 119–120.
50. This survey, described as Poll #38, was conducted by telephone on December 16 through December 21, 1975, with 2,836 adults.
51. *Gallup Opinion Index*, June 1976, p. 25.
52. Ibid., November 1974, p. 4.
53. Ibid., February 1976, pp. 9, 10.
54. Ibid., November 1972, p. 12.
55. Ibid., November 1976, pp. 16 ff.
56. During the year after Ford's defeat in 1976, some Republican leaders, such as Senator Howard Baker of Tennessee, appeared to be making serious efforts to court the black vote. See Tom Wicker, "Baker on the Run," *New York Times Week in Review*, December 18, 1977, p. 19.
57. For one account of developments in black politics well into the 1970s, see Thomas L. Blair, *Retreat to the Ghetto* (New York: Hill and Wang, 1977), Chapter 7. The title is itself indicative of the frustration which the author sees as accompanying black political successes.

SUGGESTIONS FOR FURTHER READINGS

Harry A. Bailey and Ellis Katz, eds. *Ethnic Group Politics*. Columbus, Ohio: Charles E. Merrill, 1969. A collection of readings that includes many of the well thought of articles on the subject.

Lucius J. Barker and Jesse J. McCorry, Jr. *Black Americans and the Political System*. Cambridge, Mass.: Winthrop, 1976. A useful survey relating blacks to the political process.

Charles S. Bullock III and Harrell R. Rodgers, Jr. *Racial Equality in America: In Search of an Unfulfilled Goal.* Pacific Palisades, Calif.: Goodyear, 1975. Relatively brief and to the point in its assessment of racial inequality.

Stokely Carmichael and Charles V. Hamilton. *Black Politics: The Politics of Liberation in America.* New York: Random House Vintage Books, 1967. A famous black militant and a political scientist combine to argue for a largely independent, liberationist form of black politics.

Nathan Glazer and Daniel Patrick Moynihan. *Beyond the Melting Pot: The Negroes, Puerto Ricans, Jews, Italians, and Irish of New York City.* Cambridge, Mass.: MIT and Harvard University Press, 1964. A fascinating look at New York City's ethnic groups, warts and all.

Matthew Holden, Jr. *The Politics of the Black "Nation."* New York: Chandler, 1973. Particularly good in analyzing critically some of the more extreme forms of black self-expression.

Matthew Holden, Jr. *The White Man's Burden.* New York: Chandler, 1973. Sees two "nations" evolving, one black and one white, and explores possible measures to deal with the crisis.

Faustine Childress Jones. *The Changing Mood of America: Eroding Commitment?* Washington, D.C.: Howard University Press, 1977. Traces the changing mood as manifest in surveys, elite opinion, the federal government, and education.

Mark R. Levy and Michael S. Kramer. *The Ethnic Factor: How America's Minorities Decide Elections.* New York: Simon and Schuster Touchstone Books, 1973. Includes a detailed look at ethnic voting in the 1972 elections.

Gunnar Myrdal. *An American Dilemma.* Vol. I, *The Negro in a White Nation;* Vol. II, *The Negro Social Structure.* New York: McGraw-Hill, 1964. The famous classic, originally published in 1944, is still much cited and remains worth reading.

William E. Nelson, Jr., and Philip J. Meranto. *Electing Black Mayors: Political Action in the Black Community.* Columbus, Ohio: Ohio State University Press, 1977. Examines intensively some black mayor's campaigns and their problems and prospects.

Gary Orfield. *Must We Bus? Segregated Schools and National Policy.* Washington, D.C.: Brookings Institution, 1978.

Thomas F. Pettigrew. *Racially Separate or Together?* New York: McGraw-Hill, 1971. A social psychologist, himself a southerner, thoughtfully surveys race relations and the prospects for integration. Includes an interesting comparison of anti-Semitism and anti-black attitudes.

Chuck Stone. *Black Political Power in America.* Indianapolis: Bobbs-Merrill, 1968. Examines the black vote and discusses possible strategies and their conditions.

Hanes Walton, Jr. *Black Politics: A Theoretical and Structural Analysis.* Philadelphia, Pa.: Lippincott, 1972. Historical and analytical treatment of black politics.

Kathleen Wright. *The Other Americans: Minorities in Amercian History.* Greenwich, Conn.: Fawcett Premier Book, 1969. Surveys briefly, by historical periods, the experience of America's various minorities, including blacks, Indians, Jews, Asians, and others.

9 · Social Class: Or Why the Socialists Have Failed in the United States

When the New Deal coalition was formed in the 1930s, it reflected a cleavage in mass opinion along economic lines, the struggle between the haves and the have-nots. Yet the ultimate effect of the New Deal, whatever its antibusiness rhetoric, was to save capitalism by reforming it. The citadel of capitalism again denied the socialist prophecies which, at least in their original form in Marx, saw capitalism proceeding inevitably to its destruction. Class war would intensify, mass poverty and alienation would ensue, there would be a revolution, and a socialist system would arise from the ruins of capitalism. But United States capitalism behaved otherwise. The reasons why it did tell us much about America, its masses, and its political coalitions.

The socialist critique of capitalism usually includes elements of the following: conflict between the major classes, the proletarians and the capitalists, growing class consciousness, mass poverty or at least large-scale economic hardship, growing alienation and unhappiness with the existing sociopolitical order, and a potential for revolution. This list may exclude some socialist "revisionist" ideas, but it focuses on the major themes of the rich and varied socialist tradition.[1] It is against ideas such as these that we test the American experience.

Because social classes do not exist in a vacuum, the American sociopolitical system has profoundly affected economic differences and people's reactions to them. For this reason we begin our presention with a discussion of aspects of the system in relation to their contributions to the countering of socialism. Next we look at evidence for American affluence and for the general contentedness of the population. We briefly examine the ambiguous American ideology as well. Then we examine indications of the decline of social class as an influence politically. In addition we aim some glancing blows at the subject of national priorities. Needless to say, our views are not unbiased. Readers will probably find this portrait of the nation's politics and economics different from the usual and may at least be provoked if not convinced.

Mass Influences and Their Antisocialist Implications

When we looked at the American political heritage and the contemporary political culture stemming from it, we found a consensus rooted in a core of values summarized as a Lockean liberal tradition. This consensus itself goes far to account for the system's mainstream politics in which the extremes of left and right have been effectively constrained. Neither socialists nor far-right conservatives have made much headway, either in the two main political parties or in their own splinter parties. The values of the Lockean liberal tradition that are celebrated incessantly by invoking the Constitution, the Founding Fathers, and American principles of government make life difficult for those who seek radical change. George Washington typically wins over the impassioned radicals. Whatever their failings, the American family and the nation's massive educational system evidently succeed quite well in inculcating the system's political culture. Nor should we forget that this consensual political culture has been compatible with considerable turmoil. We seem to be "a turbulent people but a relatively stable republic."[2] The republic persists, with its mainstream politics and its turmoil—and without much of a socialist tradition.

American individualism, or privatism, is also at odds with collectivist appeals to classes and to the "social" in contrast to the private. American mythology glorifies independent and self-reliant individuals who can make it on their own. America is the land of opportunity for all. In addition, Americans have tended to give individualism a private twist oriented toward self-advancement and a private life somewhat divorced from the public sector. William Watts and Lloyd Free summarized this form of individualism well in reviewing the state of the nation in the early 1970s:

In the United States, the country of individualism par excellence, there is a sharp distinction in people's minds between their own personal lives and national life. . . . As a result, they find it possible to feel that they as individuals can fare well, even though they perceive the country to be faring poorly.[3]

An individualism such as this is obviously at odds with much of socialism's heavy stress on classes and the collective. And although it is easy to romanticize and even parody this individualism, as much popular culture does, it is also easy to see how it would reinforce a capitalist system's stress on private property and competition. And we can see that this individualism, with its stress on the private self and material success, can cause indifference to those unable to "stand on their own two feet." That there could be poverty amidst abundance is compatible with the creed of self-reliance. Even if Americans are not as individualistic as they imagine, the idea is strong.

In addition to the political culture and the distinctive individualism, we should consider the nation's powerful religious tradition. The hold that religion has on much of America is in some ways at odds with materialistic conceptions of class warfare and the coming of the revolution. A religious faith is not necessarily incompatible with socialism, but it is certainly arguable that the American religious tradition has had a conserving effect that tends to reinforce the system. The argument can be made on the basis of both the individual's faith, which generally takes fairly orthodox forms, and the nation's civil religion, which blends with the government and the social system. Religion may be an important source of the reform impulse, but it is oriented largely to change *within* the system.

The American ethnic heritage is, in the main, another counterforce to ideas of the primacy of economics and the class struggle. The complex mixture of national, religious, and racial bonds obviously cuts across boundaries of class. A Mexican-American like John Salazar should, in the eyes of a Marxist, see himself chiefly as a worker and think in terms of the working class and its common interests. But Salazar was also concerned with his Latin family and his bonds with other Mexican-Americans. Similarly, many blacks have developed a group consciousness that esteems black culture and the recognition of blacks as blacks, not simply as "workers." Milton Gordon in his study of assimilation wrote that "each ethnic group may be thought of as being divided into subgroups on the basis of social class, and . . . theoretically each ethnic group might conceivably have the whole spectrum of classes within it."[4] In practice, as Gordon says, this may not always be the case, but in American society the horizontal stratifications of social class are partly countered by the vertical stratifications of ethnicity.

Regionalism as a counterforce to radicalism also has its unique American aspects. They can be seen most clearly in relation to the effects of the Civil War. This bitter war and its aftermath fostered a southern regional loyalty that was eventually to be a major element in the New Deal coalition. But within the South, ties to the Democrats tended to run through all classes. Thus in their analysis of party and class ties in the South in New Deal days, Ladd and Hadley argued that "class distinctions in patterns of partisan support apply almost exclusively to the electorate beyond the southern states."[5] By 1940 such differences were beginning to appear but were still "relatively modest." Since this period the South has changed much, with class and party differences tending to emerge. Yet through much of United States history the South's regional loyalties tended to submerge class differences and the struggle between the haves and have-nots.

Underlying all these influences, even in the poorest parts of the rural South and in the urban slums, has been the nation's relative abundance.

The Affluent American

Americans have traditionally seen themselves—and the world has seen them—as the "people of plenty." In the 1950s, when John Kenneth Galbraith published his influential book, *The Affluent Society*, he called attention to the nation's material well-being. Recognition of this idea sank in, and the lack of affluence among some was overlooked.[6] Not until the 1960s did the poverty of a segment of America gain much recognition. The protest of the 1960s also spurred analysis of income distribution and the concentration of both income and wealth among the few. As a result, it has become popular to downgrade American affluence and to highlight the deprivations and inequalities that exist. But much of America *is* fairly affluent—and contented.

To establish—or perhaps to *re*establish—recognition of the affluence of the majority we can cite again the analysis by Ben J. Wattenberg. Wattenberg frankly sought to prove that Americans have made remarkable progress economically and were even coping with adversity quite well when it occurred. But whatever the bias, he presents valuable evidence. According to figures he assembled, there has been an impressive rise in real income, measured in constant 1972 dollars from 1950 to 1972.[7] In 1950 only 16 percent of families had incomes of $10,000 and more, 36 percent were in the $7,000 and above bracket, and 59 percent had incomes of $5,000 or more. In 1972, 56 percent had incomes of $10,000 or more; of these, 45 percent had incomes of $12,000 or more. There were 73 percent at $7,000 or more and a massive 83 percent had incomes of $5,000 and above. Since these were in constant 1972 dollars there was obviously a major movement upward in incomes from 1950 to 1972. Wattenberg further argued that in 1972 dollars, $7,000 would mark the lower limits of the middle class, since that income level was the one at which people had enough money to buy essentials and some extras besides. If we accept that cutting line, then in the early 1970s nearly three-fourths of American families were middle class. Wattenberg added that even if the dividing line were moved up to $10,000, then 56 percent of families would qualify as middling. Certainly this group is much larger than the meager 16 percent of families earning $10,000 and more in 1950. (See Table 9–1.)

Table 9–1 Family Income Distribution, Constant (1972) Dollars

	1950	1960	1970	1972	1973*
More than $ 5,000	59%	73%	83%	83%	84%
More than $ 7,000	36	59	72	73	74
More than $10,000	16	37	54	56	58
More than $12,000	—	22	41	45	48

*Estimate based on a real income growth of 3.5% calculated in 1972 dollars. A calculation in 1973 dollars would push the "more than $12,000" over the 50% mark.
Source: Ben J. Wattenberg, *The Real America* (New York: Capricorn Books, 1976), p. 52.

Clearly American incomes did move up from 1950 to 1972 on a large scale. Skeptics may object that a family income of $7,000 or even $10,000 is quite inadequate to a family of two parents and several children living in a large city. But, according to Wattenberg, the total of 53.5 million families included 30.2 million who were either two-person or three-person households. Thus less than half of all families consisted of four or more people. Small families of young newlyweds or retired couples whose children have become self-supporting could certainly live on $7,000 more readily than a large family.

There is the further possibility that working wives alone have pushed up family income. Not so, counters Wattenberg. From 1960 to 1972 male income alone rose by 83 percent, while the cost of living rose by 41 percent. Real income therefore rose quite apart from the contributions of working wives. These figures further contradict economists who scoff at the rise in dollar income as an artifact of inflation. Another point of Wattenberg's is that census counts of income neglect fringe benefits such as medical insurance and other contributions by employers. These benefits do have value, though it is difficult to estimate. Unions seek them and employees accept them, and they add to the real income of millions of Americans.

Wattenberg strengthens his argument for the middle-class character of America with a National Opinion Research Center poll of 1973, in which people were asked to identify the social class they thought they belonged in. As it turned out, 4 percent identified as lower class, 41 percent as working class, and 41 percent as middle class. Another 11 percent identified as upper middle class and 2 percent as upper class. Thus 55 percent identified themselves as middle class and above. Critics may question Wattenberg's conclusions but he has certainly assembled some impressive evidence. For one thing, it is hard to deny that there has been a substantial increase in American incomes since World War II. For another, income figures from the early 1970s show that the bulk of Americans had incomes well above the poverty level. And there is evidence that the majority of Americans *see* themselves as middle class.

It is also true that the upper end of the income scale increased.[8] According to census figures cited by Wattenberg, there were slightly over 200,000 households with incomes of $25,000 a year in 1952. By 1962 there were 364,000 such households. Twelve years later, in 1974, there were some 6.4 million households with incomes of $25,000 or more. Higher yet on the scale, there were 425,000 households with incomes of $50,000 or more by 1970.

As the upper end of the income scale increased, so did the middle. In addition, there is evidence that the poverty group at the lower end declined during the 1970s. Several interesting conclusions emerged from an important Brookings Institution study that bears on this subject. For one, it was not clear that any marked redistribution of income, after taxes and expenditures, had occurred over the previous two decades. Total income and average income increased, but there was no drastic leveling as between income groups. For another, a survey of the poor did find much change over a six-year period. About 50 million people in all were poor during these six years. But in each year there was a smaller number, and the composition of the poverty group changed as people moved in and out of poverty. Changes in family composition were a major reason: the birth or departure of children, plus divorce, altered households and their needs and incomes.

Most important, the Brookings study found evidence of a major reduction in poverty when in-kind subsidies were taken into account. Most studies of poverty tend to rely upon an income standard and therefore neglect services subsidized by the government in the form, for instance, of medical care or food stamps. The authors believed that "a definition of household income that both includes the recipients' cash valuation of in-kind benefits and adjusts for underreporting of cash income would probably reflect a current poverty rate close to 5 percent rather than the official level of 12 percent."[9] In summing up their findings, the authors wrote:

> Considerable progress has been made in the past two decades toward our national income security objectives. Protection from precipitous losses in welfare due to disruptions in the earnings of regularly employed workers has greatly expanded; the financial access of the lower-income population to certain valued goods and services has been substantially improved; and major reductions in income poverty have occurred.[10]

The welfare state has been doing *some* work effectively in protecting ordinary Americans from unemployment and other hardships and in reaching out to improve the lot of the poor. There has *not* been much income redistribution, but average income has gone up and government services reduced the poverty group to about 5 percent of the population by the mid-1970s.

An enlightening perspective on income comes from an article by the economist Robert L. Heilbroner in which he attacks the "myth" that Americans are middle class.[11] His own figures—for which he relied heavily on the 1975 *U.S. Statistical Abstract*—can be used to support the contention that much of America is affluent, whether we call it middle class or something else. At the outset he referred to a significant survey by Yankelovich, "one of the most sophisticated pollsters in the country," which profiled Americans as 18 percent lower class, 61 percent middle class, and 21 percent upper class. Arguing against this survey, Heilbroner maintained that some 20 percent of Americans were poor, 40 percent were working class, 35 percent were middle class, and 5 percent were upper class. The poor had incomes of less than $7,000, the working class extended from about $7,000 to $15,000, and the rest were higher.

In making a case for a substantial number of poor and working-class people, Heilbroner also argued for the small size of the rich group. From the available evidence he estimated that perhaps 200,000 families had incomes of $100,000 or more annually and perhaps 250,000 families had assets or estates worth $1 million or more. If one assumes these two groups did *not* overlap—when in fact they must indeed overlap—then at the outside about 450,000 families could be considered rich. But this group was less than 1 percent of the more than 50 million families in America. Just under this group was the upper class. In 1974 a family with an income of $32,000 was in the top 5 percent of all families and could be labeled upper class. Heilbroner's argument was that many Americans who thought themselves middle class were really upper class and only a very few—less than 1 percent—were really rich.

Does this challenge to the "myth" of middle-class America stand up?

Not in our opinion. His own figures and some supplemental data suggest otherwise. First we might explore the highs and lows, the rich and the poor, in his income stratification. By his own account the really rich are a tiny number, less than 1 percent of all families. What he calls the upper class begins at the level of $32,000 family income and extends up. This income level looks impressive but would include some professional and business people who are likely to think of themselves as middle and not upper class. These days even a fair number of professors have such incomes, not to mention doctors, lawyers, and civil servants.

At the other end, the end occupied by the 20 percent who are poor at incomes below $7,000, Heilbroner fails to take account of government in-kind services. As we have seen, when such services are accounted for, the percentage of the poor drops to about 5. These "corrections" of Heilbroner's figures reduce the numbers at the high and low ends of the income stratification scale and enlarge the middle.

As for the middle group, Heilbroner defined the working class as up to $15,000 in income and 40 percent of the total, as against 35 percent middle class above them. Any lowering of this $15,000 cutting point obviously enlarges the middle class. In our opinion Heilbroner arbitrarily selected an excessively high working-class income standard to support his challenge to the "myth" of middle-class America. By lowering this standard to perhaps $12,000 or $13,000 we would immediately create a large and dominant group. And we would justify this change with Heilbroner's own report on the Yankelovich survey, in which over 60 percent of the respondents were classified as middle class. In short, we think the evidence proves that much of America *is* middle class.[12]

One further assessment by an economist surveying the American economic system on the occasion of the nation's bicentennial is a fitting summation. According to Arthur M. Okun:

> The result of the system has been a high standard of living for most Americans. A family with an income at the national average of about $14,000 a year today has a command over goods and services that would have put it well into the top 10 percent of the pyramid in 1948; a family with a $7,000 income—half the average—has a living standard matching that of the average family of 1948. Judged purely as a system of productive efficiency, contemporary American capitalism has to get a high grade. It needs a tune-up, and perhaps even an overhaul, but not a trade-in.[13]

Okun's perspective reinforces the evidence. Real income has moved up over the years for American families and has done so beyond the increases in money income due to inflation or to working wives. Poverty has decreased, and when in-kind services are taken into account the poor amounted to about 5 percent of the population in the mid-1970s. The welfare state also provides support for those who suffer disruptions in earnings, as by unemployment. High incomes also grew but the really rich were a tiny minority. The middle group between the poor and the rich was much the largest. And although some observers argued for a substantial working-class group, surveys suggested that most Americans were middle class.

This affluence may still impress many as insufficient. Nor do we doubt for a moment that most Americans will continue to strive for "more." But most Americans are apt to agree with Okun that any changes made be a tune-up or an overhaul, not a trade-in for an altogether different model. We can see more clearly now why socialist alternatives have had tough sledding in America.

A "Generally Contented Population"

We have looked at the deradicalizing aspects of the sociopolitical system and at the evidence for middle-class levels of affluence. Still, Americans might be dissatisfied with their lives, for whatever reasons, and such discontent would obviously provide opportunities for those who advocate radical change. Thus we need to move beyond analysis of objective data on living conditions to explore how Americans actually feel about their jobs and their lives. A large body of literature forcefully portrays the deficiencies of American society and the unhappiness of many people within the system, but we prefer to rely as much as possible on actual surveys, in which people are asked directly to describe their jobs and their lives. Such first-hand information is of basic importance, although it is often surprisingly neglected.

A good body of evidence to start with is a set of Gallup surveys over the years since World War II which asked, "On the whole, would you say you are satisfied or dissatisfied with the work you do?" In early 1949 about 67 percent reported they were satisfied.[14] The percentage satisfied rose over the years to a peak of 87 percent in 1969, then dipped. By 1973 it was 77 percent, and of the remainder, 12 percent had "No opinion" and 22 percent were "Dissatisfied." These are impressively high percentages of job satisfaction.

Supporting evidence is available in a Department of Labor monograph. Gallup surveys were cited in it and some of these were broken down for men only, ages twenty-one through sixty-five, and to exclude the "Don't know" category. With this focus on the male working population, the percentage responding as "Satisfied" for the 1963 to 1973 period ran from a low of 86 percent to a high of 92 percent. These high percentages imply that job satisfaction is greater among men who are working than for those who don't. This study also uses results from surveys by such organizations as the Survey Research Center and the National Opinion Research Center, which support Gallup's findings. For the years 1958 through 1973 the proportion of the whole working population that was "Satisfied" was at least 80 percent and in several surveys ran over 90 percent.[15]

The Labor Department study did not overlook possible changes or important variations among groups. As to the first, the authors concluded that "there has been no substantial change in overall levels of job satisfaction over the last decade." Nor did they find young workers groaning about their work more than in the past. "The much talked-about decline in the job satisfaction of younger workers over the last decade is . . . not substantiated by the seven national surveys."[16] Younger workers tend to be less satisfied with their jobs, but there was no clear evidence of any change in the amount of dissatisfaction. Nor were differences between men and women important: "Where sex differences in job satisfaction have occurred they were slight, and only intermittently were they statistically significant."[17]

As for blacks and other minorities, the picture was less clear. Their responses fluctuated, followed "no consistent pattern," and were within the margin for sampling error. On the other hand, Gallup's report on job satisfaction among nonwhites showed blacks' job satisfaction as consistently less than that of whites. The high was 76 percent in 1969; the low was in 1973, with only 53 percent "Satisfied."[18] Of this last poll Gallup warned that it was based on only one survey and was subject to a large margin of sampling error. Yet we noticed in examining ethnic politics that blacks tended to be less happy and less satisfied with specific features of their lives, including their standard of living. There is good reason to think blacks are less satisfied with their jobs. Still, at its worst, in Gallup's surveys over half the blacks who had jobs were willing to classify themselves as "Satisfied" and at times the percentage was 70 percent or more.

Should we take these reports at face value and conclude that all is well with American workers? Perhaps, but there are pros and cons to consider. One problem is the wording of the basic question. Reports of dissatisfaction *do* increase when the wording includes references to possible "attractive alternatives" or to several degrees of dissatisfaction.[19] The Labor Department monograph points out that the wording of the question utilized by Gallup and other surveys tended to produce the "highest estimate of satisfied workers." There are other possible biases too.

Workers may feel defensive about such questions and think that reports of dissatisfaction reflect upon themselves and their choice of work. Or, they may accommodate themselves by lowering expectations and demanding less of their job, and then report satisfaction. On the other hand, as the monograph mentions, there are some trends that provide grounds for high satisfaction scores. There has been a consistent movement from the occupations least liked toward those associated with greater satisfaction.[20] In addition, real wages and fringe benefits have been increasing for years, and technology and automation have improved the jobs of at least some workers. Further, management has become more "employee centered" and has sought in various ways to "humanize" work and management's role in it. Finally, federal and state legislation, whatever its limitations, has sought to improve health and safety conditions in industry.

All these considerations warn us of the complexities of measuring job satisfaction. Even so, those who expect radical change fueled by high levels of worker alienation and discontent can find little comfort in the evidence.

Opinions about the quality of American life in general are as important as opinions about work alone. Campbell, Converse, and Rodgers, in their study based upon a 1971 survey, were much concerned to devise reliable measures of life satisfaction, happiness, and the like, and these methodological interests somewhat obscure the findings themselves. But what emerges in this lengthy study is decidedly on the positive side. At the outset the authors review the "happiness reports" compiled in previous surveys from 1957 to 1972. An initial finding is that the percentage who viewed themselves as "very happy" declined from 35 percent in 1957 to 22 percent in 1972.[21] On the other hand, only small percentages labeled themselves "not too happy," running from a high of 17 percent in 1965 to a low of 9 percent in 1972. The group that described itself as "pretty happy" ranged from 52 to 68 percent. If we combine the "very happy" with the "pretty happy" group, the totals range upward from 84 percent over the years 1957 to 1972.

After reviewing these "happiness reports," the authors probed further into Americans' feelings about their lives. They devised a scale to measure "overall life satisfaction" and reported a "generally contented population . . . very similar to the impression conveyed by the responses to the happiness item."[22] Another scale measured ways of characterizing "life in general," and people could choose such desciptions of their lives as "Boring," "Miserable," "Hard," "Useless," and so on, or respond in such positive terms as "Interesting," "Easy," "Worthwhile," and so on. The result here was "a substantial piling up of responses toward the ends of the scales that would normally be considered positive, just as was the case with the global items on life satisfaction and happiness. The only slight exception is the 'easy' vs. 'hard' scale, where respondents still remain more positive than not."[23] The authors also experimented with ways to measure a general sense of well-being and to measure positive and negative aspects of specific domains of life, such as marriage, family, and work. Their final conclusion was: "Throughout, we have noted that these measures lean strongly toward positive reports: only a very limited minority of people confess to any general lack of happiness, dissatisfaction with life, or for that matter, dissatisfaction with any of the component domains of life." Indeed, the authors even add, "We are frequently asked whether we really believe that Americans are in fact satisfied with the terms of their lives as these absolute distributions seem to imply."[24] Clearly the import of this study is that Americans are a "generally contented population." And this conclusion is one that emerges from various scales and questions designed to go beyond the usual happiness reports.

Other aspects of the study reinforce this positive picture. The analysis of work, which confirms that this is one of the most important domains of life, includes a telling commentary on job satisfaction: "Many of those people who have retired from the labor force wish they had worked longer than they did." And although income was obviously a major factor in working, "a high proportion of those who work (and especially those who are white and male) say they would work even if they had all the money they wanted."[25] Not surprisingly, then, "Unemployment appears to have serious deleterious effects on the overall quality of life." Whatever the dissatisfactions of groups such as some younger workers and blacks, the jobs that people have matter in other ways than income.

Other questions probed reactions to the legal and governmental system. When people were asked about their experience of fair or unfair treatment by public officials in general, 22 percent said they were treated "very fairly" and another 56 percent said "fairly enough."[26] Combined, these responses mean that over three-fourths of the respondents felt they had been treated, in the main, fairly. Of the remainder 17 percent felt they had "not been treated very fairly," 5 percent had "not been treated very fairly at all." Upon analysis it was found that those with the most negative responses were "young black people living in metropolitan centers." This is hardly surprising. What is perhaps most surprising is that so many felt they had been treated reasonably well.

Another question was about people's sense of freedom "to live the kind of life you want to." To this catchall inquiry 49 percent said they "feel very free, " another 40 percent "feel free enough," and 10 percent "do not feel free at all."[27] Further questions explored reasons why some people did not feel entirely free, and here "the most frequently mentioned re-straints on personal freedom were laws and governmental bureaucracy. Racial discrimination was mentioned by one-eighth of these respondents, primarily blacks. Sexual discrimination . . . was not mentioned." As we would expect, those who felt there were restrictions on their freedom were generally those who felt they were treated unfairly. The groups that stood out were blacks, young people, and people in metropolitan centers. Older people, it was surmised, tended to settle into accommoda-tion with reality.

All in all, the evidence from this study so overwhelmingly portrays Americans as a "generally contented population" that one cannot help wondering if something is wrong. For one thing, there may be bias. Peo-ple do not always tell the whole truth and may give interviewers more positive responses than they actually feel. Careful analysis of these possibilities led the authors to decide that there were biases present and these "were worth knowing about where later substantive results were concerned." Yet they also thought that in the end, "Generally these ef-fects have been small."[28]

Other factors may have also influenced the results, as the authors were aware. Americans *feel* they have considerable freedom and may exercise considerable mobility in adapting their lives. One consequence is a tendency toward "progressive mobility over the life span into situations which are in an objective way 'better.'"[29] Most people do not put up with intolerable situations. They tend, instead, to shift toward situations that are more rather than less satisfactory. In contrast, there is also the "ac-commodation effect": "Where a situation is fixed for a person over a long term, there may be a tendency toward accommodation to it, reflected in gradual increases in satisfaction."[30] The authors argue that this mecha-nism best explains "the very general gains in satisfaction with age in all domains but health, as well as declines in aspiration level with age." Mobility, accommodation, and declining aspirations over the long term all help to account for the apparent contentedness of the population.

One other explanation is more judgmental and controversial. As the authors of this inquiry acknowledge, "the degree of absolute content-ment . . . seems to conflict hopelessly with other things we know about levels of public discontent in the United States."[31] Their answer is to argue that both personal discontent and public discontent are much exag-gerated. For example, even the highly visible protest of the 1960s in-volved only a relatively small proportion of the population. Against media "images of a citizenry generally up in arms" the authors argue, "It is unlikely that as much as 2 or 3 percent of the adult population ever had any active part in this movement, or that much more than 10 percent of the population had any particular psychological involvement with it." Protest tends to gain attention more than reports of basic satisfaction.

There probably *is* a margin of error present in all this evidence, but the view of Americans as a "generally contented population" is substantiated in so many ways that it must be considered an essential part of American life. Such contentedness is at odds, to put it mildly, with much socialist criticism.

The Radical-Conservative Ideology

Politically Americans tend to be dominated by a conservative ideology, albeit one that incorporates as well a radical, populist element. This attribute is much influenced by our affluence, our generalized sense of contentment, the liberal yet tradition-oriented consensus reinforced by religion, and the weakness of class bonds due to the nation's individualism and ethnic pluralism. In the area of ideology, the mass of Americans tend to think in terms that are at odds with leftist appeals for fundamental change.

Important evidence of this comes from a study that probed variations in liberal-conservative attitudes by means of surveys taken in 1964, the election year in which President Johnson faced Senator Goldwater. One scale devised by the authors, Lloyd A. Free and Hadley Cantril, measured "operational liberals." On this scale those sampled responded by indicating approval or disapproval of a number of distinct policies or programs associated with welfare state operations. Included were such programs as Medicare, Head Start, urban renewal, and the like. On most of these items approval ran well over 60 percent. Free and Cantril concluded that about two-thirds of the public could be described as "operational liberals." That is, two-thirds expressed approval of specific programs of a liberal nature and presumably voted for them.

Free and Cantril also examined another dimension of ideological attitudes with a set of quite general questions about attitudes toward individual initiative, the role of the states and the national government, socialism, and the like. On this scale about half of the respondents ranked as conservative.[32] Combining results from these two scales shows us that in 1964 about two-thirds of the American public were willing to *vote* in a liberal direction but about 50 percent of this population *thought* conservatively. The old-fashioned individualistic ethos had a strong grip on many Americans, even as they voted otherwise and the welfare state grew to major proportions. This pattern of voting one way and thinking another may be called schizophrenic, hypocritical, or worse, but it adds importantly to our understanding of why socialist appeals go unheard.

This schizophrenic outlook has persisted and perhaps became stronger in the 1970s. A survey published by the respected Institute for Social Research, at the University of Michigan, found it in a quite different context. In this instance the authors' main interest was "bureaucratic encounters," people's reactions to a variety of government services, including the employment service, job training, workmen's compensation and unemployment compensation, public assistance, hospital and medical care, and retirement benefits. Government services were "widely utilized."[33] Nearly 60 percent of the respondents reported contact with one of the service areas, and there was a "relatively high degree of satisfaction with various agencies." There were variations, but "most people were relatively satisfied with public services." Responses did not support negative stereotypes of bureaucracy as "inefficient, unfair, error-ridden" or as "irresponsible" and "authoritarian." But the authors found that "people's specific experiences were more positive than their general attitudes." Thus 80 percent felt they received fair treatment in their government contact but "only 42 percent rated government offices in general as fair." People tended to prefer that government rather than private enterprise handle a number of their problems, but at the same time they evaluated government in general "less favorably than private enterprise in most respects." Perhaps, the authors speculated, they were "dealing with an ideology of stereotypes rather than strong personal values and convictions."

Should we anticipate that in time this apparently inconsistent pattern will change? The United States is far removed from the realities of free-market capitalism. Experience with the welfare state would seem likely to drive this point home and reduce fuzzy evaluations of the government. But it had certainly not happened by 1973, if we accept the conclusions of the Michigan study. And the prevalence of an antigovernment mood all over the country during the mid-1970s, including the election year 1976, is strong evidence that this outlook persisted, perhaps even intensified. The mood held up, as did big government and the desire for its services.

There may be an element of schizophrenia at the core of American ideology. Certainly the conservative, individualistic rhetoric contains a radical, populistic strain that confounds traditional socialist thinking. Michael Harrington approvingly cites the words of an earlier social critic, Leon Samson, who formulated a socialist version of Americanism called "substitutive socialism." As Harrington explained Samson's conception, "The European ruling classes . . . were open in their contempt of the proletariat. But in the United States equality, and even classlessness, the creation of wealth for all and political liberty were extolled in public schools."[34] Harrington thought much of this rhetoric was "sincere verbiage which concealed an ugly reality," but even as myth it was real enough. Harrington further quotes Samson as contending that "the idea that everyone can be a capitalist is an American concept of capitalism. *It is a socialist concept of capitalism.*" And if Americans have a "socialist capitalism," then why should they turn to the plain, garden variety of socialism? Certainly the American ideology with its blend of conservative individualism and radical common man appeals complicates the task of those who want the public to turn toward socialism. Indeed, the strange rhetorical mixture adds to the problems of everyone who tries to understand what the public "really" thinks about the body politic.

When John Kenneth Galbraith called upon the Democrats to take up the banner of socialism and make no bones about it, he was advocating a policy that would be politically suicidal for the party.[35] Americans are willing to accept policies that extend the welfare state and have socialist overtones. But there are no indications whatsoever that party adoption of a socialist ideology would do anything but antagonize large numbers of potential supporters. To present potentially radical policies as in keeping with the views of the Founding Fathers, as well as with individualism, the private enterprise system, and the needs of the common man, reassures the public and accommodates to American-style political schizophrenia.

The Decline of Class Differences

The influences we have been discussing certainly undercut socialist appeals, but that is not all. They tend to weaken the social class differences, the struggle between the haves and the have-nots, which formed much of the basis for the New Deal coalition in its prime. If the class basis for the parties persisted, we should find that most people at the lower end of the scale of socioeconomic status—as measured by income, occupation, and education (singly or in combination)—would identify with the Democrats. And, conversely, those higher on the scale would identify with the Republicans. But the trends are otherwise. One authoritative statement of this development is the analysis by Nie, Verba, and Petrocik, who analyzed two decades of voting, from 1952 through 1972:

> In the South, class differences between Democrats and Republicans have become more pronounced; in the rest of the nation they have become less so. In each case, however, major components of the stable support bases of each of the parties weakened. The Democratic party cannot rely on the South or the northern working class. The Republican party no longer can rely as heavi-

ly on the Protestant upper middle class. . . . The class basis of the parties has been severely diminished and the race issue cuts across existing alignments.[36]

The race issue especially—but also other issues such as the Vietnam war and Watergate—did not simply cut across previous cleavages of class and party to realign people *within* the parties. In some measure they "led the public to turn against the political parties and against the political process generally." These noneconomic issues contributed, then, to the weakening of the class basis of the two major parties.

Ippolito, Walker, and Kolson reach a similar conclusion in their public opinion text:

> In terms of social class distinctions, the major parties reflect an impressive degree of heterogeneity. While it is true that Democratic identification is disproportionately concentrated in the lower socioeconomic brackets, substantial numbers of individuals in these groups do identify as Independents or Republicans. And, conversely, a significant proportion of those in the upper socioeconomic categories identify with the Democratic party.[37]

In addition, they report that, "there is evidence that the partisan implications of social class have been decreasing over time," and "the major parties provide at most a very moderate example of status polarization, and this polarization has been less evident in recent elections than it was during the Roosevelt and Truman administrations."

Still, since many people do not vote their party identification, Ippolito and his colleagues looked to other indicators of class besides voting. One of these is education, and the authors made an analysis of opinions arranged by education level in relation to nine different issues, as reported by Gallup polls. As we saw in detail in Chapter 6, there were diffferences but not necessarily consistent ones. For example, the college educated and those with only a grade-school education reacted much the same to the idea of "defense spending reductions," but the college educated, and presumably more conservative, respondents opposed reductions of spending for social welfare by 70 percent, as compared to 55 percent opposed among the grade-school group.[38] If education levels do in some measure reflect social classes, it is difficult to see any consistent clash between haves and have-nots, even on economic issues. They act most like opposed classes only on the abortion issue, a matter far removed from normal New Deal concerns.

To measure class differences by occupation the authors again used Gallup surveys. Occupations were put into three main categories and the same nine issues were used. As it turned out, each occupational group was distinctive in some way but not in a way that reflected clear class differences. On issues related to economics, such as government spending, the occupations differed little. "Few clear patterns emerge from this information," as the authors put it.[39] In Chapter 6 we touched upon these authors' discovery that manual workers did not fit the image of reactionary "hard-hat" types, that they divided much like the other groups on such issues as capital punishment, the Equal Rights Amendment, and gun registration. Again this is evidence of class heterogeneity.

We remember too that Ladd and Hadley went beyond the claim for class heterogeneity to argue that there has actually been an "inversion" of the New Deal class order.[40] Their data for the 1960s and early 1970s indicated that the haves showed signs of becoming more liberal than the have-nots. The high socioeconomic group that had been a bastion of conservatism in New Deal days was changing and by the 1970s was relatively liberal even on many economic issues. Ladd and Hadley attributed much of this shift to the changing shape of the left, as economic issues were displaced somewhat by issues related to social change and social equality. In addition, the growth of education enhanced social mobility and altered traditional class lines.

But what of the 1976 election? Could the Democratic victories in presidential and congressional contests be read as a return of the New Deal coalition and a heavily class-based voting pattern? Gerald M. Pomper's authoritative analysis inclines to the view that the 1976 coalition was a new one, but that party- and class-based voting were both important again: "For the first time in a generation, the electorate divided sharply along lines of party loyalty, with Carter gaining four of every five Democrats, and Ford doing even better among the GOP."[41] And in contrast to 1972, "Carter's candidacy reasserted . . . economic alignments by bringing the Democrats votes among those of the lower-middle class, in blue-collar occupations, with high school rather than college education, and in the less wealthy areas of the South . . . The election may indicate a renewed class basis to American politics."[42]

But Pomper compared this election with previous ones on a state-by-state basis and found "The most striking result is how different the Carter-Ford contest is from other contests. . . . We should not simply see the 1976 results as a throwback to the elections of the New Deal."[43] There was a mixture of the new and the old. Class and party were reasserted in some measure but much was different about the makeup of the Carter Democratic coalition. When we view Pomper's analysis along with the other evidence of the declining political importance of social class differences, we have grounds to conclude that the struggle between the haves and have-nots is certainly not *the* overriding issue of American politics. It remains important but must compete with many other concerns.

The Coalition, the Budget, and National Priorities

We have found that socialism has limited appeal and even social class differences show signs of declining over the years. An added issue must be fully confronted in any contemporary attempt to create a New Deal-style coalition. One of the hallmarks of New Deal philosophy was the belief that the federal government, with its enormous money-raising potential, was the basic means of attacking unemployment, health needs, and other social and economic problems. But what if it turned out that the seemingly limitless federal treasury was in fact close to its limits? Constraints on the financial powers of the national government would be a significant damper on what a New Deal coalition might wish to do. And there were signs as the 1970s progressed that it would indeed be difficult for the federal government to provide the added financial resources necessary to support effectively a much enlarged program of social spending.

Some of these signs can be read if we look at trends in governmental spending over the years since the 1950s, as described by the Brookings Institution. For example, a study of national priorities published in 1974 found that federal expenditures rose in the period 1955 to 1970 from 19 percent of the Gross National Product to 21.4 percent. Military expenditures as a percentage of GNP fell during this time but were offset by rising expenditures for nonmilitary purposes. The huge federal budgets of this era and their growth from year to year did not much increase the share of GNP spent by the federal government. Actually the big increase took place at the state and local level: "Between 1955 and 1970 state and local spending rose from 10.2 to 15.0 percent of GNP."[44] As a result, total government expenditures at all levels rose between 1955 and 1970 from 28 percent to 34 percent of GNP, and for 1971 such spending was estimated at 35 percent. Obviously government grew during this 1955–1970 period, although it grew more at the state and local than the federal level.

According to a more recent Brookings study, by the mid-1970s military spending had fallen to 24.6 percent of the federal budget and 5.9 percent of GNP. Nonmilitary spending in 1976 took fully three-fourths of the federal budget.[45] The welfare state grew as the warfare state diminished, and national priorities did in fact alter, even if less than critics of military spending might wish. With more than a third of GNP spent by government at all levels, the present economic system could hardly be described as free-market capitalism.

Less encouraging for the prospects of the new coalition's policies, however, were some predictions about the immediate future. In 1974,

"barring major changes in current tax policies and expenditure programs," the Brookings experts expected "little room for maneuver in the
federal budget during the next three years. Despite the large rise in
revenues to be expected from economic growth and the cuts in domestic
programs proposed in the 1974 budget, there are no significant discretionary resources available until fiscal 1977."[46] In effect, there just was
not much money available for new programs, at least without major
changes in tax policies or cuts in existing programs.

A Brookings Institution study that sought to project further ahead,
into the late 1970s and beyond, was similarly discouraging for those with
an interest in expanded social programs. In this report, written in 1976
by Henry Owen and Charles L. Schultze—who was to become President
Carter's chief economic adviser—several points confirmed earlier findings. One was that total federal spending had grown only slightly faster
than GNP over the previous two decades. This "masked two divergent
trends—a continuing fall in the relative size of defense spending and a
steady rise in the relative size of domestic spending."[47] This rise Schultze
attributed mostly to legislation expanding existing programs and legislation creating new programs. The Great Society legislation of the 1960s had
worked to decrease military spending and to enhance social spending.

After careful analysis of the federal budget and of projections into the
late 1970s and beyond, Schultze commented:

> There are two central messages contained in the projections. First, without a
> significant further reduction in the real level of defense spending or an increase
> in the share of GNP devoted to federal spending, little leeway is left in the next
> five years to expand domestic programs or to inaugurate large new ones. The
> leeway would be even less, indeed would virtually disappear, if it were de-
> cided to expand the real level of defense outlays modestly during the next
> several years.[48]

Finally, even on the basis of projections for a full employment economy,
Schultze could predict for 1981 only "about $30 billion in program ex-
pansion or new federal activities." Such a limited sum would hardly
allow for major new programs, such as national health care, or for
sizable additions to existing programs.

This analysis offers little encouragement to coalition supporters who
visualized the election of 1976 as a political breakthrough mandating major new social legislation. Of course Schultze, and the others as well,
could be wrong. Predicitions are always risky. Activists in the New Deal
mold might suggest new taxes or increased federal deficits to enlarge
federal spending opportunities. But the mood of the country made these
alternatives politically unpalatable, and the energy problems of the late

1970s threatened to divert both attention and resources from social programs. These Brookings Institution studies are a reminder that even the federal government has limited resources and that this condition can be a constraint on coalition activism.

The Basic Argument

We have examined socialist theories and some of the reasons why they have not been part of the American tradition. Social and economic class differences have tended to blur. Both individualism and ethnic group bonds, as well as personal and civil religion, tend to weaken class consciousness. Both the consensual political culture and regional loyalties—especially in the South—have had the same effect. Beyond these influences there is much evidence that most Americans are affluent, that the poor are a small minority and the really rich are a quite small number at the top. The distribution of income resembles a somewhat flattened out diamond rather than a pyramid with a large mass base of poor. Most Americans tend to *see* themselves as middle class when asked or when interviewers size them up. Next, a review of the evidence from surveys on how Americans see their jobs and their lives turned up surprisingly positive results. Impressively high percentages say they are satisfied with their jobs. Different ways of measuring such intangibles as satisfaction and happiness lead to the conclusion that Americans are a "generally contented population." Nor can biases and other possible limitations explain away the results, although there is some tendency for people to lower aspirations and accommodate themselves to what they cannot change. Obviously, the combination of affluence and basic satisfaction with life in the bulk of the population has made radical thought and action less attractive.

The tendency of Americans to think about politics in a schizophrenic manner further reduces the effect of radical appeals. Liberal policies tend to be supported in practice but much conservative, individualistic ideology persists in people's minds. The antigovernment attitudes widely expressed during the 1970s appear to be a continuation and perhaps intensification of such attitudes. Additionally, the "socialist capitalist" ideology of America's "people's capitalism" contradicts traditional socialist theory.

These influences have not only undercut the appeals of socialism but weakened the socioeconomic differences that originally formed the basis for the New Deal coalition. Studies of trends in class-oriented voting behavior in recent decades point to the conclusion that class-based differences in party identification and voting are weakening. Even the

Democratic victories of 1976 brought together a coalition somewhat different from that of the past. But regardless of differences, the Democrats in office faced serious budgetary constraints that made expanded social programs problematic. Even the long-established and popular Social Security system was in difficulty. There was not much leeway to act unless the Democrats were willing to proceed toward major changes in tax and spending policies that would be politically risky.

This analysis, if correct, points to several conclusions which we offer as food for thought in addressing the nation's problems in this last quarter of the twentieth century. For one, it is apparent that socialist alternatives, presented as such, will make little headway. There is much about the system that acts powerfully to counter socialist appeals and there is little reason to think these conditions will change in the foreseeable future. In the second place, social class differences appear to have suffered a permanent decline but are unlikely to disappear. Economics is of basic importance to most people and will continue to matter, and on this basis a tendency for the have-nots to support the Democrats and the haves to support the Republicans should persist. Economic crises would tend to intensify such differences. But it also appears that in an increasingly middle-class nation confronting many kinds of issues, the political conflict characteristic of the New Deal in its prime will not recur. Indeed, if Heilbroner is right the class conflict of the future may pit the major segments of the middle class, the lower middles and the higher middles, against one another. And for this conflict a somewhat different political rhetoric would presumably be in order.

However, as a third tentative conclusion we might suggest that a legacy of the New Deal rhetoric will persist. We have remarked a number of times on the amazing stability and continuity of the United States political system. George Washington, after all these years, is still "in." In a system such as this the New Deal heritage which dominated a generation of Americans will persist among some politicians and a good many voters for quite a while. It will remain alive even as the realities change. FDR and the New Deal will continue to be invoked, along with Jefferson and other national heroes. And the New Deal legacy of an active government will certainly persist, even as the nation grapples with new problems and seeks new solutions.

This legacy merits respect, but a fourth point deserves attention as in some ways counter to it. Increasingly the United States seems to confront problems for which the old ideologies, on both the left and the right, are deficient. We can never return to the days of free-market capitalism but a left that can offer only stale alternatives, such as socialism or the New Deal, is hardly much better. Perhaps it is time to set aside these somewhat dated ideologies and try to see the world anew. A healthy dose of pragmatism and some fresh thinking are in order. In this sense, too, the New Deal coalition is part of the past.

We have examined mass opinion from a number of perspectives, and have seen that in many ways mass opinion is the foundation of the system. Now we can begin to put the pieces together, to show how coalitions, elites, and masses relate and interact. When we have observed these interactions, we will have an integrated perspective from which to view elites, masses, and the system's coalitions.

NOTES

1. To define Marxism, revisionism, and the variations of socialist theory would require several other books. As an example of contemporary American Marxism, see Paul A. Baran and Paul M. Sweezy, *Monopoly Capital* (New York: Monthly Review Press Modern Reader, 1966). Vaguely revisionist books which became popular during the 1960s and later include the following: Herbert Marcuse, *One Dimensional Man* (Boston: Beacon Press, 1968); Charles A. Reich, *The Greening of America* (New York: Bantam Books, 1971). A recent text systematically applies a socialist perspective to United States government: Edward S. Greenberg, *The American Political System* (Cambridge, Mass.: Winthrop, 1977). This includes many suggestions for further reading. An important contribution to the literature on Marx and Marxism is the work of the democratic socialist Michael Harrington, *Socialism* (New York: Bantam Books, 1973).
   A Soviet Marxist would probably cringe when confronted with some American variants on socialist doctrine. We sympathize with his desire for a more orderly world and neatly defined doctrines but can do little to assuage his pain.
2. Hugh Davis Graham and Ted Robert Gurr, *Violence in America: Historical and Comparative Perspectives*, A Report to the National Commission on the Causes and Prevention of Violence, vol. 2 (Washington, D.C.: U.S. Government Printing Office), p. 628.
3. William Watts and Lloyd A. Free, *State of the Nation* (New York: Universe Books, Potomac Associates, 1973), p. 21. Note the anxious concern that Michael Harrington expresses in commenting on the "privatization" of working-class life. See his *Socialism* (New York: Bantam Books, 1973), pp. 436–437.
4. Milton Gordon, *Assimilation in America* (New York: Oxford University Press, 1964), pp. 48 ff. Harrington's *Socialism* refers to the immigrants and ethnic consciousness as one reason for socialism's failure (p. 158).
5. Everett Carll Ladd, Jr., with Charles Hadley, *Transformation of the American Party System*, 2nd ed. (New York: W. W. Norton, 1978), pp. 67 ff.
6. In fairness to Galbraith it should be said that he did single out impoverished groups of people whose condition was such that they did not share in the rising affluence of the many in the mainstream of the economy.
7. Ben J. Wattenberg, *The Real America*, rev. ed. (New York: G. P. Putnam's Capricorn Books, 1976), pp. 52 ff. The use of "constant dollars" is a method of measuring dollar values over time, to factor out changes in income levels due chiefly to changes in price rather than real increases in income. In other words, a "constant dollar" should have the same or similar buying power at different time periods.
8. Ibid., pp. 64–65.

9. Henry Owen and Charles L. Schultze, eds., *Setting National Priorities: The Next Ten Years* (Washington, D.C.: The Brookings Institution, 1976), Chapter 12, John L. Palmer and Joseph J. Minarik, "Income Security Policy," p. 526. This conclusion is similar to one reached by a Congressional Budget Office study. See "Poverty Status of Families Under Alternative Definitions of Income," Congress of the United States, Congressional Budget Office, Washington, D.C., Background Paper No. 17, Revised and Reprinted, February 1977.

10. Ibid., p. 534.

11. Robert L. Heilbroner, "Middle-Class Myths, Middle-Class Realities," *Atlantic*, October 1976, pp. 37 ff. The survey referred to relied partly on the judgment of the polltaker in assessing occupation and neighborhood and partly on the "feelings of the interviewer."

12. For an argument that is somewhat similar to Heilbroner's, see Andrew Levison, *The Working-Class Majority* (New York: Penguin Books, 1974). Levison argues that the working class is still quite large and is *not* disappearing, as the proponents of post-industrial change tend to believe. As with Heilbroner, much of the argument turns on where we should draw the line—and on what basis—between the workers or lower middle class and the middle class.

13. Okun, "Equal Rights but Unequal Incomes," *New York Times Magazine*, July 4, 1976, p. 102.

14. *Gallup Opinion Index*, April 1973, p. 8.

15. *Job Satisfaction: Is There a Trend?* (Washington, D.C.: U.S. Government Printing Office, U.S. Department of Labor Manpower Research Monograph No. 30, 1974), pp. 4–5.

16. Ibid., p. 7.

17. Ibid., p. 11.

18. *Gallup Opinion Index*, April 1973, p. 16.

19. Ibid., pp. 51–52.

20. Ibid., p. 7.

21. Angus Campbell, Philip E. Converse, and Willard L. Rodgers, *The Quality of American Life* (New York: Russell Sage Foundation, 1976), pp. 26–27.

22. Ibid., p. 34.

23. Ibid., p. 39.

24. Ibid., p. 99.

25. Ibid., p. 318.

26. Ibid., p. 277.

27. Ibid., p. 278.

28. Ibid., p. 133.

29. Ibid., p. 164.

30. Ibid., p. 485.

31. Ibid., pp. 100 ff.

32. Lloyd A. Free and Hadley Cantril, *The Political Beliefs of Americans* (New Brunswick, N.J.: Rutgers University Press, 1967), Chapters 2 and 3. An application of Free and Cantril's concepts in seeking to understand the national import of the conservatism triggered in 1978 by California's Proposition 13 tax revolt is that by Curtis B. Gans, "Conservatism by Default," *Nation*, October 14, 1978, pp. 272–274.

33. Daniel Katz, Barbara A. Gutek, Robert L. Kahn, Eugenia Barton, *Bureaucratic Encounters* (Ann Arbor, Mich.: Survey Research Center, Institute for Social Research, University of Michigan, 1975), pp. 184 ff.

34. Michael Harrington, *Socialism* (New York: Bantam Books, 1973), p. 142.

35. Galbraith, *Who Needs the Democrats: And What It Takes to Be Needed* (New York: New American Library Signet Broadside, 1970). Galbraith himself was not optimistic about the prospects for widespread acceptance of his self-styled radical alternatives, at least in the short run.

36. Norman H. Nie, Sidney Verba, and John R. Petrocik, *The Changing American Voter* (Cambridge, Mass.: Harvard University Press, 1976), pp. 347 ff.

37. Dennis S. Ippolito, Thomas G. Walker, and Kenneth L. Kolson, *Public Opinion and Responsible Democracy* (Englewood Cliffs, N.J.: Prentice-Hall, 1976), pp. 78–79.
38. Ibid., pp. 94–95.
39. Ibid., pp. 97–98.
40. Ladd and Hadley, *Transformations of the American Party System*, pp. 239 ff.
41. Gerald M. Pomper, Ross K. Baker, Charles E. Jacob, Wilson Carey McWilliams, and Henry A. Plotkin, *The Election of 1976* (New York: David McKay, 1977), pp. 73–75.
42. Ibid., p. 75.
43. Ibid., pp. 80–83.
44. Edward R. Fried, Alice M. Rivelin, Charles L. Schultze, Nancy H. Teeters, *Setting National Priorities: The 1974 Budget* (Washington, D.C.: Brookings Institution, 1971), p. 8. These sub-totals are high because of some double counting of federal grants to states and state grants to local government. The total reflecting government spending as a percent of GNP excludes this double counting of grants.
45. Joseph A. Pechman, ed., *Setting National Priorities: The 1978 Budget* (Washington, D.C.: Brookings Institution, 1977), pp. 35, 82. In 1955 defense spending was 58.2 percent of the federal budget.
46. Fried et al., *Setting National Priorities: The 1974 Budget*, p. 441.
47. Owen and Schultze, eds., *Setting National Priorities*, p. 346.
48. Ibid., pp. 356–357.

SUGGESTIONS FOR FURTHER READINGS

Charles H. Anderson. *Toward A New Sociology: A Critical View.* Homewood, Ill.: Dorsey Press, 1971. Incorporates, from a critical perspective, much analysis of the class system in the United States.

Shlomo Avineri. *The Social and Political Thought of Karl Marx.* Cambridge, Eng.: Cambridge University Press, 1968. A well written and respected introduction to the ideas of Marx.

Edward C. Banfield. *The Unheavenly City Revisited: A Revision of the Unheavenly City.* Rev. ed. Boston: Little, Brown, 1974. A famous and controversial book offering a conservative and critical analysis of such subjects as poverty.

Saul D. Feldman and Gerald W. Thielbar, eds. *Life Styles: Diversity in American Society.* Boston: Little, Brown, 1972. A set of readings on varied life styles including such unusual ones as that of the stripper.

Ada W. Finifter, ed. *Alienation and the Social System.* New York: John Wiley, 1972. Readings that sample many of the important contributions to the study of alienation.

Robert H. Haveman, ed. *A Decade of Federal Antipoverty Programs: Achievements, Failures, and Lessons.* New York: Academic Press, 1978. Readings that survey political, social, and economic aspects of antipoverty programs.

Dorothy Buckton James. *Poverty, Politics, and Change.* Englewood Cliffs, N.J.: Prentice-Hall, 1972. Analyzes the nature and extent of poverty in the United States in the context of values, institutions, and processes that tend to keep the poor in their place.

Robert J. Lampman. *Ends and Means of Reducing Income Poverty.* Chicago: Markham, Institute for Research on Poverty Monograph Series, 1971. An economist's scholarly analysis of poverty, past and present, and the effects of income redistribution.

Thomas L. Lasswell. *Class and Stratum: An Introduction to Concepts and Research.* Boston: Houghton Mifflin, 1965. Useful in reviewing the concept of class, some of the research done, and problems of measurement.

Andrew Levison. *The Working-Class Majority.* New York: Penguin Books, 1974. Levison challenges those who believe the working class is declining and also defends them from charges of authoritarianism.

Seymour Martin Lipset. *Political Man: The Social Bases of Politics.* Garden City, N.Y.: Doubleday, 1960. A much respected set of essays that explores the social bases of a modern democratic system.

Seymour Martin Lipset. *Socialism: Its Conspicuous Absence in the United States.* New Brunswick, N.J.: Rutgers University/Transaction Books, 1978. A leading sociologist examines the United States and the socialist heritage and argues that American values incorporate many of the aspirations of socialism.

Herman P. Miller. *Rich Man, Poor Man.* New York: Thomas Y. Crowell, 1971. A readable and well-researched analysis of income differentials.

Frank Parkin. *Class Inequality and Political Order: Social Stratification in Capitalist and Communist Societies.* New York: Praeger, 1971. A wide-ranging comparative analysis that is sympathetic to the quest for equality.

Daniel W. Rossides. *The American Class System: An Introduction to Social Stratification.* Boston: Houghton Mifflin, 1976. An extended scholarly analysis by a writer who considers existing inequalities excessive.

Arthur B. Shostak and William Gomberg, eds. *Blue-Collar World: Studies of the American Worker.* Englewood Cliffs, N.J.: Prentice-Hall, 1964.

Richard L. Siegel and Leonard B. Weinberg. *Comparing Public Policies: United States, Soviet Union and Europe.* Homewood, Ill.: Dorsey Press, 1977. A well-researched effort to compare and assess a wide range of public policies, including civil liberties, in socialist and nonsocialist systems.

Robert Tucker, ed. *The Marx-Engels Reader.* New York: W. W. Norton, 1972. A good one volume anthology of the basic writings by Marx and Engels with a helpful introduction.

Harold L. Wilensky. *The Welfare State and Equality: Structural and Ideological Roots of Public Expenditures.* Berkeley, Calif.: University of California Press, 1975. A valuable effort to compare and explain the levels of expenditures that occur in different kinds of political systems.

Part Three
ELITES, MASSES,
AND THE
POLITICAL
PROCESS

devoted mostly to the "shaky foundations of democracy" the masses are seen as highly intolerant, authoritarian, and prone to violence when aroused. Ordinary people, it is said, do not understand and appreciate basic values, such as freedom of expression. Controversial speakers, such as communists and atheists, are unlikely to be tolerated, and tolerance for ethnic, racial, and religious diversity is also limited. Understandably, foreigners too are regarded with suspicion, and warlike solutions to foreign policy problems are readily advocated. As for attitudes toward democracy, the masses tend to be either apathetic or, when aroused, willing to support demagogues and heavy-handed solutions. To the masses, due process of law is not a cardinal virtue.

Finally, near the end of the book, Dye and Zeigler summarize their perception of mass attitudes in a statement that is as strong as we may find anywhere: "Masses are authoritarian, intolerant, anti-intellectual, nativistic, alienated, hateful, and violent."[3] This statement is so harsh an assessment that we may wonder if we should take it at face value. But even if we allow the authors some literary license, we must still conclude that they do not think much of the abilities and morality of the mass of ordinary citizens. Other elite theorists have less hostile perceptions of the masses, but as a rule they tend to look down their noses at them.

Dye and Zeigler carry the argument a step further in stating that the deficiencies of the masses are not a temporary matter that will change with time. They marshal evidence to demonstrate that mass socialization via family, school, and work experience as adults creates people with narrow, closed minds.[4] "Working-class authoritarianism" is deeply ingrained. Given the nature of the masses, mass apathy actually *helps* democracy to survive. When demagogues arise to play upon popular passions and arouse mass activism, then democracy is threatened. Democratic values associated with the liberty and dignity of the individual come under attack. It is "the irony of democracy" that it exists for the masses but it is elites more than masses that uphold democratic values. Nor do Dye and Zeigler see any likelihood of change in the long term. On the contrary, they project a bleak future beset by the problems of increasingly scarce resources in which people will face horrendous problems of sheer survival and the need for expertise. Technological elites will increasingly supplant whatever mass influence remains and eventually relegate democracy to antiquity.

Not all elitists, we should again remind readers, would agree with Dye and Zeigler. Some of them prefer that elite rule be curbed and mass influences be enhanced.[5] Still, it is clear that the logic of the elite position is strengthened by those who develop a strong case for the incompetence of the masses.

Elections as Symbolic

The elite perspective downgrades the masses and so must not concede them much influence. Elections, above all else, are a crucial part of any political system that' professes to be democratic. Consistent elitists can hardly allow that choices made by the masses through elections act as powerful determinants of elite behavior.

Not surprisingly, Dye and Zeigler argue that elections serve chiefly as "symbolic reassurance" to the masses to help legitimate the established order.[6] The masses receive certain emotional gratifications from voting, but the elections do not determine public policy. Apart from the symbolic function, elections do, they admit, perform three lesser functions. One of these is to enable voters to participate in choosing personnel to hold office, as distinct from choosing policies. Voters may express a preference for Jimmy Carter over Gerald Ford, even if most of them know little of the issues. Second, voters may pass judgment upon *past* policies, such as an unpopular war. Such retrospective judgments may make "elites sensitive to mass welfare" but do not govern elite policies in the present or the future. Third, elections help to protect people from official abuse, as when black voters in the South won the vote and used it to moderate white racial policies. But in the main, to Dye and Zeigler elections are symbolic, and certainly not a means by which masses force elites to follow clearly expressed policy preferences.

Dye and Zeigler's view of the masses as generally incompetent is reinforced by analysis of their actual voting behavior. The typical mass voter is portrayed as poorly informed, lacking in ideology, inconsistent, and quite unable to respond to the issues. That many people are not well informed on the basic structure of the political system, the officeholders, and the issues is not hard to prove, and we mentioned some of this evidence in our discussion of mass participation. Large percentages of people are unable to name their senators and representatives in Washington and may even be confused about their terms of office. More specific questions relating to the president, Congress, the courts, and the Constitution and its Bill of Rights usually turn up uncertainty and outright ignorance. From time to time an enterprising reporter is able to write with wry humor about his experience in approaching people on the street to ask them to sign some part of the Constitution. The usual result is that many people do not know what the text is from and refuse to sign a statement of support.[7] On issues, too, there is often much vagueness, ignorance, and misperception. Dye and Zeigler cite approvingly the words of a well-known political scientist who states, "For many people, politics does not compete with sports, local gossip and television dramas." The authors then add that "many people simply have no opinion about political issues that are the subject of heated debate in the mass media."[8] Clearly the masses thus perceived are poorly equipped by their levels of information to play a significant part in elections.

Nor do the masses hold consistent and stable political opinions. The more highly educated people tend to think in ideological terms, such as liberal or conservative. And they tend to relate positions one to another, to avoid inconsistencies. The liberal normally favors the expansion of government and advocates a cluster of policies associated with welfare state measures. The consistent conservative would tend to favor limited government and the cutting of specific programs. But for the mass of people such ideological reasoning is typically lacking. They do not conceptualize and do not relate opinions, if they have them, to a pattern of belief. As Dye and Zeigler sum up, "Thus, except for a small educated portion of the electorate, the ideological debate between the elites has very little meaning. . . . The masses cannot be expected to possess an ideology."[9] Added to this limitation is the instability of mass opinions. Identification with a party persists but issue positions vary from time to time, except perhaps for a few highly controversial matters such as those associated with race. The masses lack both information and the ideological sophistication that would foster some consistency and stability, so their reactions tend to be emotional and volatile.

On this basis Dye and Zeigler argue that issues do not really count much in elections. Issues may seem to matter at times, as in the 1972 election, when George McGovern sought to present a choice in his electoral battle with Richard Nixon. But even then personalities mattered more to most people than issues. McGovern was an unpopular Democratic candidate, the most unpopular in decades. On the other hand, "Nixon was clearly a popular candidate, with positive ratings from voters of all ideological leanings." Thus even in an election that was unusual for its issue content, personalities mattered more than issues, and "it is probable that two-thirds of the electorate make a choice unrelated to the issues raised by the competing candidates or parties."[10]

Dye and Zeigler admit that elites may themselves blur the issues by failing to present clear alternatives. But basically, in this view, the trouble lies with the mass electorate. Their ignorance, lack of ideology, and instability make them incapable of using the election process to provide issue mandates that would govern elite behavior. Of course if the masses are as bad as some hard-nosed elitists perceive them to be, then their lack of policy influence via the elections may be seen as a blessing, not a fault.

Political Parties and Interest Groups

If the elections matter little, then the political parties suffer as well. A major purpose of the parties is to serve as conduits for popular demands, with the majority party organizing the government to carry out the popular will as determined by elections. Dye and Zeigler see American parties as plagued with numerous shortcomings. They tend to be dominated by activists. They fail to present real choices. They reach only a limited segment of the population. And in any case the parties have deteriorated in recent years. Much of this criticism would probably be conceded even by those with no strong elitist bias. Some observers would even argue that the criticism mistakes virtue for vice, on one point at least, for many believe that the parties work best in presenting a limited range of choices.[11]

Dye and Zeigler add a telling point, however, in citing a study of the delegates to the 1972 Democratic National Convention, which was held after party reforms had sought to reduce the power of political bosses and to enhance the representation of minorities, especially blacks and women. Whatever the intent, Dye and Zeigler cite evidence that at this convention:

> The gap between elites and masses was *wider* than usual. Seventy percent of the Democratic rank and file opposed busing, compared with 21 percent of the delegates; 69 percent of the Democratic rank and file opposed amnesty, compared with 18 percent of the delegates; 57 percent of the Democratic masses opposed a guaranteed income, compared with 26 percent of the delegates.[12]

Similarly, the party platform formulated by this convention was at odds with the masses. The real effect of party reform as catalogued by Dye and Zeigler was to increase the gap between elites and masses. It thereby added to the deficiencies of the party system as an instrument of the popular will serving the masses. In the end, from the elite perspective the weakness of the party system means that the prevailing elite consensus is not effectively challenged via strong parties presenting clear alternatives. (See Table 10–1.)

One further avenue for potential mass influence upon elites is the interest group system. Pluralists have long argued that American democracy may indeed be imperfect but does provide some counter to these imperfections via the mass of organizations people join and by means of which they express themselves. In this view these organizations add a form of representation to the public will, give people a sense of belonging, and help to bring about beneficial changes in public policy. Some in-

Table 10-1 Positions on Three Issues: Democrat Rank and File Versus 1972
Democratic Convention Delegates

	Percent Opposed	
Issue	*Rank & File*	*Delegates*
Amnesty	69	18
Busing	70	21
Guaranteed Annual Income	57	26

Source: Thomas R. Dye and L. Harmon Zeigler, *The Irony of Democracy,* 4th ed. (North Scituate, Mass.: Duxbury Press, 1978), p. 198.

terests may indeed be "bad" and pervert public policy, but to the pluralists the interest group system as a whole is beneficial.

Naturally enough, Dye and Zeigler attack this benign conception of pluralistic democracy. They argue that many people do not join groups, that group leadership reflects an elite bias, and that the result is an added force for conservatism, not change or responsiveness. They acknowledge, on the basis of a major study of people's organizational affiliations, that more than a majority may belong to some organizaton. But they counter with the argument that most who join are inactive and the active elite gives an upper-class bias to most organizations. Elites emerge to dominate the interest group system. In passing these authors admit that some organizations do not have an elite bias, and they offer the Ku Klux Klan as an example. But the Klan is an exception and most organizations, they insist, tend to enhance the gap between elites and masses. This conclusion is confimed by an authoritative study of participation in America by Verba and Nie, whom Dye and Zeigler cite approvingly and which we also cited in Chapter 4. As a rule, those who are already well off economically tend to join organizations and to be active in them, thereby adding to the advantages they already possess. Overall, in the eyes of Dye and Zeigler, the "iron law of oligarchy" described long ago by the European scholar Robert Michels tends to prevail. Every group ends up dominated by a small elite of leaders. The realities of group politics undercut the pluralist defense of interest group democracy.[13]

Other aspects of the pluralist case come under heavy fire from Dye and Zeigler. They argue that the system tends to reflect and to be responsive to conservative business interests. Mass organizations may have large numbers of people but they tend to achieve only symbolic rewards, whereas small, cohesive groups, and especially those representing business interests, achieve tangible benefits. Analysis of the energy crisis in 1973 demonstrates that oil interests tended to monopolize information, had the resources for a vigorous propaganda campaign, and provided many of the experts drawn into the government bureaucracy to cope with the problem. Even when numbers of the "have-nots" organize to pursue their interests, their organizations tend in time to become bureaucratic and status quo oriented, with a conservative influence upon their members and upon the system. They tend to attract those who are more active and interested and to that extent are already committed to the system. Then, whatever change they do achieve tends to be incremental and piecemeal rather than sweeping or radical. On point after point in their analysis of interest groups, Dye and Zeigler offer evidence at odds with the pluralists' optimistic interpretation. Elite influence and mass impotence are again revealed.

We have now followed one part of the case for elitism developed by Dye and Zeigler in their systematic analysis of mass attitudes, elections, political parties, and interest groups to demonstrate mass apathy, incompetence, and nastiness. But what of the elite itself? As they define it initially the elite is a small and unrepresentative group drawn mostly from the upper strata of society and with certain values in common. The group is not closed but admits new members only quite gradually as they are socialized into elite values. Public policy reflects these elite values, so that most lines of influence extend from elites to masses and little from masses to elites.[14] But this definition leaves much about elites uncertain.

The Concentration of Wealth and Corporate Power

Elite theories vary in content, but none of them conceives of an elite of the poverty-stricken, to put it mildly. Members of the elite are typically portrayed as quite well off financially and as associated closely with others who have great wealth. Therefore a crucial feature of the elitist case is usually an examination of corporate concentration, the concentration of wealth, and the relationship of economic elites to governmental elites. Given the size of the United States and its huge GNP, it is not difficult to come up with some impressive figures on the size of certain corporations and the great wealth of some individuals and families. Dye and Zeigler present evidence for the concentration of corporate resources in a limited number of businesses in various sectors of the economy, including industry, utilities, transportation, communications, and banking. According to their figures, among some 200,000 industrial corporations, the top 100 controlled 52 percent of all industrial assets. The five largest industrial corporations controlled 10 percent of the nation's industrial assets.[15] Among 13,500 banks, the 50 largest controlled 48 percent of all banking assets. Three banks controlled 14 percent of all banking assets. Among insurance companies, eighteen controlled two-thirds and two controlled one quarter of all insurance assets.

In addition to these corporate giants dominating sectors of the economy, there are the tie-ins formed at the top which tend to intensify corporate concentration. One of these ties is the presence of interlocking directorates. Leading executives, such as the well-known David Rockefeller of Chase Manhattan Bank, tend to sit on the boards of a number of corporations. Big corporations in turn buy stock in other corporations and exert influence upon them, whether subtle or overt. Dye and Zeigler cite some eye-catching figures: the 3,572 people listed as major officials of top corporations "controlled half the nation's industrial assets, half of all assets in communications, transportation, and utilities, nearly half of all banking assets, and two thirds of all insurance assets."

Having argued the case for corporate concentration, Dye and Zeigler marshal evidence for the concentration of wealth. One basic and rather frequently cited table presents the distribution of family income from 1929 into the 1970s. According to this table, the distribution changed but little over this fairly long period. In 1929 the lowest one-fifth of families with the smallest incomes received a meager 3.5 percent share of all family income. In 1974 this share was up only to 5.4 percent. As for the high end, the wealthiest one-fifth of families received 54.4 percent of family income in 1929. In 1975 this share was down only to 41.0 percent. From such modest changes a case can be made that little income redistribution has taken place over a period of some forty years. A critic could angrily argue that gross inequalities in incomes persisted. Indeed, Dye and Zeigler list some Americans with fortunes of $100 million and more, including the Du Ponts, Fords, and Mellons. They further observe that such huge fortunes increased from 45 in 1957 to 153 in 1968.

But perhaps the most colorful account of the "super-rich" is the book by Ferdinand Lundberg. Lundberg caustically compared the United States to a "banana republic" and then detailed the high concentration of wealth in a small number of enormously rich families. He awarded the prize for superwealth to the Du Ponts, whom he described as "250 Big Du Ponts and many Little Du Ponts." By examining the evidence available he estimated the Du Pont family fortune at many billions: "I conclude, therefore, that the financially cohesive Du Pont family is capable of throwing something around a $7.5 billion 'punch' at any time in the American political economy on the present price level."[16] Another family fortune illustrates the oddities of the tax system and what reformers regard as a major loophole. Mrs. Horace B. Dodge was listed as having a net worth in 1957 of 75 to 100 million dollars. Lundberg pointed out that she had "converted all her holdings into tax-exempt state and municipal securities."[17] For this reason she could receive literally millions of dollars each year in interest paid by these securities yet pay not a cent in federal income tax. Lundberg's book is filled with vivid details such as these. It becomes crystal clear that some Amerians are fabulously rich.

One other source, although not the work of an avowed elitist, supplements and updates this portrayal of concentration. After examining figures on income distribution, David Garson concluded, "The general picture is one in which the wealthiest one-fifth of the nation owns *three quarters* of all private wealth, while the poorest fifth owns less than one-half of one percent!" Alongside this concentration of wealth he also found much concentration in the economy.

> The top 500 or so manufacturing firms and the top 50 financial institutions dominate the economy. And they are tied together by interlocking directorships, linking economic notables in a given metropolitan area, linking corporations in the same industry, and linking corporations to banks. It is no exaggeration to state that less than 0.5 percent of the population control the American economy through the economic positions they hold.[18]

These portrayals of corporate concentration may be dramatized by taking some living examples of corporate gigantism from the mid-1970s. Our figures are from the *World Almanac* of 1978. Among banks, Bank of America led with over $60 billion in deposits. Citibank had over $53 billion in deposits, followed by Chase Manhattan with over $38 billion. At the end of the list of 101 banks, the smallest still had over a billion dollars in deposits. At the head of this list are banks with huge deposits that would obviously enable them to exercise considerable influence.

Among industrial concerns, Exxon led the list, with revenues of over $48 billion and profits exceeding $2.6 billion. Next was General Motors, with revenues over $47 billion and profits in excess of $2.9 billion. GM's competitor, Ford, had revenues of more than $28 billion and profits of almost $1 billion. Even the smallest concern in this list of the 50 biggest reported revenues of $3.6 billion.

The case for elite domination of the system often moves beyond analysis of the concentration of wealth and of corporate giants dominating the economy to include the military as a central feature of a military-industrial complex. There is readily available evidence for those who wish to examine it. The Cold War, the war in Indochina, and the continuing arms race between the superpowers have made national security issues a persisting and often dominant concern. The national government regularly spends huge sums on defense and maintains an enormous military establishment. Control of this defense establishment, including the CIA, has often been problematic. The military has advantages in information, expertise, and even in the secrecy that shrouds many military matters that make civilian control difficult. Military contracts count for much to many big companies. They tend to forge strong alliances with military counterparts in government in advocating novel and expensive weapons systems whose usefulness is hard to evaluate from outside. Some members of the military and economic elites form close personal ties and there is a blurring of the public with the private sector. Unions become drawn into support of such projects when jobs are involved. Constituency pressures affect congressmen who vote on military contracts and military bases for their districts. It used to be said of one congressman that if the government put any more military bases in his state it would sink. Supplementing these pressures are those from veterans, reserve organizations, and other military-oriented associations. They tend to support a strong military posture and will also rally in support of measures relating to military pay and fringe benefits. The military-industrial complex has become a popular target of elite critics.

Interlocking Economic and Political Elites

Given the evidence for corporate concentration and the fantastic size of some family fortunes, a further stage in the elite argument consists in tracing the "interlock" that relates economic elites to political elites. Historically an important linkage has been campaign contributions. The costs of campaigns, especially those for high office, are high and increase year after year. Adequate funds do not insure victory, but inadequate funds may insure defeat. Businessmen and wealthy individuals have interests to protect and want people in office who, if not friendly, are at least not unfriendly. For those who have large sums available to them, either from their own fortune or from corporate coffers, a hefty contribution may represent a small cost with potential for a substantial return. As Dye and Zeigler note, Richard Nixon raised roughly $60 million dollars for his 1972 reelection campaign. Indeed, they argue that, "Few candidates can even begin a political career for state or local office without securing financial support from wealthy 'angels.' "[19] The wealthy businessman W. Clement Stone backed Nixon in 1972 to the tune of about $2 million. Stewart Mott, heir to a GM fortune, was a strong backer of George McGovern. Business people tend to back Republicans but may back Democrats at the same time. Labor, and especially the large AFL-CIO federation, tends to back Democrats with money and, even more important, with a large scale-organization to register people and get them out to vote.

At any rate, the flow of money into campaigns from big corporations and rich families has been impressive and has involved large sums. The 1972 election may have been unusual because of the tactics of Nixon's

Committee to Re-elect the President, which led to Watergate, but the massive flow of campaign contributions probably differed only in degree from previous elections. Even in 1964, when Barry Goldwater ran as one who was seemingly an outsider in opposition to the Eastern Establishment, he nonetheless received large sums from wealthy members of that same Establishment.[20]

The ties between the private capitalistic sector and the public sector become strong and close. Wealthy entrepreneurs help officeholders win their positions. Once their candidate is in office, business people supply information, expertise, personnel, and a variety of services. And, of course, business interests lobby heavily to supplement their other influences. The lobbying by International Telephone and Telegraph to obtain a favorable antitrust ruling was a spectacular case in point.[21] Of this intense effort Senator Edward Kennedy observed, "The sustained and sophisticated ITT antitrust lobbying effort from 1969 to 1971 is a tribute to the advanced state of the lobbying art. Any cabinet member or White House aide who was not contacted by ITT must now be suffering from a feeling of second-class citizenship."[21]

To Galbraith the ties between business and government are so pervasive as to amount to a fusing together:

> There is a close fusion of industrial system with the state. Members of the technostructure work closely with their public counterparts not only in the development and manufacture of products but in advising them of their needs. Were it not so celebrated in ideology, it would long since have been agreed that the line that now divides public from so called private organization in military procurement, space exploration and atomic energy is so indistinct as to be merely imperceptible. Men move easily across the line.[22]

Galbraith wrote that even firms that do not sell most of their output to the government are heavily dependent upon it for regulating total demand, for underwriting risky technology, and for the supply of trained personnel. He believed that "increasingly it will be recognized that the mature corporation, as it develops, becomes part of a larger administrative complex associated with the state. Men will look back in amusement at the pretense that once caused people to refer to General Dynamics and North American Aviation and AT&T as *private* business."

Plato believed that government by philosopher kings would be for the best. Modern American elite theorists are not of one mind but many are quite critical of elite influence. Certainly it is in its nature undemocratic. Popular influences are either stifled or filtered and manipulated to create the results desired by the elite. Galbraith has argued that the technostructure exerts a pernicious influence in a variety of ways. It fosters a Cold

War ideology that sustains high levels of defense spending—without the destructiveness of actual fighting. Government spending in general maintains a high level of aggregate demand and full employment. In addition, specific demands are manipulated to create wants for all manner of material goods, whether for deodorants or cars, that go beyond genuine needs. Spending that serves the technostructure is favored. Spending for social purposes to improve hospitals, housing, city slums, and public transportation suffers. People are encouraged to work beyond need and to think of idleness as a form of evil. These values permeate the educational system to make it a handmaiden of the industrial system rather than a critic and source of independent values. Even aesthetic purposes suffer. What is useful is easily justified, but what is merely beautiful is considered valueless if not dangerous. (Even Plato would have banned the poets.) Fundamentally the system becomes one which exists for itself and subordinates all else to it, rather than existing to serve the physical needs of ordinary men and women. People become the servants of the system ostensibly developed to serve them. The imperial presidency, so celebrated and criticized since Watergate, is the fitting capstone for this pyramid of power.

The Structure of Power

In our discussion of elite theory we have drawn upon a number of sources to try to construct a plausible case for elite domination. As Dye and Zeigler see them, the masses are thoroughly undemocratic in their values and tend to be either apathetic or violence-prone. These undemocratic attitudes are deeply ingrained via the socialization process that derives from the influence of family, education, and job experience.

The masses are therefore ill equipped to take advantage of democratic processes that might otherwise constrain elites. Elections become chiefly symbolic exercises; the masses are badly informed, inconsistent and unstable, and are not able to judge and act upon the issues of the day. Political parties have decayed, do not present meaningful choices, and tend not to be representative of mass attitudes anyway. Interest groups reflect an elite bias, effectively exclude the underdog, and have a largely conservative influence that favors the status quo.

Alongside the masses, who are deemed to be incompetent, largely impotent, and a potential threat to democratic values, there is the enlightened elite. Typically they are closely associated with and may derive from economic elites. Much concentration may be found in leading sectors of the economy with a relatively few gigantic corporations dominant and these relationships in turn reinforced by interlocks among top corporate officials in different corporations. The great wealth of a small number of individuals and families adds to the other disparities in influence between the elite and ordinary people.

The interlock between economic and political elites comes about in a variety of ways, some of which may be seen in the intimate ties between business and the military establishment. The result is a blending of the private and the public sector so pervasive as to render the distinction almost meaningless. Elite influence on public policy produced a number of evils. To some the Cold War itself was a product of a misguided and self-serving elite. In any event, elite influence distorts and perverts national priorities and threatens to create a system that becomes an end in itself rather than the means to a better life for all.

In a world in which much has gone wrong, elite theory, the "view from the top," helps make sense of the world, provides a recognizable set of "devils" to blame for the troubles of the times, and may even, perhaps, provide some wry humor. And for those who have lost faith in the masses, an elite that is more or less benign may be reassuring. But whatever the advantages of elite theory in its various guises, hard-nosed and otherwise, it is not the last word. There is a good deal of evidence for a different perspective. To criticize elite theory and to develop this different perspective is our next task. Unless we can restore some of our tattered faith in the people and in self-government, we might as well end our account of public opinion at this point.

NOTES

1. Floyd Hunter, Community Power Structure (Garden City, N.Y.: Doubleday Anchor Books, 1963). First published in 1953. Among social scientists Hunter's conception of elitism became the model of the single elite and has been frequently cited in contrast to the pluralist or plural elite model. One fairly brief account of elite theorists and their theories is Geraint Parry's, Political Elites (New York: Praeger, 1969).
2. C. Wright Mills, The Power Elite (N.Y.: Oxford University Press, 1956), p. 4.
3. Thomas R. Dye and L. Harmon Zeigler, The Irony of Democracy: An Uncommon Introduction to American Politics, 4th ed. (North Scituate, Mass.: Duxbury Press, 1978), p. 374. In the second edition, Zeigler's "postscript" expressed modest hopes that far-reaching educational reform might in time enlighten the masses and thereby improve the prospects for a measure of self-government.
4 Ibid., p. 126 ff.
5. Much of the writing on elites is critical, including that of Hunter, Mills, and Galbraith. At the same time, elite theorists often express implicitly a preference for a centralized system of political and administrative structures and tend to deplore much of what they see in popular culture and tastes. One wonders how much popular influence such writers really want in their ideal political system.
6. Dye and Zeigler, The Irony of Democracy, pp. 175 ff. Readers may wish to compare the authors' treatment of elections in the fourth edition with that in the third edition. The fourth edition clearly adds an election function, that of choosing personnel.

7. An Oklahoma reporter once tried this stunt, using the Sixth Amendment to the Constitution, on the governor and some state legislators. The governor quickly recognized and signed the amendment, but some of the state legislators were suspicious, obviously unaware of what they were reading. Presumably Oklahoma is not the only state in which this might happen.
8. Dye and Zeigler, *The Irony of Democracy*, p. 162.
9. Ibid., p. 164.
10. Ibid., p. 168.
11. The importance of the electoral middle, the moderates, in determining the outcome of the election is a major thesis of Richard M. Scammon and Ben J. Wattenberg, as we noted in Chapter 2. See *The Real Majority: An Extraordinary Examination of the American Electorate* (N.Y.: Coward-McCann, 1970). Many political scientists incline to a similar view.
12. Dye and Zeigler, *The Irony of Democracy*, p. 198.
13. Ibid., p. 260. The reference is to Michel's *Political Parties*, first published in English in 1915. See Robert Michels, *Political Parties: A Sociological Study of the Oligarchical Tendencies of Modern Democracies*, translated by Eden and Cedar Paul; introduction by Seymour Martin Lipset (New York: Free Press, 1962).
14. Ibid., p. 6.
15. Ibid., pp. 95 ff.
16. Ferdinand Lundberg, *The Rich and the Super-Rich* (New York: Bantam Books, 1969), pp. 165, 169.
17. Ibid., pp. 161, 224. This quirk in the tax system infuriates reformers. But it pleases governors and city fathers, who use the issuance of such securities as an important means of raising money and defend it politically with great vigor.
18. G. David Garson, *Power and Politics in the United States* (Lexington, Mass.: D. C. Heath, 1977), pp. 177, 185. Garson argues that we need to move beyond the elitist-pluralist debate to what he calls "the political economy approach." See Chapter 12.
19. Dye and Zeigler, *The Irony of Democracy*, pp. 204–205.
20. G. William Domhoff, *Who Rules America?* (Englewood Cliffs, N.J.: Prentice-Hall, 1967), pp. 87–90.
21. Anthony Sampson, *The Semisovereign State of ITT* (New York: Fawcett Crest Books, 1973), p. 237.
22. John Kenneth Galbraith, *The New Industrial State*, 2nd rev. ed. (Boston: Houghton-Mifflin, 1971), pp. 395–396.

SUGGESTIONS FOR FURTHER READINGS

E. Digby Baltzell. *The Protestant Establishment: Aristocracy and Class in America.* New York: Random House Vintage Books, 1964. A well-written analysis, historical and contemporary, of the Protestant upper class.

Richard J. Barnet and Ronald E. Muller. *Global Reach: The Power of the Multinational Corporations.* New York: Simon and Schuster, 1975. A critical look at the multinationals.

R.B. Bottomore. *Elites and Society.* Baltimore, Md.: Penguin Books, 1970. A readable survey of elite theory and some questions of social philosophy from a socialist perspective.

Ovid Demaris. *Dirty Business: The Corporate-Political Money-Power Game.* New York: Harper's Magazine Press, 1974. An exposé of corporate misdeeds.

G. William Domhof. *The Higher Circles: The Governing Class in America.* New York: Random House Vintage Books, 1970. Domhof argues that the upper class, made up of those from the top families, schools, and other upper-class institutions, is the governing class.

James A. Donovan. *Militarism, U.S.A.* New York: Charles Scribner's Sons, 1970. A retired Marine Corps colonel critically assesses the military-industrial complex and its effect on national policy.

John Kenneth Galbraith. *Economics and the Public Purpose.* New York: New American Library Signet Book, 1973. A famous social critic extends the analysis of his *The New Industrial State* with his prescription for socializing the system.

Edward S. Greenberg. *The American Political System: A Radical Approach.* Cambridge, Mass.: Winthrop, 1977. American government from the perspective of Marxist social theory.

Michael Harrington. *The Twilight of Capitalism.* New York: Simon and Schuster Touchstone Books, 1976. The well-known social democrat renews his indictment of the failures of capitalism and the misunderstandings of Marxism.

Suzanne Keller. *Beyond the Ruling Class: Strategic Elite in Modern Society.* New York: Random House, 1963. A review of elite theory, elite types in strategic positions, and supporting data.

Kenneth Lamott. *The Moneymakers: Or the Great Big New Rich in America.* Boston: Little, Brown, 1969. Highly readable accounts of modern Americans who have made large fortunes.

Robert J. Larner. *Management Control and the Large Corporation.* New York: Dunellen, 1970. Larner concludes that control and management of the largest corporations is separated from ownership but it does not appear to make much difference.

Seymour Melman. *The Permanent War Economy: American Capitalism in Decline.* New York: Simon and Schuster, 1974. A critical account of capitalism and the military.

Mark V. Nadel. *Corporations and Political Accountability.* Lexington, Mass.: D.C. Heath, 1976. An interest group perspective that details ways in which corporations influence the political system for their own benefit.

Geraint Parry. *Political Elites.* New York: Praeger, 1969. A survey of classical elite theory and criticisms of it.

Kenneth Prewitt and Alan Stone. *The Ruling Elites: Elite Theory, Power, and American Democracy.* New York: Harper & Row, 1973. A readable review, commentary upon, and assessment of elite theory.

Bruce M. Russett. *What Price Vigilance? The Burdens of National Defense.* New Haven, Conn.: Yale University Press, 1970. A scholar presents a provocative analysis of the data available and argues the pernicious effects of defense spending.

David Wise and Thomas B. Ross. *The Invisible Government.* New York: Bantam Books, 1964. A readable exposé of the activities of the intelligence establishment.

David Wise. *The Politics of Lying: Government Deception, Secrecy, and Power.* New York: Random House Vintage Books, 1973. A highly critical account of the practices of governmental elites over the years, under both Republican and Democratic administrations.

11 · Elite Theory Criticized: The View from the Middle

Whatever the appeals of elite theory, there is plenty of evidence that does not fit it. And whether we call this contrasting perspective pluralism or something else, the evidence needs an airing. We need not put the ordinary citizen on a pedestal as the centerpiece of an idealized and unrealistic version of democracy. Nonetheless, we can show that the elite model distorts and oversimplifies a complex reality, one that does not fit either single elite theory or a pure democracy either. For there is reason to believe that the mass of people, meaning the nation's vast middle class, live pretty well and have a democratic potential, as the system itself does. In some ways the people do actually constrain elites.

The Masses as Middle Class

In turning our attention to the masses we should recall our analysis of social class in Chapter 9. There we argued that the bulk of the population is fairly affluent. An average family income of $14,000 as of the nation's bicentennial is in itself eloquent testimony to the generalized levels of material well-being that prevail. As we also noticed from the surveys cited, most Americans *see* themselves as middle class. It is true that poverty has continued to exist, but by the mid-1970s it had fallen to about 5 percent of the population when in-kind services provided by the government are counted in the reckoning. The distribution of income looked much like a flattened diamond, with most people in the middle and fairly small extremes at the top and bottom.

In addition, there is solid evidence that Americans are a "generally contented population." Certainly the evidence from job satisfaction surveys, and from the study of "the quality of American life" by Campbell and others, all adds up to a strongly positive reaction on the part of most Americans. Here we might recall too that we found the nuclear family still strong and found as well that most Americans are believers in some form of religion and think it important in their lives. Both, we may surmise, probably contribute much to the generally contented population found in the survey data.

That this kind of evidence has an impact we may see even in the eyes of an avowed critic, Herbert Marcuse, whose *One Dimensional Man* was influential among student protest leaders during the 1960s. His credentials as a critic of the system would appear to be impeccable. Yet Marcuse had to admit that modern society provides a pretty good life for many. In his words, "A comfortable, smooth, reasonable, democratic unfreedom prevails in advanced industrial civilization, a token of technical progress."[1] This admission that life was "comfortable, smooth, reasonable," even if also described as "unfreedom," is a significant admission by one who denounces the system. An affluent and generally contented population may disconcert radical critics but says much for the state of the masses.

The masses may also be attacked for their taste, or lack of it, as displayed in patterns of consumption and entertainment. The piling up of material possessions far beyond essentials and the frivolity of much mass entertainment make easy targets. Even if this criticism has merit, however, it may easily be overdone. For one thing, one suspects that many of the critics of popular taste themselves enjoy the good life and have plenty of possessions of their own. Thus they may be condemning in others a style of affluent living quite similar to theirs. In the second place, popular tastes are not quite as superficial and frivolous as may first appear. Ben J. Wattenberg, in his defense of "the real America," dug up some interesting figures on patterns of personal consumption expenditures from 1960 to 1970.[2] Expenditures for "private education" registered the sharpest percentage increase, 181 percent, followed in descending order by medical care, personal business, foreign travel, and recreation. At the low end, expenditures for food, beverages, and tobacco increased by 63 percent, and transportation by 81 percent. Those who attack mass spending habits neglect such basic trends in spending patterns.

In citing these pluses to characterize the conditions of the bulk of Americans we do not want to oversimplify, as many do in writing either to criticize or to defend the system. The system is certainly not perfect. Poverty persists, and some groups, most notably blacks and women, tend to have incomes roughly three-fifths—or less—that of white males. As average incomes have risen, a good deal of income inequality has persisted. Critics like Galbraith would continue to argue that a whole range of public services are neglected, even as private affluence swells. A great many social problems exist and may continue for the foreseeable future. While we are on this point we might also note that most Americans, no matter how affluent and middle class they may already be, still expect, by and large, to have their incomes rise further year after year. There are no signs of a "saturation" effect. Whether we think this unceasing quest for "more" is good or bad, it is a basic and powerful concern which political leaders ignore at their peril. Still, whatever the deficiencies of the system, it is difficult to depict the mass of Americans as impoverished and embittered.

Education and Democratic Attitudes

Even if most people are fairly affluent and satisfied, elite theorists can still consider them ignorant, bigoted, and authoritarian. In challenging this tendency to dwell upon the worst in the ordinary American we may counter with some of the evidence touched upon in previous chapters. For one thing, we saw in Chapter 6 that the United States devotes enormous resources to education. The proportion completing high school rose from 60 percent in 1960 to about 75 percent in the early 1970s. The proportion entering college rose dramatically, from 32 percent in 1960 to 43 percent in 1973. The masses in America obviously receive education on a grand scale and it extends upward to higher education. Formal education does not guarantee enlightenment but it is a fundamental correlate of tolerance. Unless we are able to dismiss this truly enormous educational enterprise as a colossal waste of effort, we must acknowledge that fundamental conditions for the spread of mass enlightenment have been provided.

This massive extension of formal education to so many people reinforces a second point made in our discussion of education. For there we cited some evidence which challenges the negative treatment of popular attitudes found in much social science literature and popular writing. If these writers are correct, then the workers often singled out as a reservoir of prejudice in reality differ little from other groups. We shall remind readers of some of their conclusions.

For instance Richard F. Hamilton's survey of working-class attitudes cast doubt upon the alleged hawkish, jingoistic attitudes of workers: "In the noneconomic area, in the sphere of civil rights, it was shown that outside the South there were only very small differences in attitude associated with class. Even these small differences did not support the received claims."[3] Andrew Levison supplements Hamilton's analysis with a review of national surveys and other data that lead him to write, "The vision of workers as the most conservative sector of the population, like working class affluence, is fundamentally a myth. While racism and militarism do exist, workers are no worse and perhaps even better than the middle class on many issues, and none of the problems which pitted them against blacks or students result from any 'inevitable' conservatisms."[4] Levison does not idealize the working class, but he finds them to be no worse than other Americans, a point that elite theory in its tendency to sterotype them as hard-hat bigots is often reluctant to admit. Ippolito, Walker, and Kolson added to this perspective with data from 1974 surveys on a series of issues in which respondents are arranged according to occupational differences. They refer to the sterotype of workers as reactionary but observe, "The data . . . tend to reject this 'hard hat' image."[5] All this evidence points to the lack of sharp contrasts in class attitudes politically and the inaccuracy of portraying workers as a reservoir of prejudice.

That distinctions between classes have declined is also a conclusion we reached in our analysis of social class differences in Chapter 9. There we found strong indications that social class differences in voting behavior have waned and other issues have come to the fore. Increasingly the country appears to be an amorphous middle class in which differences that arise from income, education, and occupation matter less than they once did.

One other study, cited in conjunction with our analysis of political culture in Chapter 3, contributes to this perspective on mass attitudes. In writing about democratic norms and tolerance, David G. Lawrence concluded on an upbeat note: "First of all, the 1971 public is more tolerant than previous data would lead us to expect. In almost all contexts this tolerant portion of Americans constitute a clear majority of citizens. . . Second, there is slack in the system that can be exploited by civil liberties–oriented citizens."[6] By this last Lawrence meant that many people who were not strongly in favor of civil liberties nonetheless respected the system's values and *could* be mobilized by the libertarians. They therefore represented a potential for support. The American public of the 1970s was not a teeming mass of Archie Bunkers awaiting the demagogue's inflammatory rhetoric.

Nor is this all. A brief review of some recent history reminds us that times *have* changed and reinforces Lawrence's conclusion that tolerance has increased. In the 1950s the South was still a racially segregated society and the north was no racial paradise. Much has changed since that time, even if inequalities have persisted. The protest that accompanied the civil rights movement enlarged the civil liberties of everyone. There have also been substantial changes in controls over executive actions and police powers. Presidents, policemen, and intelligence agencies operate under constraints that were not widely approved in the 1950s. Experts may dispute the kind and degree of change, but it would be hard to affirm that no change has taken place.

Nor, in this context, should we neglect Watergate, with its implications for the contrast often drawn between elites and masses. The White House and its staff have to be seen as elite territory. But the mean-spirited and vindictive lawlessness that Watergate exposed would fit nicely into some of the more malevolent portrayals of the masses. This problem led Dye and Zeigler to revise rather substantially the third and fourth or post–Watergate editions of their popular text. They had to recognize and analyze elite repression as a possibly serious threat to democracy.

Furthermore, their analysis led them beyond Watergate to historical examples of elite repression, including the behavior of former presidents in crisis situations.[7] But once elites are seen to be thus flawed, they no longer differ sharply from the masses. And this narrowing of differences is particularly true if we accept the modified perspective on mass shortcomings presented by authors such as Hamilton, Levison, and Lawrence.

It is also true, as we must emphasize here and elsewhere, that the issues have changed a good deal over time. In the 1950s and 1960s a lunch counter that flatly refused to serve blacks its hamburgers and other junk food was a clear and simple target. By the 1970s the issues were not so clear and simple. Did past discrimination justify medical schools in setting aside a number of spaces for the admission of minorities on the basis of test scores not the same as those applied to whites? Should the denial of a fee for a campus talk to Ron Ziegler, President Nixon's press secretary, be construed as censorship or not? Was Henry Kissinger in some sense a criminal who should not occupy a chair in a great university? Was opposition to gay rights in any form simply old-fashioned bigotry? Well-educated and articulate spokesmen for elite factions differed in the answers provided. That ordinary citizens should be confused, uncertain, and divided in their responses could hardly be considered chiefly a consequence of mass bigotry.

We cannot and would not try to prove that all Americans are models of tolerance, halo and all. But we believe that those who perceive the mass of Americans as a narrow-minded, bigoted lot are in error. American civil liberties seemed in general to be in much better shape in the 1970s than they were in the 1950s. And the problems that arose were often of a nature that defied simplistic explanations, including especially elitist tendencies to blame the prejudice-ridden masses.

Concern with Public Opinion

To show that the masses are relatively affluent and contented and are not a reservoir of prejudice goes far toward establishing their democratic potential. But is that potential realized? A critique of elite theory needs to show that this democratic potential is not dissipated in elections that are chiefly a "symbolic exercise." But before we evaluate the election process we want to make clear to readers that there is much about the whole system that appears designed to cater to the wishes of the masses.

In the first place, there is the plain fact of the continuing extension of the suffrage in the United States. Even Dye and Zeigler have to admit that, in the beginning the elite that drafted the Constitution held democratic ideas: "Other elites asserted the divine right of kings, while American elites talked about government by the consent of the governed."[8] And as time passed there were further extensions of the suffrage. By the 1970s virtually everyone eighteen or older could qualify to vote without regard to race, sex, or other attribute. To explain this vast expansion of the electorate over time as basically the work of an elite is possible but not plausible. It is almost redundant to add that this expansion of the franchise is thoroughly in accord with the democratic values of the political culture, values which the American elite was far more willing to accept from the very beginning than other elites.

In the second place, the structure of the system appears designed to maximize pluralism and opportunities for mass influences. The principles of separation of powers and checks and balances in the federal government—and its extension through the states down to thousands of units of local governments and special districts—defies classification in simple power structure terms. At the national level Dye and Zeigler have to admit that the checks and balances still work to pit "ambition against ambition" in the relationships between president, Congress, and courts.[9] The unseating of Richard Nixon from the nation's highest office is further proof, if any is needed, that Congress has the capacity to check the executive. At the level of the states, Dye and Zeigler acknowledge much diversity of elite structures, ranging from a single unified elite system in some states to a plural elite in highly diversified states like California.[10] And at the community level they find some single elite structures but also some plural elite communities. To recognize this complexity and diversity is realistic but does not accord well with the notion of a single elite that somehow dominates the whole.

In contemplating this structural diversity we should recall as well that much of this proliferation of government has been made elective. Many judges at the state level are selected by a process that involves the ballot, and, voters at the state and local level often pass upon issues referred to the electorate on subjects that range from the sublime to the ridiculous, from energy programs to nude bathing at local beaches. In Oklahoma voters periodically pass judgment upon the continuance of prohibition, although it is not clear the vote does much to change anyone's drinking habits one way or another. Overall, it has been said that the United States has more elections than the rest of the world combined. We see no reason to challenge such a statement. But we do question whether such extensive use of the electoral processes are best explained by a theory that minimizes mass influences.

Quite apart from this elaborate system of elections, there is the widespread use of public opinion polling. It developed in the United States and has had its most extensive application in the American environment. The use of polls by candidates and officeholders has become commonplace. We shall discuss the subject in later chapters, but for now we might note one authority's assessment: "There are more than a thousand polling organizations in the United States. . . The breadth and intensity of modern public opinion polling is matched by its influence. Pollsters have become the *vox populi*, and their work touches all our lives."[11] Jimmy Carter's pollster, Pat Caddell, was an intimate part of the Carter campaign for office and continued to work closely with the president in the White House. The TV networks used surveys of their own in analyzing the course of the primaries and the major campaigns all through 1976. A steady stream of books and articles address the "state of the nation" and try to assess the public mood. A reigning assumption is that what the public wants counts for something and had better not be ignored.

Politicians are not the only "elite" that is keenly interested in what the public wants. The business world is eager to know how consumers dispose of their incomes—and to help them do it. Consumers are bombarded on all sides, day and night, with messages that seek to gain their attention and get them to buy. The ads vary in content and taste, and not much is sacred any more. Sexy shampoos, the "champagne of beers," remedies for "jock itch"—interspersed with exhortations to clean up the environment—assault the eyes and ears of Americans on the road and at home. As John Kenneth Galbraith acknowledges, large numbers of Americans have considerable discretionary income to dispose of, and the business community, high and low, goes to great lengths to find out what people want and how they can be induced to buy. Again we have evidence of a system heavily oriented toward concern with mass opinions and actions.

In politics and in economics, the prevailing value system is one that tends to put a premium on "the people," their desires, and the need to be "responsive."[12] After all, the value consensus that is widely recognized as characteristic of the United States incorporates the values of popular self-government. There are differences of opinion as to what the people may want, but heaven help the prominent politician or business person who says, "The public be damned!" Attempts to explain away this widespread interest in mass wants and tastes as fundamentally the creation of manipulative elites appear strained and implausible. It looks as though the elite must respond to pressures beyond its control.

Elections and Issues

The system appears to cater to popular tastes, good and bad, political and otherwise, and is impressively fragmented as though democratically responsive. But we still face the question whether elections are little more than a "symbolic exercise." Admittedly some of the research on elections would support the conclusion that the electorate plays a limited role. The book that was long taken as the bible of American voting studies, *The American Voter*, in the main saw voters as not much issue oriented. Voters took part in choosing the winning candidates but did not determine the choice of public policies. This analysis troubled many political scientists and stimulated much research. By the mid-1970s authoritative studies had significantly modified the earlier findings.

The most authoritative of these studies is that of Nie, Verba, and Petrocik, appropriately entitled *The Changing American Voter*. At the outset they criticize *The American Voter* as relying upon a limited data base, chiefly that of the 1956 election, and they argue that this election was significantly different from others.[13] By contrast, Nie, Verba, and Petrocik draw upon election data that spans a period of two decades, up through 1972. They conclude that issues do matter to the public. Indeed, in the closing chapter they write:

> One of our major conclusions is that the American public responds to political issues. . . . As we traced the transformation of the American public, we found that a substantial change in the structure of belief systems had occurred. Political attitudes became more coherent after the Eisenhower years. Citizens began to evaluate candidates and the parties in terms of issue positions they presented. And this new issue coherence and concern for issues was translated into a greater connection between issue position and the vote.[14]

In this same section, Nie, Verba, and Petrocik note specifically, "We find a high level of issue consistency during the presidential years of 1964, 1968, and 1972, when there were relatively clear issue choices. But we find a similar level of issue consistency in studies conducted during non-presidential years. In other words, citizens have come to think about issues more consistently no matter what the specific electoral stimulus."

As their summary statement puts it, "The data suggest, in other words, that the public will cast an issue vote . . . if it is given a meaningful issue choice." The voters portrayed in this major study, based on a large body of data from numerous elections, are quite different from the unstable and contradictory masses of elite theory.[15] (See Figure 11–1.)

But do the voters, whether issue conscious or not, actually influence significantly the course of public policy? The formation of the New Deal coalition is a case in point. Dye and Zeigler admit that elite philosophy changed: "In the New Deal, American elites accepted the principle that the entire community, through the agency of the national government, had a responsibility for mass welfare."[16] But did the elite have much choice? The New Deal is commonly said to have saved capitalism and thereby prevented more drastic change. Surely, then, change due to

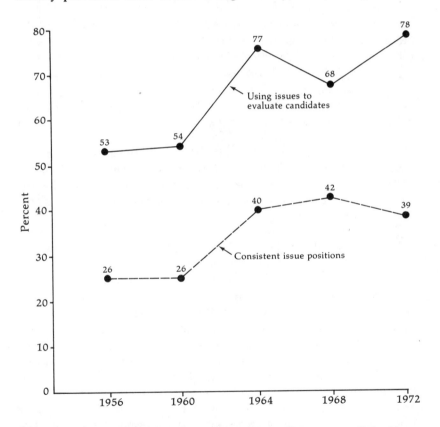

Figure 11–1 Proportion Consistent in Attitudes and Proportion Referring to Issues to Evaluate Candidates, 1956–1972

Source: Norman H. Nie, Sidney Verba, and John Petrocik, *The Changing American Voter* (Cambridge, Mass.: Harvard University Press, 1976), p. 146.

popular pressure for a government that would tackle the problems of the Great Depression was all but inevitable. FDR and the New Deal represented a response to mass pressures and the administration of Herbert Hoover had to give way. An elite which resisted such pressures would probably have found itself unemployed and a more compliant elite in its place.

Since then the welfare state has grown apace, with the Great Society legislation of the 1960s representing a continuation of the New Deal response. According to the economist Charles Schultze, military spending has been falling and spending on social programs has been rising. These social programs are in three broad categories: the "rapid expansion of retirement, disability, and unemployment compensation"; low-income assistance programs; and new social service and social investment programs. These programs, according to Schultze, arose from "legislation creating new programs or expanding the scope of existing ones."[17] In other words, they arose from political initiatives. The impact on federal spending may be seen specifically in the budget figures submitted to Congress by President Gerald Ford early in 1976. Ford had a full year in office ahead of him and the figures presumably reflect a relatively conservative ordering of priorities. The proposed budget totaled nearly $395 billion.[18] The largest single spending item was the category of "income security"—much of this Social Security—and it amounted to $137 billion. The next largest item was defense spending at $101 billion. Health spending by the federal government was budgeted at more than $34 billion. Obviously the kinds of programs associated with the New Deal and its continuation in Great Society legislation have grown a great deal.

These figures pose a problem for those who argue the dominance of a military-industrial complex. The military remains exceedingly powerful, but it is hard to see how its dominance can be claimed while the military share of federal spending has declined and social spending has grown. Furthermore, these figures do not even take account of the burst of state and local spending that has occurred in recent decades. The growth of the welfare state has itself certainly involved controversy and some measures the public might not support if they were put to a national vote. Yet it is difficult to explain away the huge sums involved in the social programs of the 1970s as totally divorced from popular pressures by ordinary Americans. The correspondence between what people want and what the government does is imperfect. But on a large scale, the macro level, we can see that there is significant responsiveness. Political coalitions rooted in the public's opinions and attitudes do matter.

The impact of the electoral system may also be seen in a small but significant way in Jimmy Carter's presidential campaign. In his travels and conversations with literally thousands of people, Carter expanded his knowledge of government substantially. He described this experience as an invaluable "learning process":

> I remember once an elderly man in Iowa . . . asked me a question about Social Security. I just didn't know the answer . . . I had to tell him I didn't know—but then the first thing I did was find out. And I wrote him a note explaining it. That's what I mean about an education . . . I would often send 40 or 50 hand-written notes a week to people who had asked me questions. I wouldn't take a million dollars for that experience.[19]

The election process educates the candidates as well as the people. A system that forces those who seek its most powerful office to campaign among the voters in this manner is taking its democratic "myths" quite seriously.

When we take account of the system's democratic values, the institutional fragmentation, the pervasive electoral processes, the public opinion polls, and the consumer-oriented economy, then add to these the voter's issue consciousness and the responsiveness evident in the growth of the welfare state, we have weighty evidence that the people's opinions *do* matter. An elite that must go to such lengths to pacify the masses must certainly be subject to mass pressures.

Interest Groups

What, then, of interest groups as reflecting largely elite concerns—while the masses dally with their pleasures? The contention that most Americans do not become active members of organizations is hard to deny. But the interest group system does reflect impressive diversity. For example, organized labor is one powerful interest in this system. Late in 1973 the leadership of the nation's major union organization, the AFL- CIO, spoke of the desirability of electing a veto-proof Congress in 1974.[20] Interestingly enough, observers outside of labor had no inclination to scoff: big labor was widely seen as having enough political muscle to make the prospect a serious matter.[21] Any group with the power to entertain such an objective seriously must be ranked as a major force on the national scene. But it does not fit easily into standard elite notions of a business-dominated elite. Similarly, the difficulty experienced by the government in coping with the prolonged coal strike during the hard winter of 1977–1978 fails to fit explanations that assume the power and success of business interests.[22]

And if labor poses a problem, the civil rights movement is even more difficult to accommodate. Blacks, and especially those in the South, were as far outside the system and its Establishment as any group could be.

Their legacy of slavery followed by segregation and subordination clear-ly relegated them to the bottom of the heap. Yet the civil rights move-ment of the 1950s and 1960s, largely led and manned by blacks, shook the nation.[23] Of the widely publicized Birmingham demonstrations in 1963, Dye and Zeigler write, "Thus, Birmingham was the beginning of a new militancy of all classes of blacks."[24] These elite-oriented authors try to explain away the Civil Rights Act of 1964 as largely symbolic. Yet they add that it resulted in some "tangible gains" and compare it with such historical documents as the Emancipation Proclamation. Indeed, Dye and Zeigler accord this whole movement an importance that belies much of what they say elsewhere, especially about interest groups and the futility of underdog activity.

Nor do other consumer- and reform-oriented interest groups fit easily into an elitist version of pressure groups. Ralph Nader is not just an or-dinary citizen yet it would be hard to classify him as a part of a business-dominated Establishment. Michael Harrington has given Nader high praise: "Ralph Nader and his colleagues have organized extremely effec-tive campaigns to limit the sovereign power of the big companies and forced safety reforms in the automobile industry."[25] Similarly, Common Cause, which has had a significant influence in reforming the political process, must either be accommodated or explained away. These and other examples could be multiplied. For our purposes it is not necessary to argue that such groups really encompass the masses. Common Cause's claim to be "the people's lobby" is self-serving rhetoric. The group has only a few hundred thousand members and makes no pretense of polling the public at large to determine what the majority of "the people" want.[26] Nonetheless, this reform group, supplemented by others, does add signif-icant diversity to an interest group system that defies simplistic views of a totally business-dominated Establishment.

The Rich Are Rich but the Government Is Richer

We began our challenge to elite theory by examining the conditions of the masses, the political processes that reflect elements of democratic pressures, and the diversity of the interest group system. We need now to deal with what many critics perceive as the heart of the theory, the mat-ter of concentrated wealth and corporate power. Lists of millionaires and multimillionaires are impressive. The average citizen who works for a living and barely stays ahead of the bill collector may look with a jaun-diced eye on the luxurious life style that goes with great wealth. He may feel at times, as Lundberg does, that the United States is a "banana republic" in which a few are super-rich and the masses toil for modest rewards. But a banana republic the United States is not. Most Americans are relatively affluent. It is true that fairly little income redistribution has taken place over the last generation or so, but the size of the pie as a whole has clearly grown and average incomes have, in the main, gone up.[27] As for the poor, the expansion of the welfare state since the 1960s, a consequence of political initiatives, helped spread benefits beyond the middle class to the disadvantaged. We have a system with a large middle range of incomes and a small percentage who are poor.

At the other end of the scale are those families with great wealth. Still, as we noticed in Chapter 9, they are a tiny percentage of population alongside the extended middle class. And even their great riches would not go far in adding to government resources for major new programs. Thomas R. Dye summarily states, "If the personal wealth of every one of America's 150 centimillionaires were *completely confiscated* by the government, the resulting revenue (about $3 billion) would amount to less than *one* percent of the federal budget for a *single year!*"[28] Personal wealth is simply not on the scale of corporate and governmental resources.

Robert L. Heilbroner makes a similar point in the short but interesting analysis that we touched upon in Chapter 9. In his figures the really rich and the upper-class families together amounted to 5 percent of all families and held about 15 percent of all income. These people obviously had large sums at their disposal and could afford amenities others dream of. But, Heilbroner argued, if all this group's "surplus income" were taken from them, it would not be enough to bring the working class to parity with the middle class.[29] In future, Heilbroner believes, growth will have to slacken because of limited resources and pollution. Without growth revenue to provide the "more" that workers and the poor expect, political conflict will arise between the lower portion of the income scale and the upper middle class. The basis for this prediction confirms Dye's conclusion that the riches of those at the upper end of the income scale would not provide sufficient resources for significant income redistribution were it all somehow available. The many Du Ponts, big and little, about whom Lundberg has written so sharply do not have the resources to make much difference to the massive levels of spending required by the modern welfare state.[30] There are some mighty rich Americans, it is true, but there is also a huge middle class that dilutes the concentration of wealth.

Corporate Power in Perspective

In addition to the concentration of wealth, there is the matter of corporate concentration in the economy. To many critics of the system, corporate size and corporate power to dominate the economy are *the* major issues. We do not deny that it is possible to compile some impressive figures on corporate size, but it is also true that the whole system is enormous, as some figures illustrate. In 1975 the Gross National Product amounted to about $1,500 billion in constant 1972 dollars. Of this total $973 billion was accounted for as personal consumption expenditures; another $339 billion consisted of government purchases; and gross private domestic investment accounted for $184 billion. It is also of interest to note the percentage shares of national income by type. The category of compensation of employees accounted for more than three-fourths of national income, 76.9 percent. Corporate profits stood at 7.6 percent, proprietors' income at 7.5 percent, and rental income at 1.9 percent.[31] Thus in standing back to look at the system as a whole, we find that GNP is truly enormous, personal consumption accounted for about two thirds of GNP, and employee compensation amounted to about three-fourths of national income. In a system said to be dominated by giant corporations, consumers and employees did quite well.

Figures on the federal government add to this perspective. For 1975 the federal budget outlays totaled about $324 billion, a sum far greater than that of any corporation. The cabinet departments spent huge sums. Health, Education and Welfare led with outlays of about $112 billion, followed by Defense with $87 billion. Treasury had an outlay of $41 billion, most of it for interest on the national debt. Figures on sources of government revenue were also revealing. Individual income taxes in 1975 accounted for about 53 percent of federal revenue.[32] Employment taxes, primarily Social Security, pulled in nearly 24 percent. Corporation income taxes totaled less than 16 percent. Therefore, the consumption, compensation, and income taxes of large numbers of ordinary Americans involve larger sums by far than those relating to the business world alone. There is big business, it is true, but there is a big economy, a big government (and many lesser governments), and there are many, many ordinary consumers and employees whose wages and incomes amount to far more than corporate contributions.

Critics further charge that big business is able to use its economic and polticial clout to extort unreasonable profits from the public. The charge has an obvious populistic appeal but it is possible to raise doubts. For one thing, polls on the subject usually reveal that the public has much inaccurate information on corporate profits and tends to judge them to be much higher than they actually are. One example is the analysis by a businessman, John Q. Jennings. He reported a poll by the Opinion Research Corporation as finding that the public believed the split between employee costs and profits (after deducting all costs other than those for employees) was 25 percent to 75 percent respectively. On the other hand, Jennings points out, official Department of Commerce figures reported that employees actually got 88 percent and corporate net profits constituted 12 percent.[33] The discrepancy here between popular perceptions and the authoritative source is enormous.[34]

Similar contrasts between perceptions and authoritative figures may occur even among government elites. In late 1977, during the struggle over President Carter's proposed energy program, *Newsweek* reported that the 1976 profit margins of five different industries ranged from 3.6 percent for steel to 9 percent for drugs. Oil and gas stood at only 5.2 percent. John O'Leary, then deputy-designate to the Secretary of the Department of Energy, reacted with disbelief: "They only show you the pea under one of the shells—and there are two more shells." By various means, O'Leary argued, the big oil companies were able to understate their profits.[35] O'Leary and other critics of big business may be right. But figures from sources usually considered reputable indicate that profit margins are not high. And if they are not, then we must question the thesis that corporate concentration and corporate power are as great as the critics would have us believe.

A related issue is the matter of capital formation for investment purposes. Investment provides the jobs and other economic necessities, including energy, for the future. A low rate of investment would seem to be contrary to the interests of big business in its quest for profits and to imply that corporate concentration is less than critics are willing to recognize. Many authorities have indeed argued that capital investment in the United States is low, perhaps shockingly low. Edgar Speer of U.S. Steel, appearing on ABC's Issues and Answers program, said, "We're only investing 16 percent of our gross national product into the machinery of our economy, where our competition abroad is investing anywhere from 19 percent of their GNP upwards to over 30 percent."[36] A recent congressional inquiry reported that United States economic growth from 1960 to 1973 was seventh among eight highly developed nations. Only the United Kingdom, with an economy often described as ailing, recorded a lower growth rate. A table comparing the same eight nations on measures of "Role of capital accumulation in economic growth, 1960-73," presented figures that put the United States at the very bottom.[37] If such figures accurately represent what they claim to represent, they do little to support claims to corporate concentration and power.

Questioning of corporate concentration may be carried one step further with a brief example, the automobile industry. Four large companies dominate American production: General Motors, Ford, Chrysler, and American Motors. GM is an enormous company and has the largest share of the market. Still, consumers have a wide range of American models available. Nor are they constrained to buy only American models. They also have available a variety of foreign-made cars from Europe and Japan. By the latter part of the 1970s the foreign competition was substantial and had become an influence upon the design and production of American made cars.[38] In addition, the American industry was under considerable pressure from the government to produce cars that were safer, more pollution-free, and more energy efficient than earlier models.[39] Consumers, it is true, continued to gripe about the automobile industry.[40] Yet these pressures from abroad and from the national government, all bearing upon a major industry with substantial concentration, mean that there are important constraints on corporate power that raw figures on corporate gigantism do not reveal.

We have countered the case for corporate concentration by arguing that the economy is huge and so is the government. Personal consumption expenditures and employee compensation loom large in the economy, as do individual income taxes among all taxes. Business profits are less than many, including some government elites, believe them to be. Investment, capital formation, and economic growth are low, perhaps dangerously so. And one major industry characterized by concentration is subject to a variety of pressures that constrain corporate power. Corporate concentration in this perspective is neither as great nor as powerful as critics, who gleefully cite lurid examples, are willing to recognize.

Interlocking Corporate Elites Questioned

An important aspect of the concern with corporate concentration is the belief that the top personnel in the corporate world "interlock" or overlap, and that these people in turn interlock with top governmental personnel. A figure like David Rockefeller, who sits on the governing boards of a number of different corporations, would be an example of a corporate interlock. If it could then be shown that top corporate personnel tended to move into key positions in government, the case for the pervasive influence of corporate concentration would be reinforced.

However, Dye's further and perhaps more refined analysis of elitism casts some doubt on such conclusions.[41] Since Dye is associated with an elitist perspective, it is especially significant that he found "clear evidence of specialization among institutional leaders." Eighty percent, he concluded, were "specialists" who held only one post rather than interlocking with many other positions. In addition, "There is a great deal of upward mobility in American society, as well as 'circulation of elites.' Only 12 percent of the top corporate elites inherited their position and power; the vast majority climbed the rungs of the corporate ladder." And, "There are multiple paths to the top. Our top elites were recruited through a variety of channels. Governmental leaders were recruited mainly from law and government; less than one in six were recruited from the corporate world. Military leaders were recruited exclusively through the military ranks, with the exception of the civilian leadership in the Defense Department."[42] Here, then, is evidence that significantly modifies the theories of those who think of the world of big corporations as joined together at the top and as also interlocked pervasively with government elites. Relationships do exist but much "specialization" and mobility occur, and elite recruitment includes multiple paths to the top. Certainly this suggests that what actually transpires is more complex than many critics of corporate concentration recognize.

Dye also cited studies of the attitudes held by top corporate officials. In these studies they emerge as relatively enlightened and, broadly speaking, part of the "liberal establishment":

> Despite popular images of ultra-conservative or reactionary corporate leadership, available evidence indicates that these leaders share the liberal, public-regarding philosophy: they are prepared within the boundaries set by the profit system to support public-regarding activities, under the rubric of "corporate consciousness" or "social responsibility." Top corporate leaders are interested in maintaining a stable and ordered domestic society. They also favor an end to the Cold War, improved relations with communist nations, less reliance on military solutions to world problems, and increased world trade and technical cooperation.[43]

The corporate elite here pictured appears to be made up of fairly benign types who are able to live with the welfare state and with international communism. The hard-line Cold War views of Galbraith's version of the elite, the technostructure, do not receive much support.

Even the imperial presidency, which some critics have visualized as the capstone of the system's power structure, was brought down significantly during the 1970s. The War Powers Act of 1973 curbed the president's use of American forces abroad. The Budget and Impoundment Control Act of 1974 strengthened congressional influence on the budget. By law and by other means presidential discretion in using and abusing intelligence agencies, the FBI, the IRS, and other elements of the executive establishment was restrained. Public financing of the presidential elections, applied for the first time in 1976, dampened the flow of cash from corporations and wealthy individuals. Imperial pretensions were further demoted by the presence in the White House of that newcomer to Washington, Jimmy Carter.[44] Nor should we forget the media, especially the quality press led by *The New York Times* and *The Washington Post*, and the courts. Both played major roles in exposing Watergate and promised to continue serving as vigorous checks on any president who aspired to imperial trappings.

In Defense of Middle-Class America

In challenging the "view from the top" we have argued that most Americans are affluent and generally contented, as even critics such as Marcuse admit. And if popular tastes often seem deplorable, we did find that people spend much on such essentials as education. Nor do the masses bear type-casting as a collection of Archie Bunkers. The country has spent great sums to make education available to all, even up into higher education, and education is widely recognized as a fundamental contributor to democratic attitudes. Declining social class differences, improvements in civil liberties and civil rights, Watergate as an elite misadventure that cannot be blamed on the masses, plus the complexity of some recent civil liberties issues, all testify to an absence of sharp differences between elites and masses. The nation's big middle class does have a democratic potential.

This democratic potential relates to the system's pervasive concern with public opinion. Virtually everyone eighteen or older is able to vote. Checks and balances, plus the dispersion of the government through a multitude of lesser governments and special districts, bespeak pluralistic diversity and responsiveness to popular opinion. The number and frequency of elections, alongside the pervasive polling, further adds to the argument for responsiveness. Combined with these factors is the more recent work on elections, which concludes that issues matter to the people. The rise of the New Deal in the 1930s and its extension in Great Society legislation in the 1960s, as military spending tapered off, is hard to explain as divorced from popular pressures. And a brief analysis of interest groups points up the presence of groups representing labor, blacks, and consumers. These reflect a pluralistic diversity not easily accounted for by theories of a business-dominated establishment.

As for the concentration of wealth, we have argued that most Americans by far are middle class and the rich are, in spite of their often conspicuous spending habits, a small number of people. Their wealth would not go far at all in financing major new social programs. Political conflict in the future may pit the upper middles against the lower middles as the latter clamor for "more." In dealing with corporate concentration, a check of the figures for 1975 revealed that personal consumption accounted for close to two-thirds of GNP. And compensation of employees accounted for three-fourths of national income. Individual income taxes made up 53 percent of revenue and corporate income taxes hardly 16 percent.

On a related issue, the rate of capital investment, the figures show that, since 1960 at least, the United States has had either the lowest or one of the lowest rates of capital investment and economic growth of any of the major industrial powers. Taking the automobile industry as an example of corporate concentration, we have seen that government pressures to alter auto design on behalf of safety, pollution, and energy considerations, as well as competition from abroad, all serve as significant constraints on these corporate giants. Big business has to cope with big government and a good many other constraints these days.

As for the interlocking of corporate and government elites, Dye's analysis of the matter calls into question the supposed tying together of the corporate and governmental. For Dye found among corporate elites considerable upward mobility, circulation of elites, and much specialization rather than interlocking. He found multiple paths to the top of the elite system, and government service itself provided much of the top elite in government. Furthermore, his analysis of the ideology of corporate elites found their attitudes to be such that they could live easily enough with the welfare state and international communism. Nor is it possible to point to an imperial presidency as the capstone of an elite-dominated power structure. The presidency continued to be a powerful office, but legal and political constraints thrown up during the 1970s set significant bounds to presidential discretion.

As we finish this critical evaluation of the elite perspective the curious reader may wonder where the argument leads. We have developed the deficiencies of the elite model at some length. And we have admitted that the old fashioned ideal of pure democracy, in which all participate directly, is a fine ideal but is hopelessly unrealistic. Do we then fall back on pluralism? Perhaps, but quite possibly not. The single elite and plural elite models occur in many forms and with almost endless variations. But there are indications that these models, whatever their flexibility, need to be enriched with further alternatives.

G. David Garson, whom we cited in conjunction with evidence for corporate concentration, proposes moving beyond elitist and pluralist positions as they have been known.[45] Thomas R. Dye, in his further analysis of "who's running America," appears to be searching for an alternative to elite theory. He finally states that there is insufficient evidence for either the pluralist or elitist models.[46]

But if the argument appears to be shifting, it is still not clear how much of a role the masses play in the system. Here we might usefully point to some tentative conclusions that follow from our own assessment. In the first place, most Americans are pretty well off economically and seem to be satisfied with their jobs and quality of life. They enjoy an impressively high level of well-being and may do so with minimal political involvement. If the political system exists to serve the people, then most Americans are pretty well served by theirs.

In the second place, the system provides multiple access points for those who wish to exert themselves to become involved. Qualifications to vote are minimal, the election process encompasses an enormous range and variety of offices, and it is often possible to vote directly on issues. No other system offers the number and variety of elections that the United States makes available to the ordinary citizen, whether in voting for the president or for the local dog catcher. And this opportunity to vote pervades much of the nation's voluntary group life as well. The potential for responsiveness to popular pressures, even if underutilized by the voters, pervades the system as one of its basic traits.

In the third place, much effort is put forth by political and economic elites to determine via public opinion polling what it is the people do want. Thus, whether people vote or not, intensive efforts are made year in and year out to determine popular attitudes and desires. Without doing anything other than pursuing their normal workaday lives, ordinary citizens will have their opinions tapped and assessed more or less constantly by the system's elites. Elites attempt to manipulate public opinion but they do not ignore it.

Fourth, there is reason to believe that elite manipulation has its limits. In some matters, at least, what the mass of people want the elite must try to provide. Here we have not sought to point to any one election as definitive proof of mass pressures but we have pointed to the rise of the welfare state over the decades. One might argue that elites led the way, but is it difficult to believe that *any* elite could have successfully blocked this kind of legislative program indefinitely. Elite self-interest no doubt furthered the welfare state but it is hard to see that the elite, in the end, had much choice.

A fifth point is closely related to the fourth. Elites must respond positively to some, at least, of the people's wishes. But they must also avoid certain policies widely recognized as highly unpopular. The masses set some limits on the alternatives that elites might otherwise feel free to pursue. In the wake of Vietnam, elites—and the imperial presidency as an aspect of the elite—lost the option of using American fighting men in a conflict abroad. This constraint may fade in time, but while it lasts it sets bounds to what presidents might do in a form that was not applicable to activist presidents such as John Kennedy and Lyndon Johnson. There are also some constraints on domestic policy, relating to such touchy subjects as taxes, race, severe reductions in the use of the automobile, and the like. The list could easily be extended. Elites must pay heed to what it is clear the people do *not* want—or risk their own position in a confrontation with an angry public.

A sixth point in our assessment of the role of the masses draws upon an element of the pluralist defense of interest groups. Even if we acknowledge that the mass of people do not become active members of organizations, it is nonetheless true that considerable variety does occur in the interests represented. To argue that only business interests are successfully represented is no longer true, if it ever was. Labor, blacks, consumers, reformers, and a host of other interests now have some manner of representation and have had some success. This diverse interest group system, even if imperfect, supplements the representation available through other channels and adds another element of responsiveness.

What results from this reassessment of the role of the masses is certainly far from pure democracy—however one might try to define that. Yet it is certainly at odds with single elite theory as well. It best fits the pluralist position, although it differs from the usual form of pluralism in its account of the middle-class masses. Elites do matter a good deal, even if constrained in some respects by mass desires and by the *potential* for popular responsiveness.

In the end the main problem seems to be popular indifference, rather than domineering elites in a system of concentrated corporate and political power. There is much democratic potential that the people do not use. They live well in the main and all too many of them have little or no interest in politics and issues. They *do* have much faith in the system and seem to expect things to work out well enough, whether the mass of people are active politically or not. Ironically, it appears that elites are much more concerned about public opinion than the mass of ordinary citizens are. The focus on the private and personal world of the individual, and his family and friends, without much concern for the public sector and its problems, is perhaps the most fundamental shortcoming of all. Such a reaction makes it difficult to mobilize support for attacks on the nation's problems. In a sense the system makes it all too easy for the individual to do well for himself and his family without much heed to the system's well-being, including the well-being of those less fortunate than himself.

But whatever the problems of privatism and political apathy, we have shown that the system has much potential for popular responsiveness and does respond. In this context we may now examine the political parties, interest groups, the media, and the experts who work so hard at selling their candidates to a seemingly indifferent public.

NOTES

1. Herbert Marcuse, *One Dimensional Man* (Boston: Beacon Press, 1964)
2. Ben J. Wattenberg, *The Real Majority*, rev. ed. (New York: G. P. Putnam's Sons Capricorn Books, 1976), p. 85.
3. Richard F. Hamilton, *Class and Politics in the United States* (New York: John Wiley, 1972), p. 519.

4. Andrew Levison, *The Working-Class Majority* (New York: Penguin Books, 1974), p. 169.
5. Dennis S. Ippolito, Thomas G. Walker, and Kenneth L. Kolson, *Public Opinion and Responsible Democracy* (Englewood Cliffs, N.J.: Prentice-Hall, 1976), p. 97.
6. David G. Lawrence, "Procedural Norms and Tolerance: A Reassessment," *American Political Science Review*, LXX (March 1976), 100.
7. Thomas R. Dye and L. Harmon Zeigler, *The Irony of Democracy: An Uncommon Introduction to American Politics*, 4th ed., (North Scituate, Mass.: Duxbury Press, 1978), pp. 17, 21. Readers interested in pursuing the matter might read the first chapter of the second edition and note the contrast in the attention given to elite repression in the later or post-Watergate editions.
8. Ibid., p. 37.
9. Ibid., p. 232–234.
10. Ibid., pp. 326 ff.
11. Michael Wheeler, *Lies, Damn Lies, and Statistics: The Manipulation of Public Opinion in America* (New York: Dell Publishing Laurel Editions, 1976), pp. 11 and 12.
12. Of course there are those on both the left and the right who do challenge this value system in various ways. In general, such people do not win many elections or sell many products, but they contribute to a lively process of national self-analysis without which we should certainly be less well off. Galbraith's ideas might be disastrous for the Democrats politically, but he is surely one of the nation's most interesting—and witty—social critics.
13. Norman H. Nie, Sidney Verba, and John R. Petrocik, *The Changing American Voter* (Cambridge, Mass.: Harvard University Press, 1976), pp. 3 ff.
14. Ibid., pp. 348–349.
15. See also Gerald Pomper, *The Voter's Choice* (New York: Dodd, Mead, 1975), p. 214, in which Pomper concludes that "Issue preferences have also become coherent. Voters grasp the connections between policy questions, rather than reacting to each matter separately. Their outlook is more integrated."
16. Dye and Zeigler, *The Irony of Democracy*, pp. 84–85. Note especially the statements at the top of p. 83 rationalizing elite reaction to the turmoil abroad during the 1920s and 1930s and the "restlessness of the masses in America." It should be noted that this restlessness did not lead to "elite repression." Instead, the elite changed its philosophy.
17. Charles L. Schultze, "Federal Spending: Past, Present, and Future" in Henry Owen and Charles L. Schultze, eds., *Setting National Priorities* (Washington, D.C.: Brookings Institution, 1976), pp. 228, 235, 346. Schultze uses figures on "nonrecession GNP," but for our purposes the exact figures matter less than the trend and the proportions, overall, in military and nonmilitary spending.
18. *Congressional Quarterly Weekly Report*, 34 (January 24, 1976), 120–121.
19. *New York Times*, October 31, 1976, p. 34.
20. Federation president George Meany expressed the idea in his address to the Tenth Constitutional Convention. See *Proceedings of the Tenth Constitutional Convention of the AFL-CIO*, Bal Harbour, Fla., October 18–23, 1973, vol. 1, p. 28.
21. Labor did well in the elections of 1974 but did not attain a veto-proof Congress. According to figures released by the AFL-CIO, the federation's Committee on Political Education endorsed a total of 422 candidates for House and Senate seats in 1974. See *Proceedings of the Eleventh Constitutional Convention*, vol. 2, p. 350. The figures may be inflated but nonetheless indicate large-scale political activity.
22. Most elite theorizing gives only passing attention to labor, or none at all. John Kenneth Galbraith discusses unions at some length and says that the "industrial system has now largely encompassed the labor movement." See *The New Industrial State*, 2nd rev. ed. (Boston: Houghton-Mifflin, 1971), p. 282.
23. One account of these activities in the South, where blacks had to overcome the worst obstacles, is in Harry Holloway's *The Politics of the Southern Negro* (New York: Random House, 1969).
24. Dye and Zeigler, *The Irony of Democracy*, pp. 347–348.

25. Michael Harrington, *Socialism* (New York: Bantam Books, 1976), p. 372. One account of Nader that evaluates him critically is Charles McCarry's *Citizen Nader* (New York: New American Library Signet Books, 1973).
26. In fairness to Common Cause it should be said that they do poll their own members from time to time. These surveys ask members to respond to a list of possible issues and to rank them.
27. Whether there has been or not is partly a matter of judgment. One writer notes that the income shares of the bottom two quintiles of poorest families rose from 13 to 16 percent and that the concentration ratio measuring inequality fell from 49 in 1929 to 40 in 1962. He states that some writers found this change so striking that they "have referred to it as an 'income revolution.' " See Edward C. Budd, *Inequality and Poverty* (New York: W. W. Norton, 1967), p. xx. As Budd adds, most of this change had taken place by the end of World War II.
28. Thomas R. Dye, *Who's Running America?* (Englewood Cliffs, N.J.: Prentice-Hall, 1976), p. 38.
29. Robert L. Heilbroner, "Middle-Class Myths, Middle-Class Realities," *Atlantic*, October 1976, pp. 38–41.
30. Perhaps several words of caution are in order. For one thing, the fortunes of the super-rich may not be as great as outsiders, even informed outsiders, believe. Howard Hughes's fortune seemed to melt away after his death, even though it is still quite large. Second, these great fortunes certainly make a great difference to those who have them and they may "make a difference" economically and politically at all levels, national, state, and local. Heilbroner is trying to demonstrate their limited scale relative to the system as a whole.
31. U.S. Bureau of the Census, *Statistical Abstract of the United States: 1976* (97th edition), Washington, D.C., 1976, pp. 394, 397.
32. Ibid., pp. 233, 238.
33. *New York Times*, November 10, 1974, Business and Finance, p. 14.
34. A similar kind of discrepancy cropped up in a consumer survey reported in a news magazine. The respondents estimated profits on sales, after deducting all costs and taxes, at an average of 17 cents and a median of 13 cents. The article cited government figures as giving an actual profit margin of 5 cents on the sales dollar. See *U.S. News and World Report*, February 20, 1978, p. 18.
35. *Newsweek*, October 24, 1977, p. 39.
36. Associated Press dispatch in the *Daily Oklahoman*, September 5, 1977, p. 20.
37. "Tax Policy and Capital Formation," Task Force on Capital Formation of the Committee on Ways and Means, by the staff of the Joint Committee on Taxation, April 4, 1977 (Washington: U.S. Government Printing Office, 1977), pp. 45–47.
38. "The United States manufacturers are lowering prices and putting more extras onto their small cars for the express purpose of meeting Japanese competition." See "Competing in a Tougher World Auto Market," *New York Times*, International Economic Survey, Section 12, February 5, 1978, p. 26. This article states that automobiles account for 26 cents of every retail dollar.
39. "The industry's creative processes haven't been dealt a death blow but gone are the days when engineers had a free hand in developing the kind of cars they felt the public wanted." See "Federal Hand Guides Detroit," *New York Times*, Special Fall Automobile Section, Section 12, October 16, 1977, p. 1.
40. Note the low ranking of the automobile industry in the consumer survey reported in *U.S. News and World Report*, February 20, 1978, p. 18. If cars account for 26 cents of each sales dollar, the industry has a huge public and that public has its discontents.
41. Dye, *Who's Running America?* This study used biographical data for over 5,000 institutional elites, gathered, Dye assures us, "painstakingly" with the help of students.
42. Ibid., pp. 211–213. Elsewhere (pp. 65–69) Dye comments upon the downgrading of the military, especially by the 1970s. His most telling observation contrasts the experience of General Dwight D. Eisenhower with that of General William Westmoreland, U.S. commander in Vietnam. Eisenhower, after his military success in World War II, went

on to become president; Westmoreland suffered defeat in his bid to become governor of South Carolina.

43. Ibid., p. 214.
44. Note the attempt by Dye and Zeigler in the fourth edition of *The Irony of Democracy* to interpret Jimmy Carter's winning of the presidency as essentially in accord with their conception of a liberal- and business-dominated Establishment.
45. G. David Garson, *Power and Politics in the United States* (Lexington, Mass.: D. C. Health, 1977), Chapter 12.
46. Dye, *Who's Running America?* p. 215.

SUGGESTIONS FOR FURTHER READINGS

Frank M. Andrews and Stephen B. Withey. *Social Indicators of Well-Being: Americans' Perception of Life Quality*. New York: Plenum Press, 1976. The authors carefully analyze surveys from the early 1970s and report that most Americans have positive assessments of their lives.

Peter Bachrach. *The Theory of Democratic Elitism: A Critique*. Boston: Little, Brown, 1967. The author is critical of the tendency for democratic theorists to accept elements of elitism in their modern versions of democracy.

Edward C. Banfield. *The Unheavenly City Revisited: A Revision of the Unheavenly City*. Rev. ed. Boston: Little, Brown, 1974. In a well-known work a conservative skeptic argues that critics have exaggerated some of the nation's domestic problems.

Angus Campbell, Philip E. Converse, Warren E. Miller, and Donald L. Stokes. *The American Voter: An Abridgement*. New York: John Wiley & Sons, 1964. The voting study that long dominated the field as the basic reference. This abridgement, published with the approval of the authors of the original, contains the essentials in a condensed and more readable form.

Robert A. Dahl. *Who Governs? Democracy and Power in an American City*. New Haven, Conn.: Yale University Press, 1961. A classic statement of the pluralist power structure position by a leading political scientist.

M. Stanton Evans. *Clear and Present Danger: A Conservative View of America's Government*. New York: Harcourt Brace Jovanovich, 1975. The author attacks liberalism and liberal perceptions of what is wrong with the system.

Doris Faber. *Enough: The Revolt of the American Consumer*. New York: Dell Laurel-Leaf Library, 1973. Describes what Farber calls the Consumer Revolution and some of its successes.

John W. Gardner. *In Common Cause: Citizen Action and How it Works*. New York: W. W. Norton, revised edition, 1973. The leader of a major public interest group expresses his philosophy, attacks special interest politics, and discusses Common Cause activities.

Robert T. Golembreivski, Charles S. Bullock III, and Harrell R. Rodgers, Jr. *The New Politics: Polarization or Utopia?* New York: McGraw-Hill, 1970. Readings with a double-edged perspective that includes both challenges to the system and those who in some measure defend it.

John Guinther. *Moralists and Managers: Public Interest Movements in America*. Garden City, N.Y.: Doubleday Anchor Books, 1976. Traces a variety of public interest movements historically down to the present and suggests that they have had a significant impact.

V. O. Key, Jr. *The Responsible Electorate: Rationality in Presidential Voting, 1936–1960.* Cambridge, Mass.: Harvard University Press, 1966. Key, a respected political scientist, here argues, in a phrase that has since become famous, "voters are not fools."

Robert G. Lehnen. *American Institutions, Political Opinion and Public Policy.* Hinsdale, Ill.: Dryden Press, 1976. Analyzes mass opinion in relation to governmental institutions and concludes with a defense of participation by the ordinary person.

Jonathan Moore and Janet Fraser, eds. *Campaign for President: The Managers Look at '76.* Cambridge, Mass.: Ballinger, 1977. An edited transcript of discussions by the people who managed the campaigns of various candidates in 1976.

Ralph Nader, ed. *The Consumer and Corporate Accountability.* New York: Harcourt Brace Jovanovich, 1973. A famous consumer advocate presents case studies in problems of corporate accountability and suggests solutions.

Norman H. Nie and Kristi Andersen. "Mass Belief Systems Revisited: Political Change and Attitude Structure," *Journal of Politics*, 36 (August 1974), 540–587. Argues from careful analysis of elections since the 1950s that the electorate displays significant issue consciousness and attitude consistency.

Richard L. Siegel and Leonard B. Weinburg. *Comparing Public Policies: United States, Soviet Union, and Europe.* Homewood, Ill.: Dorsey Press, 1977. Compares public policies of eight major nations across a broad range of policy areas.

Leonard Silk and David Vogel. *Ethics and Profits: The Crisis of Confidence in American Business.* New York: Simon and Schuster Touchstone Books, 1976. The authors report on a series of conferences with many of the nation's top business leaders, who spoke off the record about their beliefs, needs, and frustrations.

James A. Stimson. "Belief Systems: Constraint, Complexity, and the 1972 Election," *American Journal of Political Science*, 19 (1975), 393–417. Briefly reviews the dispute over voter rationality, then carefully probes the 1972 election to show that many voters had fairly consistent opinions.

James L. Sundquist. *Politics and Policy: The Eisenhower, Kennedy, and Johnson Years.* Washington, D.C.: Brookings Institution, 1968. Sundquist, a Democrat in the New Deal tradition, examines the steps leading up to the Great Society legislation of the 1960s and in the process relates issues and elections.

Ben J. Wattenberg and Richard M. Scammon. "Black Progress and Liberal Rhetoric," *Commentary*, 55 (April 1973), 35–44. Argues that blacks have made real progress toward equality and marshals some impressive data to support their case.

Harold Watts and Felicity Skidmore. "An Update of the Poverty Picture Plus a New Look at Relative Tax Burdens," *Focus*, 2:1 (Fall 1977). (*Focus* is the newsletter of the Institute for Research on Poverty, Madison, Wisconsin). The authors use 1976 figures to present in condensed form an analysis of income redistribution and its impact.

12 · People and Parties: Party Decay, Candidates, and Interest Groups

In criticizing elite theory we concluded that the system has a powerful, although imperfectly realized, democratic potential. There are elites and they are influential, but the public has more opportunities for influencing and constraining elites than it generally chooses to exercise. Privatism usually prevails.

The tendency for most people to focus on their personal concerns to the neglect of the public sector poses a problem for those who seek to influence large numbers of people. Political parties are supposed to play the major role in mobilizing the popular will to guide national leadership. The old New Deal Democratic coalition in its prime did so. But the political parties have declined over the years, as have the old clear-cut party coalitions. And as the Democratic and Republican parties declined, other institutions and processes took their place. In this trade-off the gainers were: the campaign managers and their experts hired to do what parties could no longer do adequately; interest groups seeking direct access to the government; and the media, which we shall examine in the next chapter. This shift did not occur in isolation, but was due to certain social and economic changes.

The Decline of the Parties

The transformation of the party system is seen by some close observers of national trends, such as Ladd and Hadley, in the perspective of broad social changes. The term "postindustrial society" has gained some currency in describing these changes, which include many of the developments we have been discussing.[1] The United States has become an increasingly middle-class society. Education levels have risen. Incomes have gone up. There has been some shift in jobs, with a tendency for the number of dirtier menial jobs to decline as white-collar jobs increased. Increasingly people work with their brains rather than their hands, even in the more routine kinds of white-collar work.

A major consequence, according to Ladd and Hadley, has been an expansion of the "intelligentsia," those who work with their minds. Communication, including the use of the media, has expanded. And so has the role of the mind workers as adversaries, a posture often adopted by intellectuals in other times and places. The part the media played in exposing Watergate made national heroes for a time of Bob Woodward and Carl Bernstein. It served, on balance, to enhance the role of the intelligentsia and their perception of themselves as adversaries. But the government grew alongside the growth of the intelligentsia. Ladd and Hadley even argue for an expansion of expectations, an "entitlement" revolution. People criticize the government but also expect much from it in support of the way of life they want. The "more" that people demand plagues politicians and intensifies the problems of making political coalitions. Voters have become more independent and more demanding than they used to be.

Observers dispute the nature and extent of postindustrial change, but there is little dispute about the weakening of political party identification. DeVries and Tarrance in their analysis of the ticket splitter were among the first to point out the importance of this form of electoral behavior.[2] In the past the voters made up their minds on how to vote by taking account of the following, in rank order: party identification; group affiliation (religion, race, etc.); candidates; and, last, issues. The ticket splitter applied a different ranking: candidates; issues; party; and then group. Ladd and Hadley followed this decline of party voting well into the 1970s, with an analysis of different kinds of elections, state as well as federal. They found, "All measures lead to the same conclusion. There has been a long-term decline of party allegiance, and a dramatic drop-off over the last decade."[3]

The authors of perhaps the most authoritative voting study available, Nie, Verba, and Petrocik, concluded their analysis of surveys covering twenty years of voting with a sketch of a politics of "individuation" in an evolving "post-partisan era":

Membership in a population group no longer predicts political behavior very well; region, class, religion are still associated with party affiliation and the vote, but not as closely as they once were. Nor does party affiliation predict political behavior well; fewer have such affiliation and fewer of those with affiliation follow it. The individual voter evaluates candidates on the basis of information and impressions conveyed by the mass media, and then votes on that basis. He or she acts as an individual, not as a member of a collectivity.[4]

Oddly enough, this individuation in voting did not mean voters were apt to be casual or incoherent in their choices:

> At the same time, the electorate has developed a more coherent set of issue positions and uses those issue orientations as guides in voting. The result is that voters in presidential elections are more likely to vote for a *candidate* on the basis of the candidate's personal characteristics and/or the candidate's issue positions than they are to vote on the basis of long-term commitment to a political party.[5]

Voters have become "more coherent," not less so, and they tend to vote as individuals rather than as members of groups. These voters sound much like DeVries and Tarrance's ticket splitters. The importance of the mass media in conveying "information and impressions" to such voters is apparent.

Nie, Verba, and Petrocik closed their study with a remarkable comparison, one drawn from the "monumental work on politics in the one-party South" by the late and highly regarded political scientist V. O. Key. The prevailing pattern in the politics of the Old South up through World War II Key found to be a one-party factionalism heavily centered on personalities. There were no coherent, stable parties in the usual sense. The Democrats dominated and political struggles took place within this amorphous, dominant party. It was these struggles, with fluid and somewhat ad hoc coalition ties formed around personalities and without much regard to issues, that Key described. Nie, Verba, and Petrocik argued for the contrast between the issue-oriented voter their study found and the southern voter of the past, but they nonetheless believed that national politics up into the 1970s displayed a "tendency . . . in the direction of the kind of factionalism Key found to characterize the South."[6] With the decline of political parties an increasingly individualistic and issue-oriented electorate emerged in a "post-partisan era" of "issue-based factions." (See Figure 12–1.)

The election of 1976, with Democratic majorities in Congress and a Democrat winning the White House, at first blush appeared to establish a return to party-oriented voting. But the appearances could be deceptive. Pomper's analysis of the election, to which we have referred earlier, warned that 1976 was *not* a resurgence of the old New Deal coalition. There were similarities, but the components—other than blacks and the unions—were somewhat different, for the Carter vote drew upon the

Figure 12–1   Trends in Party Affiliation

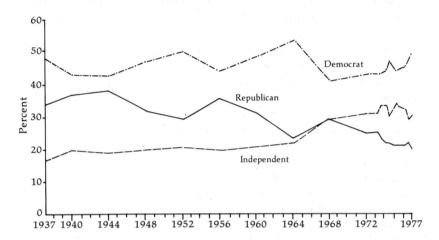

Question: *In politics; as of today, do you consider yourself a Republican, Democrat or Independent?*

Year	Democrat	Republican	Independent
1937	48%	34%	17%
1940	43	37	20
1944	43	38	19
1948	47	32	20
1952	50	29	21
1956	44	36	20
1960	48	31	21
1964	53	24	23
1968	41	29	29
1972	43	26	31
March–May 1973	43	26	31
May–August 1973	43	24	33
March–June 1974	44	23	33
July–October 1974	47	23	30
March–May 1975	44	22	34
Sept–November 1975	45	22	33
March–May 1976	46	22	32
August–October 1976	48	23	29
May–July 1977	49	20	31

Source: "Opinion Roundup," *Public Opinion*, 1 (March/April 1978), 23; data from AIPO (Gallup) Surveys of March 1937, November 1937, September 1940, September 1944, September–November 1948, October–November 1952, September–November 1956, September–November 1960, August–November 1964, September–November 1968, May–August 1972, March–May 1973. May–August 1973, March–June 1974, July–October 1974, March–May 1975, September–November 1975, March–May 1976, August–October 1976, May–July 1977.

South, the Protestants, the suburbs, and the small towns more than Democrats usually have. Carter won narrowly and, with some exceptions, his vote was spread widely across many population groups, not concentrated in a relatively few of them. Gallup's election analysis reported that white voters, only, slightly favored Ford over Carter and more than half of them split their tickets.[7]

Ladd and Hadley, in their review of the 1976 returns, cite an unusual but remarkably authoritative source in arguing the theme of change underlying the appearances of a Democratic party victory.[8] The source is none other than Pat Caddell, the pollster who worked for Jimmy Carter and who after the election prepared a memo interpreting the results. As quoted by Ladd and Hadley, Caddell warned about the desire to "reconstruct" the New Deal coalition. He admitted that the traditional Democratic groups had in some measure supported Carter but felt that their support could not explain Carter's victory. The "nontraditional" groups supporting Carter included white Protestants, the better educated white-collar people, and rural and small-town voters. In this his analysis sounded much like that of Gerald Pomper. Caddell also warned that the Democrats could no longer depend upon a coalition based chiefly on economic division. Prosperity and a middle-class society had produced a nation of "haves," in the main, to whom the old issues and the rhetoric that accompanied them did not have much meaning. Again we see invoked the theme of a changing society and an altered political process, in which the old political party differences were no longer especially meaningful.

In acknowledging this trend we should not leave the impression that party identification, Democrat or Republican, no longer matters at all. It has been and will probably continue to be one of the basic motivations for a sizable bloc of voters, even if half or more are willing to split their tickets. Yet while party identification remains important, it is not likely that there will be a resurgence of party feeling. For if the authors we have cited are correct, broad social and economic changes in American society bear much of the responsibility for the decline in party identification. A selective, independent, ticket-splitting electorate appears to be a natural development within a postindustrial society.

Reform as Weakening Party Organization

As the changes associated with postindustrial society lessened voters' allegiance to political parties and increased candidate and issue concerns, party organizations weakened. Paradoxically, party reform also contributed to this decline. This was particularly true of the Democrats, the party that has claimed the allegiance of a plurality of voters over the years.

During the 1960s and 1970s the Democrats initiated a number of reforms designed to reduce the power of political bosses and to make the party more broadly representative and responsive. Reformers felt that leaders such as President Lyndon Johnson and his supporters imposed their own policies—including an unpopular war—on the party and held down the representation of minorities and women.

Richard L. Rubin has examined this party reform movement at some length and is especially critical of "reformist, issue-oriented activists of the New Politics wing of the party." He believes they have come to hold a "disproportionate share of the mass mobilizing power within the party" and to use this power both to promote the "ideological content of party politics," thereby escalating intraparty conflict, and at the same time to increase the demand for "primary oriented internal democracy."[9] This has weakened the party's power brokers who had traditionally mediated conflict. Overall Rubin argues, "The rapid development of competing political groups to challenge 'regular' party authority, the step-level growth in the number and force of hitherto unorganized claimant groups, and the increased volatility of media-oriented political opinion have all added substantial disaggregating pressures that work against the reconciliation of internal party demands." In short, the Democrats experienced a good deal of dissension within the party, and the role of the media in channeling political opinion directly to the public added to the conflict. Rubin's judgment confirms the opinions of those who have argued that much of the Democratic party reform debilitated rather than rejuvenated the party.

Ladd and Hadley pursued an analysis of the landslide elections of 1964 and 1972 to argue that they were not accidents but reflected, instead, the crumbling of the parties. Their conclusion is that "the unnatural landslides of 1964 and 1972 were not unnatural after all. Rather, they appear products of the emergence of a new dynamic in American national politics. . . . The old dynamic seems to have been upset."[10] Like Rubin, they believe that issue-oriented activists committed to a "programmatic politics" have gained strength relative to the traditional party loyalists. The weakened parties thus become liable to take-overs by committed activists. These are apt to be a minority in their own party and a decided minority in the public at large. With an unrepresentative minority in control of one of the major parties, the public tilts by the numbers toward the more representative party and a landslide results. This rationale is a persuasive one in accounting for the two landslide elections, one by the Democratic candidate and the other by the Republican, within an eight-year period.

While reform-minded activists weakened the political party system internally, campaign reforms legislated by Congress contributed to a weakening of the role of the parties in elections. For that matter, these reforms had a number of consequences contrary to what the reformers presumably sought. The respected columnist David S. Broder has written discerningly about the impact of these reforms on the 1976 elections, pointing out that this was the first time the presidential contest was publicly financed. The intention was to cut down on the influence of special interests and the fat cats who could channel large contributions to favored candidates. If the regulations worked as intended, the influence of big givers would decline and that of ordinary citizens would rise. But as Broder sized up the campaigns, what happened in some ways worked against increased popular participation. For one thing, the public funding available amounted to "legally induced poverty." Both candidates were forced to "curtail travel and personal appearances in favor of catching voters wholesale through television ad campaigns—thus increasing the dependence on the mass-media manipulation which the reformers abhor."[11]

Broder went on to say that because of "the limits on what party organizations can raise and spend" for their national tickets, "the campaign as a living presence will virtually diappear . . . from those states which are not targeted for special attention by the candidate organizations. Already, many of the normal activities that provide opportunities for citizen involvement . . . have been shut down by the financial curbs." At the time he was writing, in early October 1976, roughly a month before the election, the campaigns were drying up in some parts of the country. Again there was an adverse influence on participation and on the role of the political parties.

Constraints on campaign contributions also increased the advantages that incumbents have in congressional elections. As Broder saw it, the new law regulating campaign financing tended to discourage private contributions, although they were still legal under specified conditions in congressional contests. The reduction of private contributions would likely damage challengers more than incumbents, given the advantages enjoyed by incumbents. Congressional incumbents were already likely to win reelection when they sought it: about 90 percent of House incumbents seeking reelection usually win. Reforms that enhance the advantages of those already so heavily favored are surely strange reforms! Interest group funding increased but became more likely to go to heavily favored incumbents. As for the political parties, insofar as reform aided incumbents, it tended to strengthen those already in a position to be independent of party obligations.

On the other hand, the law governing presidential elections created a bizarre complication for those who sought to link their congressional campaigns to the presidential campaign. Congressman Ed Koch, seeking reelection in New York City in 1976, found out the hard way. The traditional campaign button listing his name with Carter and Mondale created a problem that stalled the Federal Election Commission for weeks. Public financing only was supposed to support the presidential elections, but the button might be viewed legally as in itself an added contribution.[12] The anxiety that the law provoked and the awareness that its regulations could be a problem probably discouraged others from seeking such linkages with the party ticket.

Related to these effects of reform and reformers in tending to weaken the parties is Andrew S. McFarland's explanation of the rise of reform-minded public interest groups.[13] In this category McFarland included Common Cause, the Ralph Nader activists, and others supporting consumer and environmental causes. According to McFarland's analysis, these activists lacked the New Dealers' faith that government could institute great social reforms. They were, McFarland emphasized, skeptical. And they also tended to believe that special interests exercised undue influence. Yet they retained enough optimism to believe they could achieve reform through cause-oriented organizations working in ad hoc coalitions to achieve specific objectives. This view of reformers is reminiscent of Nie, Verba, and Petrocik's comments on the emergence of "issue-based factions" in the "post-partisan era." It would appear that reform groups, however laudable their goals, diverted the energies of activists from the parties and tended to splinter them by creating cause-oriented temporary coalitions.

Weakening Party Control of Nominations and Campaigns

As the parties weakened they lost control over both nominations and campaigns. Increasingly their place was taken by candidate-centered organizations that drew together a host of hired experts. Robert Agranoff, a political scientist who has also served as a political consultant, has described much of this process quite well. As candidates perceived the parties' inadequacies they turned to other sources for help. First they went to advertising people for themes and messages, then to pollsters for information about the electorate's opinions. Soon the need for other kinds of experts became apparent: "specialists in direct mail . . . journalists to formulate news releases, television documentary producers . . . voting behavior researchers . . ."[14] As the scale and expense of campaigns grew, management skills and technology were needed to supply the professional campaigns that candidates wanted. Agranoff has specifics:

> A survey of the 208 candidates running in statewide constituencies in 1972–73 revealed that 168 of them employed the services of at least one hired consultant: 61 of 67 Senate candidates; 38 of 42 gubernatorial candidates, 30 of 37 attorney general candidates, 20 of 32 state treasurer candidates, and 19 of 31 secretary of state candidates. A recent *National Journal* study of United States Senate candidates indicated that of the 67 candidates with opposition, 62 employed advertising firms, 30 hired professional media consultants, 24 used national polling firms, and 20 acquired the services of a campaign management and public relations firm.[15]

As he sized up the situation, the use of "political consultants" in one form or another was becoming the "normal practice for most high visibility offices."

At the outset Agranoff characterized this new style of campaigning as differing in four ways from previous campaigning. For one, it was candidate centered.[16] The emphasis in the campaign lay on electing the candidate, not the party and its ticket. Second, this style differed from the old in the professionals utilized. Party professionals had given way to the "advertising and public relations man, the management specialist, the media specialist, the pollster." Third, these specialists in turn brought their skills to bear in systematic research. Accustomed to conducting product research on which to make marketing decisions, they transferred their research and decision-making skills to the electorate and the political process. Fourth, the new mode of campaigning included communication through a variety of media. The party organization was still used but communication channels were enlarged to vary the means of reaching the public. Electronic media were used most of all.

Thus Agranoff explained, "The air waves and the computer are performing many of the voter contact activities that the campaign workers once undertook. Radio, television, and the computer letter are replacing in importance the campaign poster, button, and bumper sticker that once symbolized the American political campaign."[17]

Changes in control are equally visible in the nominating process. Statewide presidential primaries, a popular reform of earlier days that has been much expanded recently, have contributed like the others to a weakening of the parties. As described by Agranoff, "Presidential aspirants now stimulate news coverage of their activities, seek nationwide television coverage of states with primaries, and use private and public polls to demonstrate their standing with the electorate, in order to place early pressure on party leaders and delegates to support them."[18] This process, in which candidates pitch their appeals directly to the people and the delegates, is far removed from the fabled smoke-filled room in which city and state political bosses at one time decided nominations. Jimmy Carter's successful run for the Democratic nomination in 1976 fits into this wide-open pattern of party nominations. He began as an outsider, an unknown from the Deep South. He was "Jimmy Who?" And he was the most conservative of the many Democratic contenders, with the exception of the maverick George Wallace. As early as 1972 he began planning his appeals to the media, to the public, to party convention delegates, and to prominent politicians.[19] His well-organized and well-executed campaign, incorporating skillful media appeals, carried him to victory inspite of his initial disabilities as an outsider and a southerner. He made himself the leading Democrat and the organization had no choice but to accept him when the national convention met in mid-1976. The following year, as the Democrats debated further changes in party rules, one state chairman looked back upon the election process to comment ruefully that "the primary process as such is destructive of party cohesion. When candidates get elected because they're on the tube, they're responsible to everybody. And therefore, they're responsible to nobody."[20]

As parties lost control over nominations they lost control as well over campaign issues. As Agranoff summarizes this trend:

> Today's candidates ordinarily have a predetermined set of issues that they make known early, and these issues are often carried forth from their initial quest for nomination. In the era of the candidate-centered campaign, the evil of the party organization is often an issue in the campaign. Milton Shapp's primary slogan was "The Man versus The Machine." Once elected, officials are no longer as dependent on the party organization for renomination and reelection, and thus they no longer fear being "dumped" for disloyalty. Members of the party-in-the-government are more free to select issue positions for personal reasons, such as their own values, constituency pressures that are contrary to official party position, or calculation of their re-election effect. . . . powerful candidates within the party structure can and do insist on the party taking the positions that they wish to advocate.[21]

In 1976 Carter's moderation disturbed some of the eminent Democrats closely identified with the New Deal heritage, but it was Carter's desires that shaped the campaign.

Agranoff attributes the development of the "candidate organization as we know it today" to the Kennedys, beginning with John Kennedy's 1960 campaign for president. But he considered CREEP, as Nixon's 1972 Committee to Re-elect the President was known, the most famous of the candidate-centered organizations. It was organized entirely apart from the Republican National Committee, and as described by Agranoff it was awesome:

> It had a number of divisions, including public relations (press relations, press advance, candidate surrogate advance), media (including its own advertising agency), direct mail (including seven computer centers and four district mail centers), information (including affiliated polling groups), state operations (including ten regional headquarters, 250 telephone centers in twenty-three states, and hundreds of paid fieldworkers), group divisions (youth, labor, ethnic, minorities, and many others), a vote security division, and, of course, the most famous security division, whose operatives were apprehended breaking into Democratic headquarters in the Watergate compex. CREEP had a headquarters staff of 355, plus over 300 regular volunteers.[22]

Furthermore, according to this account, the Nixon people did not trust party regulars in many precincts to carry out contact work, so they appointed many of their own and brought the others under CREEP control. This organization set up outside the national committee existed to reelect Richard Nixon, not to support a party and all of its nominees. CREEP may have been a bit unusual. Certainly the famous security division responsible for Watergate was somewhat unusual, or so we have been frequently assured. But as a candidate-centered organization that dominated the campaign processes it was pretty much in tune with its times.

Another striking example of this new style of campaigning is William Singer's attempt, in 1975, to oust Richard Daley as mayor of Chicago. One would not expect a mayoral race to be a prime example of advanced campaign techniques. But as Agranoff assessed this campaign:

> Singer had more than issues. He had a full-time staff of 45, 10 district headquarters spread about the city, about 2,000 regular and highly committed volunteers, and coverage of nearly all 3,211 precincts during the voter canvass and on election day. Moreover, Singer spent about $200,000 on polls-based television advertising, with commercials prepared by David Garth, a New York consultant.[23]

Singer was unsuccessful, but Agranoff says that his approach and techniques have been increasingly used by others in "displaying party independence." A display of party independence is obviously not cheap, but cost may be a minor factor for some who feel the call to public service.

Interest Groups, PACs, and the Coin of the Realm

As the parties deteriorated and the campaign managers often took over their functions, the interest group system flourished. Interest groups have always been a prominent part of the cluttered United States political scene. Muckrakers for generations have righteously exposed "special interests" and condemned their insidious influence. Yet an increasingly middle-class society has become ever more diversified and has produced interests of all kinds that are willing and able to seek access to those in office. And in recent times this flourishing thicket of interests has included a healthy growth of public interest groups. Common Cause could even claim to be the "people's lobby" busily working to save the country from the other interests. This kind of diversity accords well with a pluralistic version of the political system. A "post-partisan" politics of "issue-based factions" sounds like a system in which interest groups play a major role, whether called people's lobbies or special interests.

One student of interest groups, Carol S. Greenwald, found that in 1974 there were some 12,600 national nonprofit associations in the United States. These ran the gamut of activities: among the leading groups 23 percent represented trade and commercial organizations, 35 percent represented a range of health, education, science, and social welfare organizations, and nearly 10 percent were cultural in nature.[24] This list in its size and variety helps establish the pervasiveness of interest groups in the system. It does not tell us which ones are most active politically. Elsewhere Greenwald tries to suggest the scale of lobbying activity: "Sophisticated observers estimate 5,000 to 10,000 practicing lobbyists in Washington who are interested in domestic issues, only 1,000 registered officially in 1974. Registration records also show . . . 11,432 foreign government lobbyists . . . and 600 executive branch 'legislative liaison' (read 'lobbyists') including twelve from the Executive Office."[25] Interest group lobbying is readily apparent but—often by intent—hard to trace politically.

Common Cause has, however, compiled some pertinent information on interest group electoral activity. According to its figures, "In last year's Congressional elections, special interest groups poured an unprecedented $22.6 million into House and Senate campaigns—nearly double the $12.5 million they had 'invested' in 1974."[26] Of course 1976 was a presidential election year and 1974 was not. Still, if these figures are correct, interest group political activity increased sharply over a very short time. Direct contributions by corporations and unions have long been prohibited, but changes in the federal law in the 1970s permitted the formation of Political Action Committees, or PACs. Interest groups could form such committees to raise money and give it to candidates under specified conditions. The number of PACs soared from 516 in 1974 to 1,166 in 1976, according to Common Cause. The Republican national chairman, Bill Brock, thought PACs were the "newest and fastest growing factor in American politics," and he formed a new division in his party to work with PACs to assist the flow of interest group money into party politics.

Common Cause examined these PACs by category and concluded that "labor union PACs" continued to be the single largest interest group contributors to congressional candidates, with a total of $8.2 million. The AFL-CIO federation was the largest single labor source followed by maritime-related unions. Business groups were second only to labor in their giving to congressional candidates; they had nearly tripled their contributions, from $2.5 million in 1974 to $7.1 million in 1976 campaigns. A group of realtors alone increased their contributions to more than $600,000 in 1976. Agricultural interests were active as well. Dairy interests that had been stung by some Watergate-related revelations of their political contributions were "back in business as usual," Common Cause reported. Health interests contributed heavily, with a total of $2.7 million in 1976, including $1.8 million from the American Medical Association alone. As Common Cause pointed out, the medical profession has long had an interest in the possible enactment of national health care legislation. When the groups with total contributions of over $1 million in the last three elections were listed, the AMA was first, with over $4 million. The AFL-CIO was next, followed by the dairy committees, United Auto Workers, maritime-related unions, the National Education Association, the International Association of Machinists, and the United Steelworkers of America.

The pattern of giving in 1976 was selective, Common Cause found. Congressional leaders and members of key committees did well. John Rhodes, Republican leader in the House, received $98,000 in special interest funds. House Democratic leaders Jim Wright and Daniel Rostenkowski each got at least $40,000. Common Cause cited a New York Times report which explained that the "dairy lobby gave to members of the agriculture committee, the maritime unions to those on the maritime committee and the teachers' lobby to members of the education committee." Members of the congressional committees that dealt with taxes also usually fared well in contributions, even though some held safe seats and faced nominal opposition.

One other pattern of note was the tendency for the PACs, like other interest groups and the general public, to favor incumbents. Incumbency and large contributions did not insure success, as Senator John Tunney's loss in California in 1976 proved. But much of the time they did make the difference.

That money counts and reform may have mixed effects is suggested by columnist David S. Broder's report on a Federal Election Commission survey of "key people" in some 850 House and Senate campaigns in 1976. Most incumbents won and most challengers lost, as we would expect. Most importantly, however, there was agreement on all sides that the 1974 law passed in the wake of Watergate increased the advantages of an incumbent. Even the incumbents who drafted the law agreed by a margin of 3 to 2 that their " 'reform' measure . . . made them even more immune from effective challenge."[27] This finding should serve, surely, as a reminder that reform may be more elusive and many-sided than reformers anticipate.

Common Cause, with its well-known bias against "special interests," may tend to exaggerate, but their figures on interest group money flowing into the political process are impressive. The astounding increase in PACs just from 1974 to 1976 clearly means that interest groups have seized upon the opportunity the law opened to them.

Common Cause likes to "view with alarm" the special interests attracted to the government like flies to honey. But what of the public interest groups themselves? We have argued that reform- and consumer-oriented groups add significant diversity to what is really a pluralistic political system. And on our understanding of postindustrial society, they may be seen as a natural outgrowth of it. As we have seen, they consist of middle-class people who reject the usual party politics, special interests, and the compromises that "violate" principles. They are activists who choose to pursue issue-oriented causes on behalf of those they perceive as underrepresented. From the 1960s on such groups have flourished and become a significant force in national affairs. Common Cause, which itself lobbies heavily against special interests, has at times ranked at or near the top in the lists of totals spent on lobbying in Washington in a given year.[28] The reformers themselves have become part of an interest group system that they often condemn. They justify themselves as a counterforce checking the "special" interests, but from the perspective of the system as a whole they add significantly to an interest group system that has grown while the parties falter.

Some Interest Groups in Action

The growth of interest group activity was increasingly apparent as the 1978 elections approached. A *New York Times* reporter, John Herbers, wrote, "Some Administration officials and members of Congress believe they are standing in the center of a great free-for-all effort to exercise political leverage on the federal government. There have always been lobbying pressures; the difference now is that there are many more activists sounding off on more issues."[29] And they had discovered direct mail as a means of raising money. Herbers said there were more than 1,600 committees of all kinds engaged in such activities and the number was "still growing," and he too mentioned the debilitation of the parties and the tendency for candidates to rely on interest groups rather than their party.

Among interest groups active in the political process, the AFL-CIO has the largest and possibly the most influential organization of all.[30] Certainly the federation has to be considered a major power on the national scene, and its political arm, the Committee on Political Education—known simply as COPE—has been so successful that it is a model emulated by other groups.

This well-developed political organization, which federation president George Meany frankly described as a "political machine," did not form by accident. Labor has long played a part in the national political scene, but in 1960 it began political work in a big way. Over the years COPE worked hard at getting union members and their families registered, and it compiled their names in a form that could be used by labor activists all across the country. Union leaders are given political training and are expected to mobilize their members. The federation leadership helps lay campaign plans. Every election year COPE endorses hundreds of candidates for Congress. By their own account, in 1974 they endorsed 422 candidates seeking House and Senate seats, and this figure does not include COPE's extensive operations at the state and local level. But most of COPE's endorsements require only nominal support. It actually concentrates on perhaps eighty to a hundred contests, which become the focus of labor's energies in seeking, with its allies, to elect a friend or defeat an enemy. National headquarters provide many services in aid of campaign field work and of the large and influential labor lobby.

Labor's willingness to develop a "political machine" to support the unions and their collective bargaining may differ only in degree from that of other interest groups. Business-based political activities are on the increase too, and Watergate exposed the seamy side of some of these operations. The penalties against some corporations and their officers for illegal activities probably reduced business politicking for a time, but business-related Political Action Committees boomed during the mid-1970s and afterward. Labor can marshal the voters but business can marshal the money. For example, according to one report, General Electric "solicits its 540 top executives, and about two-thirds participate, contributing about $70,000 a year."[31] Some corporations even use "payroll withholding plans for their executives." With money rolling in from business organizations, "corporate PAC growth . . . put business in nearly the same league with organized labor as contributors to Congressional campaigns." Some people worried that if the trend continued, by the 1980s corporate PACs could "dominate Congressional politics."

Business lobbying takes many forms, and Mark V. Nadel has put together an extended account of them.[32] One form of influence he titled "Musical Chairs," to describe the interchange of personnel between government agencies and the corporations those agencies regulate. According to Nadel, in 1975 a congressional study found that "at least 350 officials on the nation's regulatory agencies once worked for the industries they now regulate." The Food and Drug Administration alone included a hundred officials who had once worked for drug or chemical companies, companies whose products the FDA regulated. Critics of such practices admit that the government thus acquires expertise not readily available otherwise, but they raise questions about the loyalties of industry experts called upon to regulate the very corporations they once worked for.

Nadel also cites a form of influence that had not been much discussed until recently: the system of advisory committees for government agencies. Set up to give administrators access to expertise from outside government service, these committees expanded over the years to become a formidable number, 1,439, by 1973. The huge Health, Education and Welfare Department alone had 367 such advisory bodies. Nadel acknowledged that many of these were not directly business related, but he regarded them as a "formalized lobbying process" and quoted Ralph Nader with approval as charging that the advisory committee system granted special interests a means of access to administrators that ordinary citizens lacked. This access built into the bureaucratic process would of course supplement other channels of corporate influence via contributions and appointments.

One form of business influence that is hard for other groups such as labor to match is advertising. Corporations after all have the money to spend on expensive TV, magazine, and newspaper ads, and may use them to foster a false image. According to Nadel, a 1970 study of environmental advertising in magazines like *Newsweek*, *Time*, and *Business Week* found the biggest spenders to be the industries with the most acute pollution problems, especially "electric utilities and iron and steel, petroleum, paper, and chemical firms." The usual tone of such ads was to portray a major corporation as a sterling defender of pure water and air and of nature's creatures. What the firm actually did in many cases was quite different. Such ads were of course meant to foster favorable public opinion and so forestall unfriendly government regulation.

Corporations manifestly exert much influence on the political process and there is evidence such efforts are on the upswing, not in decline. But in a system characterized by weakened parties, candidate-centered organizations, and a flourishing interest group system, there is much competition for the goodies available.

People, Parties, and Interest Groups

Political parties are traditionally thought of as the main means of marshaling the popular will to guide the government, but changes in American society have changed the parties profoundly. For convenience, we may sum up the emerging pattern as one of a postindustrial society. Politically a major implication is that voters have become less party oriented and incline to be independent, selective, and demanding. Party identification does remain as a major influence upon voter behavior, and on the face of it the Democratic vote in 1976 appeared to reflect a resurgence of the old New Deal coalition and a halt to the decline in party identification. Examination of the vote, however, suggests that it depended crucially upon "nontraditional" groups whom the candidate and the issues brought into the Democratic column, momentarily at least. And meantime the forces associated with declining voter support for the parties persist: a large middle class that is affluent and relatively well educated, but increasingly diversified and somewhat cynical and distrustful. An individualistic rather than a group-oriented or party-oriented voting pattern has been on the increase and appears likely to persist and possibly increase.

We can trace the process of change in the deterioration of the major party organizations. Reforms, especially those of the Democrats in the 1960s, opened the party to issue-oriented activists who compounded the problems of party unity. Reforms in campaign law further weakened party participation in the conduct of elections and probably strengthened incumbents more than their challengers. The effect, on balance, would be likely to loosen party influence, such as it is, on incumbents. Added to these developments is McFarland's analysis of the reform-minded supporters of interest groups associated with consumer and environmental causes. McFarland found them to be skeptical of traditional political party institutions and processes and of big government itself, but optimistic enough to back certain causes through ad hoc coalitions of like-minded activists. Instead of revitalizing the political parties, they have enlarged the interest group system.

As these and other pressures battered the parties, they lost much control over both nominations and the general election campaigns. Increasingly candidates won the nominations on their own, as Jimmy Carter did with a campaign that began in earnest in 1972. Later on, nomination in hand, the candidate used the party label to shape his own strategy and issues. In some cases candidates ran against the "organization," a strategy akin to Carter's anti-Washington theme in 1976. In place of the party, candidates turned to campaign managers or political consultants. For a fee consultants could create an organization with a number of specialized skills, all managed with heavy reliance on the media and especially television.

The weakening of the parties enhanced the role of interest groups, and interest group money and Political Action Committees grew at an amazing rate during the 1970s. Their activities tended to favor, selectively, incumbents and those in key leadership positions. Reform groups, such as Common Cause, added a further dimension to an already diverse interest group system. At times Common Cause has itself ranked at the top of groups filing lobby expenditure reports, but the political machine of the AFL-CIO ranks as probably the largest and possibly the most effective. Business bounced back from the trauma of Watergate to multiply corporation-based PACs and to enhance business lobbying with an arsenal of weapons including appointments, advisory committees, and image-oriented advertising. Business, labor, and consumer activists were part and parcel of a muscular interest group system that both supplemented and in many ways undermined the parties.

This pluralistic diversity could be seen as healthy and beneficial. It could also be seen as creating an ungovernable political system. Certainly it has made for a complex form of coalition politics. And it has enhanced the role of the media.

NOTES

1. Everett Carll Ladd, Jr., with Charles Hadley, *Transformations of the American Party System*, 2nd ed. (New York: W. W. Norton, 1978), Chapter 4. The account of postindustrialization that we give in the text is both abbreviated and colored by our own perspective. Daniel Bell is credited with developing the concept initially.
2. Walter DeVries and V. Lance Tarrance, *The Ticket-Splitter* (Grand Rapids, Mich.: Wm. B. Eerdmans Publishing, 1972). The subtitle, *A New Force in American Politics*, describes the authors' message.
3. Ladd and Hadley, *Transformations of the American Party System*, p. 329.
4. Norman H. Nie, Sidney Verba, and John R. Petrocik, *The Changing American Voter* (Cambridge, Mass.: Harvard University Press, 1976), p. 347.
5. Ibid., p. 346.
6. Ibid., p. 355.
7. *Gallup Opinion Index*, December 1976, pp. 16 ff.

8. Ladd and Hadley, *Transformations of the American Party System*, pp. 300–301.
9. Richard L. Rubin, *Party Dynamics* (New York: Oxford University Press, 1976), pp. 174, 181.
10. Ladd and Hadley, *Transformations of the American Party System*, pp. 358–359.
11. David S. Broder, syndicated column, *Norman* (Okla.) *Transcript*, October 6, 1976, p. 6.
12. *New York Times*, September 19, 1976, p. 37. One has to read this article—and reread it—to believe it. The technical questions posed by the reform law in application to this normally innocent and desirable campaign practice are almost mind bending. But it was a serious business. According to this story, two of the commissioners thought the campaign buttons were illegal and ought to be banned.
13. Andrew S. McFarland, *Public Interest Lobbies: Decision Making on Energy* (Washington, D.C.: American Enterprise Institute for Public Policy, 1976), Chapter 1.
14. Robert Agranoff, *The New Style in Election Campaigns*, 2nd ed. (Boston: Holbrook Press, 1976), pp. 24–25.
15. Ibid., p. 8.
16. Ibid., pp. 4–6.
17. Ibid., p. 26.
18. Ibid., pp. 11, 12.
19. Martin Schramm, *Running for President: A Journal of the Carter Campaign* (New York: Simon and Schuster Pocket Books, 1977). Note the "Jordan Memo" of November 4, 1972, outlining Jimmy Carter's campaign for the Democratic nomination in 1976, in the chapter "Running for President."
20. Broder, syndicated column, *Norman* (Okla.) *Transcript*, August 17, 1977, p. 6.
21. Agranoff, *The New Style in Election Campaigns*, pp. 13, 14.
22. Ibid., p. 15.
23. Ibid., p. 7.
24. Carol S. Greenwald, *Group Power: Lobbying and Public Policy* (New York: Praeger, 1977), p. 16.
25. Ibid., p. 334.
26. Common Cause, *Frontline*, April–May 1977, pp. 3–8.
27. Broder, syndicated column, *Norman* (Okla.) *Transcript*, May 1, 1977, p. 6.
28. *Congressional Quarterly Weekly Report* 32: 3 (July 27, 1974), 1947 ff. Among the twenty-five top spenders that filed lobby spending reports for 1973, Common Cause led the list. It topped the list in 1972 as well. Common Cause, it might be added, probably complies with lobby law regulations much more carefully than many other lobbies. Some do not even bother to register.
29. *New York Times*, March 27, 1978, p. 1.
30. For a more extended analysis, see Harry Holloway, "Interest Groups in the Post Partisan Era: The Political Machine of the AFL-CIO," *Political Science Quarterly* (forthcoming).
31. *Congressional Quarterly*, 36 (April 1978), 849–854.
32. Mark V. Nadel, *Corporations and Political Accountability* (Lexington, Mass.: D. C. Heath, 1976), Chapter 3, especially pp. 54 ff. The whole book is an extended study of the forms of corporate influence on the political process.

SUGGESTIONS FOR FURTHER READINGS

David W. Abbott and Edward T. Rogowsky, eds. *Political Parties*. Chicago: Rand McNally, 1978. Readings that include many of the important articles written over the years on the condition of the party system.

Robert Agranoff. *The Management of Election Campaigns*. Boston: Holbrook, 1976. A systematic, detailed analysis of what goes into election campaigns by one who has been a political consultant.

Herbert E. Alexander. *Financing Politics: Money, Elections and Political Reform.* Washington, D.C.: Congressional Quarterly Press, 1976. A leading authority describes fund-raising practices and comments on the reform legislation of the 1970s.

Daniel Bell. *The Coming of Post-Industrial Society.* New York: Basic Books, 1973. Bell argues the case for the emergence of a new kind of social system that no longer fits the ideologies, such as Marxism, that have often been applied.

Frank B. Feigert and M. Margaret Conway. *Parties and Politics in America.* Boston: Allyn and Bacon, 1976. A major text that thoroughly covers its subject.

A. Lee Fritschler. *Smoking and Politics.* 2nd ed. Englewood Cliffs, N.J.: Prentice-Hall, 1975. Interest groups and bureaucratic politics.

Mark J. Green. *The Other Government: The Unseen Power of Washington Lawyers.* New York: Grossman/Viking Press, 1975. An exposé focused on the influential lawyers in the nation's capitol.

Carol S. Greenwald. *Group Power: Lobbying and Public Policy.* New York: Praeger, 1977. An extended analysis of group activities all through the political system.

Stephen Hess. *The Presidential Election.* Washington, D.C.: Brookings Institution, 1978. A discussion of presidential leadership and the process by which we select national leaders.

Russell Warren Howe and Sarah Hays Trott. *The Power Peddlers: How Lobbyists Mold America's Foreign Policy.* New York: Doubleday, 1977. A somewhat unusual focus on lobbying and foreign policy.

William R. Keech and Donald R. Matthews. *The Party's Choice.* Washington, D.C.: Brookings Institution, 1976. Political scientists carefully examine the ways that presidential nominations have been won over the years.

William J. Keefe. *Parties, Politics, and Public Policy in America.* Hinsdale, Ill.: Dryden Press, 1976. A fairly brief, readable text that deals with the problems and hard times on which the parties have fallen.

Austin H. Kiplinger with Knight A. Kiplinger. *Washington Now.* New York: Harper & Row, 1975. A lively and well-informed account of the Washington activities of a wide range of people and organizations.

Theodore J. Lowi. *The End of Liberalism: Ideology, Policy, and the Crisis of Public Authority.* New York: W. W. Norton, 1969. A thoughtful and critical analysis of interest group pluralism.

Lester W. Milbrath. *The Washington Lobbyists.* Chicago: Rand McNally, 1963. A political scientist who interviewed many lobbyists sizes up their role in the political process.

Nelson W. Polsby and Aaron Wildavsky. *Presidential Elections: Strategies of American Electoral Politics.* 4th ed. New York: Charles Scribner's Sons, 1976. Two respected scholars examine the stages in the process by which candidates seek the nation's highest office.

John E. Sinclair. *Interest Groups in America.* Morristown, N.J.: General Learning Press, 1976. A brief, readable account of interest groups, with a good annotated bibliography.

Frank Smallwood. *Free and Independent.* Brattleboro, Vt.: Stephen Greene Press, 1976. A Dartmouth political scientist took the plunge into politics, served a term in the Vermont State Senate, and the result is an extremely readable and interesting book.

Judith G. Smith, ed. *Political Brokers: People, Organizations, Money and Power.* New York: A Liveright/National Journal Book, 1972. Readings that focus on the political activities, in and out of Washington, of a variety of groups.

George Thayer. *Who Shakes the Money Tree?* New York: Simon and Schuster, 1974. A lively account of campaign finance practices.

Martin and Susan Tolchin. *To the Victor: Political Patronage from the Clubhouse to the White House.* New York: Random House Vintage Books, 1971. A fascinating inside look at city, state, and national politics that dwells upon the importance of patronage in getting things done politically.

David B. Truman. *The Governmental Process: Political Interests and Public Opinion.* New York: Alfred A. Knopf, 1962. The classic analysis of interest groups in American politics.

L. Harmon Zeigler and G. Wayne Peak. *Interest Groups in American Society.* 2nd ed. Englewood Cliffs. N.J.: Prentice-Hall, 1972. One of the important texts on the subject.

13 · The Media: From Quality Press to Campaign Spots

A society with weak parties, countless factions, and a demanding, if somewhat cynical, electorate is one in which there is much for the media to do. No one is clearly in charge, whether it be a strong political party coalition or an entrenched single elite. In this diverse and complex system, communication is essential. The American media for communications are as varied as the population, but the quality press and the television networks are probably the most important in influencing large-scale political opinion. Even this statement, however, needs to be assessed in terms of the many and contradictory theories that have been developed about the influence of the so-called mass media.

Theories of the Media

One media theory is well represented by C. Wright Mills, with his view of the United States as dominated by a "power elite." The masses, as he portrayed them, were little more than putty molded by the elite. The power of the media was such that they did not just filter people's experience of "external realities."[1] They went far beyond that to enter "into our very experience of our own selves." These means of communication provided us with "new identities and new aspirations" and with "models of conduct." Poles apart from this theory is the colorful analogy proposed by the skeptical political scientist V. O. Key: "The flow of the messages of the mass media is rather like dropping a handful of confetti from the rim of the Grand Canyon with the object of striking a man astride a burro on the canyon floor."[2]

Reposing somewhere between these extremes is the concept of the media as agenda setters. What it amounts to is the "ability of the media to structure our world for us . . . . the mass media may not be successful much of the time in telling us what to think, but the media are stunningly successful in telling their audience what to think about."[3] On this theory the media do not shape our "identities" and "aspirations," as Mills thought, but they do call our attention to subject matter that they transmit. In doing so they create an "agenda" that the media audience thinks about. This agenda-setting role is a modest concept of media influence, but most students of political socialization would probably agree that the mass media are a good deal less influential than the family and the educational system. By the time people reach adulthood they are pretty well formed and are hardly likely to be changed much by what they see in a newspaper or on TV. In Key's words, "The messages of the media do not strike the isolated and atomistic individual; they strike, if they reach their target at all, an individual living in a network of personal relationships that affect his outlook toward the objects of the external world, including the mass media." Key surmised that "group forces on balance provide a net resistance to those messages calculated to maintain the status quo."[4] The media are important, but their role is bounded by the complex pressures of a pluralistic system. They may help set the public agenda, but they do not mold the masses.

The Quality Press as the Nation's Agenda Setter

The nation's press includes a good many newspapers and news magazines, but some matter much more than others. And those that matter to activists, leaders, and informed citizens do so because of their quality and the quality of their readership, rather than mass circulation. Some people see a "liberal establishment" centered in on the nation's leading newspapers, magazines, and radio and television networks. This elite is thought to exert a pervasive influence which extends in the first instance to other elites and then percolates down through the nation. Former Vice President Spiro Agnew acquired much notoriety with such charges in 1969, and similar accusations appear from time to time. In its harshest form, criticism by conservatives visualizes a small group of people, none of them elected or directly accountable to the public, who set national policy and even determine trends in manners and morals. Defenders of the media react by scoffing at such sweeping accusations and advising a quick rereading of the First Amendment. If the conservative critics are right, the media system is dominated by liberals and is able to do more than set the nation's agenda.

One view of the power of the press comes from a memo written by Hamilton Jordan, when he was helping to plan Jimmy Carter's presidential campaign. Late in 1972 Jordan wrote:

> Like it or not, there exists in fact an eastern liberal news establishment which has tremendous influence. The views of this small group of opinion-makers in the papers they represent are noted and imitated by other columnists and newspapers throughout the country and the world. Their recognition and acceptance of your candidacy as a viable force with some chance of success could establish you as a serious contender. . . . They could have an equally adverse effect.[5]

Having singled out this "small group of opinion-makers," Jordan followed up with specific recommendations. One was that his boss "review and read portions of the *New York Times, Washington Post, Wall Street [Journal]* and other national selections every day. Despite its liberal orientation and bias, the *New York Times* is the best paper in the country and possibly the world." Carter was also urged to foster relationships with political columnists he already knew and to get to know others. As Jordan saw it, the path to the presidency included the courting of the "opinion-makers" associated with the major newspapers.

Theodore H. White gives another and stronger version of the elite press as a liberal establishment. In his account of the 1972 election he described the election itself as a struggle between Richard Nixon, on the one hand, and the adversary press and media on the other. While Nixon sought to win the people to a conservative agenda, the press fought to create a liberal one. As White forcefully expressed it, "The power of the press in America is a primordial one. It sets the agenda of public discussion. . . . It determines what people will talk and think about.[6]

At the head of the elite press establishment White put *The New York Times*, the "hometown newspaper of all men of government, all men of great affairs, and all men and women who try to think. In the sociology of information it is assumed that any telephone call made between nine and noon anywhere in the executive belt between Boston and Washington is made between two parties both of whom have already read *The New York Times* and are speaking from the same body of shared information."[7]

The *Times* was the "bulletin board for the editors of the great news magazines, who speed their correspondents to the scene of any story the *Times* unearths." Furthermore, it was the "bulletin board of all three national television networks, whose evening news assignments, when not forced by events themselves, are shaped by the ideas and reportage in the *Times*." Local editors and TV producers read the *Times*, and it was also the "bulletin board" for book publishers in deciding what books to nourish or discourage. In all, according to White, the *Times* reported what was "important to know" about finance, music, clothing, advertising, drama, and business, as well as politics. It was read in the White House and read in capitals across the world as soon as available.

In all of this, White made it clear that in his opinion the values pervading all *Times* reporting were broadly liberal ones that often opposed Nixon and what he represented. Nixon in turn hated those "liberal bastards" and what they were trying to do.[8] In his account White dramatically portrays an elite press establishment ranged against Nixon and undoubtedly captures some of the real hostility felt by these adversaries. But he wrote well before the full weight of Watergate revelations took hold. One wonders if he would have written in the same vein a few years later. In any case he probably exaggerated the influence of the liberal press establishment in general and *The New York Times* in particular.

What Leaders Read

But to fault White is not to conclude that he is totally wrong. A data-based study of what national leaders read does lend some support to the notion of a liberal press establishment. In this study, by Carol H. Weiss, a sample of national leaders reported on their reading habits.[9] The sample included people from major governmental and corporate institutions, as well as media, labor unions, and major voluntary associations. Curiously enough, the super-rich proved to be the hardest sector of this leadership sample to reach and interview. Still, the overall rate for completion of interviews was good: 545 respondents representing 70.5 percent of the sample. We therefore have an unusual glimpse of the actual reading matter that circulates among this elite.

One finding was the primacy of the *Times*: "The reading matter they most have in common is *The New York Times*. . . . It comes closest to being the national newspaper of the national elite." Other papers fared well among certain sectors. The *Wall Street Journal* was much read by businessmen and labor leaders. In Washington the *Washington Post* was widely read among members of the executive branch, Congress, labor leaders, media leaders, and voluntary association leaders. More than 90 percent of the Washingtonians in the sample read the *Post*, and Weiss described it as the "primary newspaper" of the city's officialdom. But three-fourths of them read the *Times* as well. Quality papers in various cities across the country also drew considerable mention. Even so, among all the columnists read by these leaders, James Reston of the *Times* ranked well ahead.

The "very heavy magazine readership" in the group put *Newsweek, Time,* and *U.S. News and World Report* at the top. Economic leaders read *Business Week* and *Fortune.* Interestingly, *The New York Times Magazine,* a supplement that appears each week in the Sunday edition, moved from seventh to third place for "regular" reading as distinct from occasional reading. Executives in the communications media were especially heavy magazine readers; in addition to the big four, these leaders listed magazines with a literary-cultural orientation: *New Yorker, Saturday Review, Harper's, Atlantic, Esquire, New York Review of Books*— magazines that tend to be on the left or middle, not the right.

Conservatives are afraid the liberal press may be more than an agenda setter and may actually alter opinions. The study of leadership reading matter included questions about opinions on many subjects, domestic and foreign. In general, Weiss found, "Reading *The New York Times* or the *Washington Post* and 'intellectual' magazines is associated with liberal opinions, and reading *The Wall Street Journal,* general and news magazines, and business magazines is associated with more conservative opinions. This pattern tends to hold up even when occupational sector is controlled." A similar kind of relationship was found in specific sectors for corporate leaders, multimillionaires, and leaders in Congress and the political parties, although at times the relationship was not strong. Weiss cautiously avoided inferring cause-and-effect. Possibly these leaders were more liberal than their peers to begin with and simply picked newspapers they found congenial. But these findings on their face lend support to the charges of conservative media critics.

One further important finding in the Weiss study is not altogether expected. The study asked these leaders about the "most valuable sources" of "information and ideas" they relied upon in respect to the *"single national issue"* that they had been concerned with in recent years. Responses varied and economic leaders, for instance, tended to rely heavily upon their own sources of information. Yet the media came in for impressive mention. Weiss concluded, "Despite their positions of leadership in society and their concentration on issues central to their functional responsibilities, leaders rely heavily on the media for information. . . . The media are society's conduit." And the media also "seem to serve as a link among members of different sectors, reporting news, ideas, opinions, even purposeful leaks when other communication channels are closed or clogged." In each sector the leaders tended to rely a good deal upon information from sources in that sector. Nonetheless, it is apparent that the media, and especially the prestige press led by the *Times* and the *Post*, matter a good deal.

The role of the quality press in agenda setting, as it applies specifically to TV news broadcasting, is clearly confirmed in Edward Jay Epstein's study of the NBC news organization:

> Network news is reactive to other media in the sense that it depends almost wholly on them (especially the *New York Times* and AP and UPI wire services) for its basic intelligence input about the news of the day. . . . outside sources establish a basic agenda of possible stories for the networks. . . . producers are judged in their news coverage by their superiors on the basis of what the "competition" and the *New York Times* featured as leading stories that day . . .[10]

The result is a news "consensus" derived from sources outside the networks, led by *The New York Times* and the wire services.

Apart from the news consensus of the moment, new categories of news emerge and again we find the quality press in the fore. Epstein reports that producers claim to have a "news sense." But they also constantly "attempt to survey the press—notably the *New York Times*, especially the Sunday 'Review of the Week' section, *Time*, *Newsweek* and the *Washington Post*—for 'news trends.'"[11] The "news sense" of the producers gets a good deal of help in spotting breaking stories.

On the other hand, Epstein acknowledges that the network news producers do exercise considerable discretion. The news consensus established by the *Times* and other sources encompasses more stories than TV can possibly broadcast each day. Still, it is clear that what the quality press, led by the *Times*, considers "the news" will be known and heeded by others in the media and beyond.

These studies of the media and the role in it of the quality press surely warrant the opinion that Hamilton Jordan's advice was sound. There is a liberal press establishment that tends to establish a news consensus and thereby create a news agenda or national bulletin board. This press is read by the nation's leaders, for whom it serves as a conduit and also as a linkage in a process that supplements their own specialized sources of information. It is possible but less certain that the liberal leanings of this elite press influence their readers.

Muckrakers and Agenda Setting

Discussion of the impact of the press would hardly be complete without attention to its adversary role and especially to what is often called muckraking. The role of *Washington Post* reporters Bob Woodward and Carl Bernstein in uncovering Watergate is a good recent example. The American press tends to pride itself on its independence and the willingness of news reporters to uncover failings of institutions and of individuals, whether presidents or small-town mayors. Muckraking is not confined to the quality press by any means, and some muckrakers are able to—indeed, may have to—function as free-lancers. Yet the Woodward and Bernstein discoveries gave fresh impetus to the adversary posture of the quality press and its muckraking reporters. Defenders and liberal critics of the quality press may deny that there is really much liberal bias in its reporting, but the adversary role of the press and its muckraking is widely and proudly defended.

Leonard Downie, in his book about the "new muckrakers," remarks that the "great upsurge of investigative reporting during the past decade has considerably influenced the course of the nation."[13] The exposés of Watergate and other misdeeds of the Nixon administration are at the top of Downie's list of influences, but he has many other famous examples. For instance, Seymour Hersh of *The New York Times* exposed the My Lai massacre, the secret bombing of Cambodia, and, later on, domestic spying by the CIA. To Downie this kind of reporting represents a golden era of muckraking that goes well beyond the influence that Lincoln Steffens, Matthew Josephson, Ida Tarbell, and the other original "muckrakers" had. Today's muckrakers are more numerous and reach a larger audience via newspapers, radio and even TV. They have been so successful as to stimulate a market for investigative reporting in and of itself, as we can see in local newspaper and TV station investigations of consumer problems such as food prices, auto repairs, and dirty restaurants. And it was apparent that some of the young people attracted to journalism had in mind a career similar to that of Woodward and Bernstein.

The quest for an exposé and a news beat means hard work and tough reporting but it has its own rules. Jack Anderson, the Pulitzer Prize–winning independent muckraker, does not print sex stories with no discernible impact on national affairs.[14] Anderson also recognizes and respects the very different category of "legitimate national secrets." He and his assistants do not themselves steal documents but feel they have the right to decide whether to publish what comes into their possession. As for sticking to the truth and nothing but, Anderson said simply, "We try not to lie." But he admitted after all that "I might tell a white lie" and that he and his staff "dramatized" their reports. The muckraker accepts certain rules but at times may bend or even break a few to get results.

The muckraker as an intense adversary out to get his scandal comes through in Downie's impressions and quotations. Jack Anderson "clearly saw himself as the leader of the pack of watchdogs he would like to see unleashed on the national establishment." Woodward reveled in the raking of the muck: "It's almost a perverse pleasure. . . I like going out and finding something that is going wrong or something that isn't the way other people are saying it is, and then putting it into the newspaper."[15] Hersh solicited his responses to his stories and was outraged if the wrongdoing he exposed was not corrected. These muckrakers represent a prominent extreme of the adversary role, but there is an element of the latter in much of the press.

The local press tends to be conservative, as studies of editorial endorsements in national elections normally reveal. But at the same time they tend to share in the national news consensus created by the elite newspapers and the wire services. Much of their national and international news is from such sources, even if they have Washington correspondents of their own.[16] Like the network news producers, however, local editors have much discretion over what they publish and the prominence they give it. Like the quality press nationally, the local papers may be influential agenda setters in their communities, and some are local powers in their own right. The local press and TV matter a good deal to those who want to be on the local agenda and to those who monitor that agenda.

The quality press does matter. And at times, as a muckraking adversary, it has had a spectacular impact on the nation's agenda. The exposure of Watergate will presumably be passed down to future generations as one of the glories of the American press. But TV, its news programming, and its audience are another realm. To track the agenda-setting impact of the Big Three networks—the National Broadcasting Company, the Columbia Broadcasting System, and the American Broadcasting Company—is a more difficult matter.

TV News and Its Constraints

That commercial television differs in many ways from a quality newspaper like *The New York Times* is hardly an astounding revelation. Edward Jay Epstein concluded from his analysis of the NBC news department that the differences were in some part due to constraints, chiefly organizational ones, on TV operations. He summarized these under a number of headings, beginning with economics.[17]

TV news broadcasts are expensive and the cost factor becomes a basic organizational constraint. For one thing, because nobody knows for sure that good, fresh news will sell and add to their profitability, the networks lack incentive to develop extensive reporting services. In any case, TV reporting, with a camera and crew, is much more cumbersome and expensive than the lone reporter with his note pad or tape recorder. Timothy Crouse, in his *The Boys on the Bus*, dramatizes the burdens of TV news coverage with a quotation from Roger Mudd of CBS: "You've got all that claptrap equipment. . . . You're always worrying about this shot or that shot and you can't quite concentrate on what the candidate is saying . . . and you're thinking *Oh Christ, we ran out of film!*"[18] This "claptrap" obviously holds down a reporter's mobility. It is also expensive to send out on assignments, so producers hesitate to commit their TV crews unless they can be quite sure the story will materialize. On the other hand, because of TV's split-second scheduling, the story mustn't materialize for too long. The networks tell us that viewers complain bitterly if news or other special material displaces, for example, a scheduled football game. Hence the use of brief news "flashes" rather than immediate in-depth coverage. Epstein found that the natural consequence was a tendency to assign reporters to fairly predictable and well-scheduled events. Presidential news conferences, conventions, and speeches met these conditions well. Closely related to predictability was the tendency to rely upon well-established news sources, such as top officials in the Pentagon and other executive and legislative branches. News producers played it safe in another way, by centering their work in a few large metropolitan centers, especially New York and Washington. Film crews might be sent elsewhere, but the cost involved and the risk of not getting a good film story inhibited such assignments. Producers try to make the news look "national" but most of it always comes from a few large urban centers.

Over the long haul these constraints have worked to push TV producers toward reliance on news generated by others. Thus we have the TV producers turning to the news consensus established by the quality press, especially the *Times, Post*, and wire services. Downie describes the way this worked with the early Watergate stories in 1972, quoting the findings of the Massachusetts Institute of Technology's Network News Study Group. One member of the study group, which monitors nightly news programs, remarked that TV coverage amounted to a "fairly straight serving of headlines from the *Washington Post*." In general there was "little original reporting" and "almost nothing" that could be called investigative reporting. Downie added that much the same kind of TV news reporting on Watergate persisted during 1973 and 1974, though he noted efforts at first-hand investigative reporting,[19] especially by CBS's "60 Minutes." Not surprisingly, most of the exceptions he cited consisted of specials rather than regular news broadcasts.

Financial constraints are bad enough, but another major constraint is the notion of "audience flow." The idea is to keep the audience tuned in to the same channel all along. If interest flags during the news, the audience may switch, and once tuned to another channel, watchers may stick with it. Since the major news programs are scheduled in the early evening, before the prime-time shows, a news broadcast that led to massive switching would be in trouble. The news must therefore be attractive, packaged to appeal to audience tastes.

The packaging of the news as entertainment leads to several emphases. The producers want good "visuals," scenes that hold the eye. TV reporters are "above all else trained to search for a good picture."[20] Action is better than inaction. This may mean a focus on violence or at least on competition. The dramatic and the vivid count for more than the correct but colorless. This also means that complex problems need to be reduced to something fairly simple and recognizable. There is no time for a lengthy lecture on the complexities, the ambiguities, and the shadings. This need for the brief, forceful presentation leads to a "fictive" quality in news stories. They should have an "opening, a middle, and an ending" like a story: "rising action, a climax, then falling action; conflict and then apparent resolution."[21] If the "show" is successful, the audience remains tuned in; if not, the ratings drop and there is a shake-up in the news department.

At ABC News, for example, the ratings fell and in February of 1975 reached a low of 19 compared to ratings of 27 and 28 for CBS and NBC. ABC brought in a new manager, Avram Westin, who made changes that boosted the ABC ratings.[22] According to *The New York Times*, Westin's conception of audience reactions was that viewers were interested in what affected them most directly, and that they wanted the news presented simply and clearly. Thus he stressed domestic economic news over foreign policy and emphasized careful editing and the use of visuals. Graphics, including key quotes from a story, were projected on the screen behind the anchor man. Here it would seem that the news agenda depends more upon the standards of show business than of good journalism.

A third distinct pressure—which Epstein does not think causes serious distortion—is the need to provide local affiliates with *national* news. Government regulations require all stations to inform their audience in this area. To meet this need, a local event is made an example of some national trend or theme. Drought ravaging a region's crops is related to the national food supply or to consumer prices.

One further constraint is the government's requirement that the networks meet certain standards of fairness. In practice this means trying to insure balanced coverage. To present one side of a controversy alone may violate such standards, so efforts are made to present some contrast in viewpoints. According to Epstein, in the TV format this goal may produce blandness but may also enhance conflict, even demagoguery. There is no time for lengthy, balanced presentations; vivid, colorful, and forceful statements are at a premium. Each spokesman has only a sentence or two in which to distill his position and drive it home. The networks maintain the appearance of neutrality but reality "out there" may be squeezed into artificially intensified opposites.

If Epstein is right, the organization of TV news production puts severe limits on what broadcast journalists can do, and overall it fosters a tendency to package the news to be visually appealing. We seem to be quite some distance from the news priorities of the quality press.

TV News and the Audience

If TV news production is long on visuals and short on investigative reporting, what does the audience absorb from this news format? There are not many serious, systematic studies of the effects of the broadcast media, but one study of TV coverage of the 1972 election is an exception. Its authors relied mainly on two kinds of evidence. One was a set of hour-long interviews with some two thousand voters whom they treated as a panel and interviewed three different times during, and at the end of, the 1972 election campaigns. The second body of data was a content analysis of the evening newscasts by ABC, CBS, and NBC during the year, plus every televised political commercial of the two major presidential candidates during the 1972 national election campaigns. The authors warn us that, strictly speaking, their conclusions apply only to general election campaigns. Still, the networks put a good deal into the campaigns, and whatever shortcomings we find here are not likely to be miraculously corrected in their noncampaign coverage.

In the first place, the networks do a bad job of covering the candidates' positions on the issues. Issues are not ignored but are "rarely" the sole topic. The focus is on the "horse race" and the hoopla,[23] views of crowds and talk about who is leading and who is slipping. The authors see this as an "impossible learning situation."[24] Issues are seldom and fleetingly mentioned, and the context, with the dramatic visuals always in the foreground, is distracting. Viewers who depend upon such news coverage to inform themselves on the issues face frustration. (See Table 13–1, which shows that the situation had not changed much by 1976.)

On the other hand, the candidates' paid ads were useful. There was an emotional "image" content to the ads, but people who relied mainly on

Table 13-1 Press Coverage of the 1976 Presidential Campaign*

	Network Evening News		Los Angeles Times		Erie (Pa.) Times		Time and Newsweek	
The Horse Race:								
Winning and losing	62%	16%	51%	17%	57%	25%	55%	19%
Strategy, logistics, and support		22%		19%		18%		28%
Appearances and crowds		24%		15%		14%		8%
The Substance:								
Candidates' issue positions	24%	10%	30%	13%	24%	6%	31%	9%
Candidates' characteristics and backgrounds		6%		7%		7%		13%
Issue-related (e.g., party platforms)		8%		10%		11%		9%
The Rest:								
Campaign events calendar	14%	2%	19%	4%	19%	6%	14%	3%
Miscellaneous (e.g., election procedures)		12%		15%		13%		11%
		100%		100%		100%		100%

*Figures based on random selection of at least 20 percent of the coverage by each news source. Figures include opinion and analysis as well as regular news reports.

Source: Thomas E. Patterson, "The Media Muffed the Message," *Washington Post*, December 5, 1976, p. B-1.

TV and those who relied mainly on newspapers had "nearly identical impressions"[25] of McGovern. The authors of this study, Thomas Patterson and Robert McClure, assess the impact of TV image making rather modestly: they do not find Marshall McLuhan's dictum, "the medium is the message," to be true. Furthermore, "Voters arrive at their image of a candidate by judging where he stands politically and by assessing his significant accomplishments and failures." Voters were not fools. As to political advertising's potential for manipulation, roughly 3 percent of the electorate was vulnerable and not all of these could be labeled "victims of advertising manipulation."[26] All in all, Patterson and McClure found little reason to fear the image-making content of political ads.

Most surprisingly, the issue content of political advertising was found to be quite beneficial:

In fact, during the short period of the general election campaign, presidential ads contain substantially more issue content than network newscasts. This information is particularly valuable to people who pay little attention to the newspaper. Advertising serves to make these poorly informed people more knowledgeable. . . To put it bluntly, spot political commercials educate rather than hoodwink the voters.[27]

The authors recognize that this conclusion overturns the conventional wisdom. They counter by pointing out that "simplicity, repetition, and coordinated sight and sound . . . communicate effectively the issue messages of televised political ads."[28] The paid ads focus on a message and hammer at it repeatedly, while newscasts cover many items and cover them lightly. The typical newscast covers fifteen to twenty separate stories. Even so, the total information would fit comfortably, with room to spare, on the front page of a good newspaper. Effective political learning via TV requires, according to Patterson and McClure, involvement with live events that are interesting and that dramatize the issues involved. They cite the example of Governor George Wallace standing in the doorway of the University of Alabama, blocking the black students out. Wallace himself was using this incident to make a point.

But a great deal of television news does not lend itself to this treatment, and the pressure for good visuals tends to outweigh issue content. Campaign coverage, particularly, fails to provide the conditions for rational electoral choice. Patterson and McClure recognize the agenda-setting potential of TV news coverage but conclude that the potential is not realized.[29]

Patterson and McClure tell us that TV newscasts are ineffective. Michael J. Robinson carries the case a step further, to argue that the newscasts foster "videomalaise,"[30] the tendency to become cynical, frustrated, and despairing and to end up less enamored than ever of the social and political system. In his study Robinson used controlled experiments, survey data, and writings about the characteristics of the American broadcast media. In general Robinson found that TV news viewers were significantly associated with negative reactions toward the system. He even suggested that the rise of the "social issue" and George Wallace's emergence as a national figure were in part a result of the way the broadcast media deal with public affairs.

Another part, certainly, came from the audience, which was a large one. Robinson reports that by the early 1970s nearly two-thirds of the American public relied on TV for much of their political information. Many of these people used no competing sources of information, such as magazines, newspapers, or local opinion leaders, and many were not well educated. TV news was reaching an audience that went well beyond the elite groups that relied upon the quality press and had multiple sources of information. One other aspect of the explanation for videomalaise is the believability of television. People like Walter Cronkite ranked high in the viewers' esteem. They were not seen as manipulators who consciously distorted the news. (See Table 13-2.)

Table 13-2   Public Attitudes Toward News Media, 1959–1976*

Most Believable	1959	1971	1976
Television	29%	49%	43%
Newspapers	32	20	21
Other media	22	19	18
Don't know, no answer	17	12	18

*1959 and 1971: "An Extended View of Public Attitudes Toward Television and Other Mass Media 1959–1971," a report by the Roper Organization to the Television Information Office; 1976: NBC poll reported in the *Washington Post*, January 9, 1976.
Source: Adapted from Robert Sherrill with James David Barber, Benjamin I. Page, and Virginia W. Joyner, *Governing America* (New York: Harcourt Brace Jovanovich, 1978), p. 177.

This large and somewhat impressionable audience received its news from a medium that tended to stress certain qualities. Themes were singled out and emphasized in the visuals that TV sought so ardently. These visuals tended, Robinson believed, to stress the negative as well as conflict and violence. This encouraged an anti-institutional or anti-Establishment outlook. Here Robinson added that studies comparing American journalism with that of other countries found these qualities, and that within American journalism, TV tended to exaggerate them. Thus Robinson argued that American journalism tended to focus on the negative. What was normal was not news. What went wrong was. Aggression, conflict, and violence were especially newsworthy. Our violent society is amply reflected in its news coverage. No wonder Patterson and McClure found that campaign coverage focused on the "horse race," the conflict, rather than the issues. According to Robinson, the third characteristic, anti-institutional bias, relates to "Naderism." When Ralph Nader announces that a General Motors product is bad, it is news and is well covered. When someone else claims that most GM products are good it is apt to be ignored. Here Robinson explains that the bias is not so much liberal or conservative as it is anti-institutional. When policies work, whether they be liberal or conservative, they are not news. When there is fault to be found with policies and institutions, then there is news.

This assessment reminds us of the muckraking that we found associated with but not confined to the quality press. TV journalism does not itself create much news, but it does pick up and transmit news generated by others. And the quest for the punchy, eye-catching visual accentuates the negative aspects of American reporting generally. The large but somewhat casual viewing audience may not learn from TV news, but it may adopt attitudes of cynicism, distrust, and frustration which it then transfers from the trusted newscasters to the system's institutions. Videomalaise.[31]

At this point we are far removed indeed from the quality press and its elite audience. Perhaps our observers of TV news production and its audience exaggerate the weaknesses. Certainly commercial television is a popular target. Nonetheless, these studies warn us that much of what TV does depends heavily upon news others gather, and that the audience may either fail to get the message altogether—as in candidates' issue positions—or may become cynical and skeptical. We may be disappointed that so little of the public agenda gets through, but there is little reason to fear TV in its news form as a powerful instrument of elite control manipulating a puttylike public.

Whatever the limitations of TV, candidates depend heavily upon it in seeking to put themselves on the public's agenda. How they work and scheme to do so is our next topic.

The Media, the Campaigns, and the Voters

Life is complicated and life in postindustrial society is especially so. The United States political system has election processes built into it on an enormous scale, as we noted in Chapter 11. In election years the nation typically has hordes of candidates scrambling hard to win a place on the public agenda. Their campaign consultants , or "political consultants" as they prefer to be called, set up candidate-centered organizations that rely heavily on the media, especially TV, to reach voters. The decline of the parties has also enhanced the role of political reporters, especially in screening candidates in the early stages of a campaign.

In effect, the political reporters help to create a public agenda of viable candidates, as specialists like Hamilton Jordan well know. Timothy Crouse writes forcefully: "Now the press screened the candidates, usurping the party's old function. By reporting a man's political strengths, they made him a front runner; by mentioning his weaknesses and liabilities, they cut him down. . . . The press was no longer simply guessing who might run and who might win; the press was in some way determining these things."[32] The small group of national political reporters who dominate this process are even called, by one of their number, the "screening committee." By their coverage of potential candidates they help to determine who becomes "viable" and who does not.[33] Crouse wrote with an eye to presidential elections. But the press all across the country is in a position to screen potential candidates at all levels by the way it handles news about them.

Screening supplies an agenda of candidates—when it works. But an electorate that is demanding, independent, and somewhat cynical is not easy to cope with. In describing the care and feeding of the ticket splitter, DeVries and Tarrance show what candidates and their organizations can do. Ticket splitters are inclined to put their confidence in the kinds of communications that candidates cannot control. For TV this means an inclination to believe newscasts and documentaries more than candidate advertising. In making up their minds about voting they look first to the candidate, then to issues, then to party, and finally to group affiliation.[34] Therefore, paid ads addressed to the ticket splitter need to stress the candidate first and foremost and then his or her issue positions. Party and group affiliation may be mentioned but do not ordinarily have priority. And appeals to the ticket splitters are the most important, partly because they will probably decide the election, and partly because those who vote a straight party ticket will probably do so regardless of campaign rhetoric.

Nor can it be assumed that what ticket splitters want is fixed for all time. Campaign managers need to know about shifts in issue concerns and revise their strategies accordingly. To find out about such shifts requires polling, with the results constantly fed back into the campaign. The campaign as visualized by DeVries and Tarrance becomes a process of continuous communication between the candidate and his experts, on the one hand, and the voters on the other.

DeVries and Tarrance describe these techniques concretely in their account of William Milliken's 1970 campaign for governor of Michigan. One of two Republican governors who won in the Midwest, Milliken received 50.7 percent of the vote as against the usual statewide Republican average of just over 40 percent. One of the novelties of his campaign was the division of the state into "media markets." Since ticket splitters relied on news media for their information, it made sense to divide up the state according to TV, radio, and newspaper coverage. Media markets took the place of the traditional governmental divisions, and "weathervane precincts" in them were checked continually in telephone interviews:

> For example, air and water pollution was considered an especially pressing problem in the Kalamazoo and Traverse City media markets, while crime and drugs were considered most important in the Flint and Detroit markets. The assignment of the Milliken [TV] spots was related to rank order of the issues among undecided voters within each of the fourteen media markets. The commercials were adjusted every two weeks during September and October to reflect the changing concerns about the state's problems among the ticket-splitters.[35]

On the national scene, one of the most famous descriptions of campaign media management is Joe McGinnis' account of the "selling" of Richard Nixon in 1968. The book abounds in examples of the packaging job, but the underlying philosophy was best clarified in a memo by Raymond K. Price, one of the speech writers. McGinnis placed a high value on Price's effectiveness and quoted him a good deal.

Price began with the assumption that most people use "reason . . . to support prejudice. . . ." There was therefore a "gut reaction" created by the "chemistry" of voter response to the candidate. Yet voters responded not to the candidate but to the "image." "It's not what's *there* that counts, it's what's projected—and carrying it one step further, it's not what *he* projects but rather what the voter receives. It's not the man we have to judge, but rather the *received impression*. And this impression often depends more on the medium and its use than it does on the candidate himself."[36] This line of thought carries us into an eerie world of "gut reactions" and "images" that depend heavily on the medium rather than the candidate. Selling a candidate this way intensifies the manipulative, the irrational, and the potential for deception.

Yet this same election allows us to see the limits of selling candidates. Nixon won but almost did not. The basic problem, as his staff saw it, was Nixon's personality: "There were certain things people just would not buy about the guy." And McGinnis added as his own commentary, "The perfect campaign, the computer campaign, the technician's campaign, the television campaign, the one that would make them rewrite the textbooks, had collapsed beneath the weight of Nixon's grayness."[37] It is also reassuring to be told, as McGinnis acknowledges, that Nixon "did not trust television" and refused to watch himself, even on a newscast.[38] The "selling" of candidates has its limits, since voters will "buy" only so much.

Nixon's campaign in 1972 was considerably different. For one thing, this election brought forth CREEP. Jeb Stuart Magruder, who effectively managed much of the massive Nixon enterprise, gives an insider's glimpse of what happened.[39]

The process began in 1971, with an extensive program of polling under the direction of Robert Teeter of Market Opinion Research, in Detroit. Expecting a close election, the pollsters chose a number of states for early special attention. The first interviews, about 13,300, were in December 1971, in all the target states. These provided basic information for their strategy in the primaries and a baseline for measuring opinion changes. There was a second wave of polling in June and July, in the same states, and a third in August. The fourth wave included continual telephone polls in the target states in the last six weeks of the campaign.

This polling supplied a wealth of information. According to Teeter, past party voting is the "single most important factor which affects the presidential vote." But true to DeVries and Tarrance's research, the party liners were largely fixed in their voting and, as Teeter observed, the election would be "decided by independents and ticket-splitters." Magruder found from polls that "people saw Nixon as informed, experienced, competent, safe, trained, and honest. He was not seen, relatively speaking, as warm, open-minded, relaxed or as having a sense of humor."

This information supplied Magruder and his associates with their basic strategy: to stress Nixon's performance, not his personal appeal. With the popular Eisenhower it was possible to use slogans such as "We Like Ike." With Nixon they could say "You Need Nixon" but not "You Like Nixon." The polling even showed them that the slogan "Now More Than Ever" had greater voter appeal than "President Nixon for President." Democrats made much of the absence of Nixon's name—as though his supporters were ashamed of him—but the polls showed that Nixon was respected, not beloved. This candidate-centered campaign needed to accentuate experience rather than personality.

Polling results led to another aspect of strategy: they would stress reinforcement rather than persuasion. Nixon had been on the political scene a long time. He was well fixed on the public agenda so most people had long since made up their minds about him. In the circumstances, to try to persuade large numbers of people to change promised a low yield. Instead, "We would, rather, stress getting our decided pro-Nixon voters to the polls. We would, in short, stress organization, not persuasion . . . As the campaign progressed, we continually cut back our advertising and put more money into storefront headquarters, telephone campaigns, direct mail, get-out-the-vote programs." TV was not entirely neglected, but organization and the use of the telephone and direct mail were relied upon more than usual.[40] Expert research and planning on a large scale directed this campaign, and, as in 1968, the political consultants were successful. As before, however, there were limits to what they could sell in marketing their product.

The reformer George McGovern, who opposed Nixon in 1972, relied heavily on media "exposure." With a relatively unknown candidate— and without a Watergate slush fund—the Democratic campaign managers tried, often unsuccessfully, to manipulate the broadcast media for their man. As Theodore H. White described his campaign, "media events" were staged day by day to capture regular coverage by the TV evening news. "The traveling campaign is based on media markets—and the candidate's imperative is to expose himself to television networks for three shots every day, plus a few more exposures aimed at local or regional evening news shows at eleven o'clock."[41]

One McGovern media event was a scene of the candidate seated on a bench in a cafeteria eating with a night shift just before they went to work. This visual was of course meant to identify McGovern with blue-collar workers, but unfortunately, whatever its visual merits, it was staged too late in the day for the national news. Another media event, a midday speech in farm country on a sunny day, with a backdrop of high grain silos, was successful. The speech was effective and the timing was right for the evening news. "Every national network will have to use it," White wrote. McGovern had the benefit of a good visual, but one wonders if many undecided voters saw it and decided forthwith to support McGovern.

The use of media events carries us naturally into the realm of news management as an art form practiced with diligence and enthusiasm. De-Vries and Tarrance pointed out that the all-important ticket splitters did not much trust paid political commercials. But to get reporters and editors to cover a candidate free of charge requires some special skills. Voters may be skeptical and wary but those who handle the news are apt to be more so. Two writers who studied TV coverage in a number of state-wide campaigns have compiled a set of rules, with explanations, that instruct the aspiring candidate and his staff in the handling of news coverage. Rick Neustadt and Richard Paisner begin by quoting a successful gubernatorial candidate as saying, "TV news is the most important part of the campaign. No one really believes the paid ads any more."[42]

Some of the advice was funny but revealing. One example was Senator Birch Bayh, of Indiana, whose home-state polls showed him hurting on the gun control issue. His staff drafted a statement saying he opposed controls on all but Saturday Night Specials. They also flew him to pistol ranges in the state to shoot target practice and read his statement. The not very subtle message was: "Bayh likes guns, you like guns; you like Bayh." This visual was effective but his opponent's was not. Mayor Richard Lugar of Indianapolis announced his plan to barnstorm the state on a train by setting up toy tracks in front of his chair and running a Lionel racer around it as he spoke. In this case the visual message that got through was: "The mayor is a child."

Another tartly phrased example deals with the problem of answering questions on TV. The well-prepared candidate, the authors made clear, should have his own "finely honed" statement ready to offer at once. This prepared visual is the one the candidate wants shown, not the other, less prepared responses. To insure the use of the prepared statement the candidate should make other visuals unusable. That can be accomplished if the candidate gives "an answer they cannot use," perhaps a long-winded statement that the film editor will cut. The candidate was further warned to "end the session quickly." Otherwise there was a chance the camera might catch something newsworthy but unflattering. A display of temper would give the reporter a juicy visual but ruin the candidate's carefully cultivated image.

There is much about this whole approach that appears cynical and manipulative, but the TV news, whatever its limitations, is not simply the product of candidate manipulation. Overall, the public is apt to suffer more from superficial treatment of the news than from manipulation and demagoguery.

News management by candidates and TV news people may count for a good deal, but Jimmy Carter's campaign for the presidency in 1976 demonstrates that political advertising can work too. Carter planned long and well and the results paid off in the creation of good ads. Joseph Lelyveld, checking into the media aspects of the campaign, described how "Carter learned his lines not as advertising copy but on the stump in the early months of 1975 when his tireless candidacy went largely unnoticed. Lines that went well were kept. What fell flat was dropped."[43] Carter had his staff, including the film crew, with him. Together they graded performances and weeded out those with less than an A. "For instance, there were four separate takes of what Rafshoon [Carter's media expert] calls the 'if I ever' bit." The reference is to Carter's famous campaign statement, "I'll never tell a lie, I'll never make a misleading statement." To come across with the right kind of statement about not lying took practice.

The placement of TV ads to capture certain kinds of audiences watching their favorite programs worked wonders for Carter in Florida, a key state in his strategy. After the primary Bev Ingram, who worked for Carter in Florida, hung up an office sign that proclaimed, "'Hee Haw' and 'Lawrence Welk' did it." Mostly blue-collar workers watched the first and senior citizens the second, and the ads helped pull the blue-collar and old folks' vote. With his staff resources, planning, and testing, Carter was able to make effective use of TV advertising. But it was not easy. It took many well polished "A" performances to push Carter to the fore on the crowded public agenda.

Use and Abuse of the Media

At the outset we presented contrasting theories about the media and proposed that the concept of agenda setting probably fit best of all. Neither Mills' monolithic power elite nor Key's extreme skepticism accounts very well for what actually occurs. Postindustrial society has reduced the role of the parties and enhanced that of the intelligentsia and the media as well. But whatever the media does to influence the public agenda depends importantly on both the media and the public.

A quality press exists and is read by the nation's leaders. It serves as both a conduit for information and part of a system of linkage for the exchange and development of ideas. Those who read this press, especially *The New York Times* and the *Washington Post*, tend to have more liberal opinions. We cannot be sure whether the press causes these opinions or a process of self-selection occurs. This press in turn creates a "news consensus" which operates upon other elements of the media, including news departments of the networks.

This quality press further tends to set trends in new ideas and categories of news. The success of recent muckrakers has highlighted the adversary posture of much of the American press. It has influenced the public agenda and encouraged investigative reporting as a press function. In general the quality press and its opinion makers function successfully as agenda setters. Their audience is comparatively small but influential.

Television news is another matter. The expense of TV coverage and the fear of losing "audience flow" hold the networks back in the news area. These financial constraints, and others, channel them in the direction of dramatic portrayals of relatively predictable events. ABC's alteration of its news format in 1975 reflects the tendency for TV news to become sports events and show business.

Patterson and McClure found that news reports on the 1972 election highlighted the horse race and the hoopla. Issues were so poorly covered that viewers gleaned more information from political ads than from the news. The image content of the ads designed to appeal to voter emotions did not seem to be a serious threat. Voters tended to judge candidates on their experience and accomplishments. But overall, TV news coverage did not contribute much to the agenda needed for a rational electorate.

Robinson argued that TV news actually fosters "videomalaise." Large numbers of people watched and many of them relied only on television. They trusted TV news but found much of it disturbing. What was bad was news; confrontation and violence came to the fore, and so did an anti-institutional bias. Cynicism, frustration, and despair increased, and because these viewers believed TV news and newscasters, they transferred their emotions to society and to political institutions.

Still, whatever the limits of TV and other news media, candidates for office must use them. Candidate-centered organizations, created by political consultants to do much of what parties can no longer do, rely heavily on the media.

In the early stages of our numerous election campaigns, when the candidates begin to present themselves, we find political reporters in a key role. They screen candidates and may well have great effect on which campaigns will continue and which will go down the drain as failures. These reporters do much to shape the agenda of candidates that the public will in due course become aware of.

As for the campaigns themselves, the process of appealing to the wary, ticket-splitting voter described by DeVries and Tarrance is difficult. It is necessary to locate the ticket splitters, find out what their concerns are, then watch for changes. As voters' concerns and opinions change, the candidate needs to know it and alter his appeals accordingly.

Two of Nixon's presidential campaigns showed that the "selling" was considerable but within bounds. Nixon won in 1968 but his poor TV personality made him hard to sell. In 1972, finding that people had strong opinions about him, his managers cut back on trying to persuade people to change and concentrated on getting out the vote of those known to be favorable. In that election McGovern's struggle to create "media events" for favorable news coverage was a reminder that media manipulation is hard to avoid.

Public skepticism is so far advanced that news management may take the place of heavy TV advertising. Neustadt and Paisner's funny, hard-nosed rules alert us to the potentials and the hazards of news management. The best-laid plans may go awry, as when a candidate trying to look dedicated to his campaign ends up looking childish. News management may be essential to get the aspiring candidate fixed on the public agenda but it is not likely to be easy. In passing we also looked briefly at Carter's successful candidacy, in which careful long-range planning and practice resulted in grade A performances on film.

In the end, what we have is a media system that is complex and potentially quite influential but often is not. The quality press certainly matters, but it is read by people who are themselves sophisticated and who have multiple sources of information. The muckrakers at times are major forces in drawing attention to the deficiencies of American society, and they represent some of the best in American journalism. But their pride in uncovering faults may lead to an accent on scandal rather than the investigation of basic, long-term, and slowly developing problems. Commercial television news is harder to assess as a contribution to the public agenda. It does not originate much news, and at times it leans toward sports-reporting and show-business styles, rather than journalism. Overall, it fails to provide the viewing public with a clear, issue-oriented agenda.

As for the media in the campaigns, this too is a mixed bag. Political reporters appear to screen candidates, for good or for ill, with some effectiveness. The political consultants certainly try to manipulate voters. But it requires skill and ample resources, and at best it works some of the time under the right conditions.

None of our evidence suggests any reason to cower in fear of the media's alarming potential for damage. The communications media are powerful influences among many powerful influences. They need to do a more effective job of presenting the public agenda to the public at large. Admittedly that job is not an easy one, and wisdespread privatism and cynicism do not make it easier. These aspects of American life are more disturbing for the long run than any media excesses. It is reasonable to speculate that the media's unfulfilled potential may reflect deficiencies in American society at large. With this thought in mind we may turn to a final examination of coalitions, elites, and masses.

NOTES

1. C. Wright Mills, *The Power Elite* (New York: Oxford University Press, 1956), p. 314.
2. V. O. Key, Jr., *Public Opinion and American Democracy* (New York: Alfred A. Knopf, 1961), p. 357.
3. Lee B. Becker, Maxwell E. McCombs, and Jack M. McLeod, "The Development of Political Cognitions," in Steven H. Chaffee, ed., *Political Communication*, vol. 4 (Beverly Hills, Calif.: Sage Publications, 1975), p. 38. This article includes a good review of the literature, past as well as present, on media effects.
4. Key, *Public Opinion*, pp. 366–367.
5. Martin Schram, *Running for President: A Journal of the Carter Campaign* (New York: Pocket Books, 1977), pp. 64–65.
6. Theodore H. White, *The Making of the President, 1972* (New York: Bantam Books, 1973), p. 327.
7. Ibid., pp. 346–348.
8. Jeb Stuart Magruder, *An American Life: One Man's Road to Watergate* (New York: Pocket Books, 1975), p. 61.
9. Carol H. Weiss, "What America's Leaders Read," *Public Opinion Quarterly*, 38 (Spring 1974), 1–22.
10. Edward Jay Epstein, *News from Nowhere* (New York: Random House, 1973), p. 37.
11. Ibid., p. 150.
12. According to Timothy Crouse, "Once a story hits page one of the *Times* it is certified news and can't be ignored." See his *The Boys on the Bus* (New York: Random House Ballantine Book, 1974), p. 78. Crouse recounts the tale of a leak planned by a member of a senator's staff to reach the *Times* and thereby become "certified."
13. Leonard Downie, Jr., *The New Muckrakers* (New York: New American Library Mentor Book, 1976), pp. 7, 275.
14. Ibid., p. 185–187.
15. Ibid., p. 15.
16. Donald L. Shaw and Maxwell E. McCombs, *The Emergence of American Political Issues: The Agenda-Setting Function of the Press* (St. Paul: West Publications, 1977). The authors studied the *Charlotte* (N. C.) *Observer* closely and at one point sum up as follows: "Hard-pressed news editors grow accustomed to pulling information from the Associated Press and United Press International wires to fill their news space and keep local audiences informed." (p. 34.).
17. Epstein, *News from Nowhere*, pp. 259 ff.
18. Timothy Crouse, *The Boys on the Bus*, p. 154. Elsewhere Crouse gives the cost of a two-hundred-word TV news story as $5,000 (p. 161).
19. Downie, *The New Muckrakers*, pp. 264 ff. An interesting exception that proves the rule and also highlights the media status system is in Crouse, *The Boys on the Bus*, p. 185. During 1972 CBS decided to investigate charges by George McGovern that the

Nixon Administration mishandled a grain deal with Russia, with the result that insiders profited greatly. The resulting TV report was so good that reporters on *The New York Times* called to say that CBS had covered the story better than the *Times*. Crouse remarks that "no form of praise meant more to the network people than recognition from the *Times*. Cronkite was elated." Crouse adds that this kind of original investigative reporting did not continue for long.

20. Crouse, *The Boys on the Bus*, p. 153.
21. Epstein, *News from Nowhere*, p. 363.
22. *New York Times*, April 13, 1975, Arts and Leisure, Section 2, p. 1.
23. Thomas E. Patterson and Robert D. McClure, *The Unseeing Eye* (New York: G. P. Putnam's Sons, 1976), p. 20.
24. Ibid., p. 58.
25. Ibid., pp. 72–73.
26. Ibid., p. 135.
27. Ibid., p. 23.
28. Ibid., p. 120.
29. Ibid., Chapter 4, "Network Evening News and the Public Agenda."
30. Michael J. Robinson, "Public Affairs Broadcasting and the Growth of Political Malaise: The Case of 'The Selling of the Pentagon,'" *American Political Science Review*, 70 (June 1976), 409–432. A summary is on p. 430.
31. Readers may feel that Robinson exaggerates his case. But he does pinpoint at least an aspect of popular reactions to much news. In the news world there is talk of "happy news." Some local TV stations have consciously tried to lighten their treatment of the news to overcome the depressing effects of the straight, hard news coverage.
32. Crouse, *The Boys on the Bus*, pp. 39 ff. Note also the section on the columnist David S. Broder, pp. 90 ff. Broder admitted that he consistently underestimated George McGovern's candidacy. The screening was not always successful.
33. See also Broder's analysis, "Political Reporters in Presidential Politics," in Charles Peters and Timothy J. Adams, eds., *Inside the System*, 3rd ed. (New York: Praeger, A Washington Monthly Book, 1976). Broder here expands upon the functions of political reporters. He sees them as doing much more than simply transmitting information.
34. Walter De Vries and V. Lance Torrance, *The Ticket-Splitter: A New Force in American Politics* (Grand Rapids, Mich.: William B. Eerdmans Publisher, 1972), pp. 74 ff.
35. Ibid., pp. 106–107.
36. Joe McGinnis, *The Selling of the President 1968* (N.Y.: Simon and Schuster Pocket Books, 1970), pp. 30–31.
37. Ibid., p. 166.
38. Ibid., p. 79.
39. Magruder, *An American Life*, pp. 178 ff. Magruder looked back upon the 1972 campaign as the "best-planned, best organized presidential campaign in history" (p. 321). Magruder admitted bias, but of course he is not the only one with a bias on this subject. We willingly leave the final and more objective assessment of this election to historians. The public financing of presidential elections that began in 1976 may make what Magruder did in 1972 impossible to duplicate ever again, whatever its pros and cons.
40. The statement represents the main thrust of the campaign but there were exceptions, such as the Democrats for Nixon group. See Magruder, *An American Life*, pp. 316 ff. An account of the efficient Nixon headquarters and its various divisions is in White, *The Making of the President, 1972*, pp. 435 ff.
41. White, *The Making of the President, 1972*, pp. 413–415.
42. Rick Neustadt and Richard Paisner, "How To Run on TV," *New York Times Magazine*, December 12, 1974, p. 20.
43. Joseph Lelyveld, "The Selling of a Candidate," *New York Times Magazine*, March 28, 1976, pp. 66 ff.

SUGGESTIONS FOR FURTHER READINGS

Robert Agranoff. *The Management of Election Campaigns*. Boston: Holbrook Press, 1976. Includes a number of chapters about the media.

Benjamin C. Bradlee. *Conversations with Kennedy*. New York: Pocket Books, 1976. A gossipy, revealing account of newsman Bradlee's relationship with John F. Kennedy as president.

Alan L. Clem. *The Making of Congressmen: Seven Campaigns of 1974*. North Scituate, Mass.: Duxbury Press, 1976. Separate chapters describe the campaigns of a number of congressional candidates.

Delmer D. Dunn. *Public Officials and the Press*. Reading, Mass. Addison-Wesley, 1969. Examines public officials and the press in Wisconsin in assessing the impact of the press.

Gary Paul Gates. *Air Time: The Inside Story of CBS News*. New York: Harper & Row, 1978. A look inside CBS by a man who once worked there and went back to interview extensively for this book.

Roy Hiebert and others, eds. *The Political Image Merchants: Strategies in the New Politics*. Washington, D.C.: Acropolis Books, 1971. Reports from a conference at which many experts in the subject discussed their work.

Sidney Kraus and Dennis Davis. *The Effects of Mass Communication on Behavior*. University Park, Pa.: Pennsylvania State University Press, 1976.

David A. Leuthold. *Electioneering in a Democracy: Campaigns for Congress*. New York: John Wiley, 1968. An analysis of congressional elections in the Bay Area of California.

John E. Mueller. *War, Presidents, and Public Opinion*. New York: John Wiley, 1973. An important study of presidential leadership in times of conflict that reaches some unexpected conclusions, as in comparing reactions to the Korean and Vietnam wars.

Harold Mendelsohn and Irving Crespi. *Polls, Television, and the New Politics*. Scranton, Pa.: Chandler, 1970. Focuses especially on the possible influence of the media and the opinion polls on election day.

Joseph Napolitan. *The Election Game and How to Win It*. Garden City, N.Y.: Doubleday, 1972. One of the well-known image makers describes the application of his talents in campaigns.

Dan Nimmo and Robert L. Savage. *Candidates and Their Images: Concepts, Methods, and Findings*. Pacific Palisades, Calif.: Goodyear, 1976. An academic exploration of image making and research on the subject.

Dan Nimmo. *The Political Persuaders: The Techniques of Modern Election Campaigns*. Englewood Cliffs, N.J.: Prentice-Hall, 1970. Focuses on the rise of the campaign mangers and their work.

Dan Rather with Mickey Herskowitz. *The Camera Never Blinks: Adventures of a TV Journalist*. New York: Random House Ballantine Books, 1977. Rather, the well-known CBS TV newsman, coauthors a running account of his life as a reporter, from his origins in Texas to his clashes with the Nixon Administration.

Donald L. Shaw and Maxwell E. McCombs. *The Emergence of American Political Issues: The Agenda-Setting Function of the Press*. St. Paul: West

Publications, 1977. Reviews other studies and reports on a North Carolina study of the influence of the media in the 1972 election.

James C. Strouse. *The Mass Media, Public Opinion, and Public Policy Analysis.* Columbus, Ohio: Charles E. Merrill, 1975. Attempts to relate media, opinion, and policy.

Hunter S. Thompson. *Fear and Loathing on the Campaign Trail '72.* New York: Popular Library, 1973. Thompson, a correspondent for *Rolling Stone*, supplies a thoroughly unconventional perspective on the 1972 campaign.

14 · The Democratic Potential Unfulfilled

As we opened our inquiry an imaginary Socrates asked us what we meant by public opinion. We answered by explaining our organizing concepts: coalitions, elites, and masses. Our Socratic type might now complain that the elaboration of these ideas carried us through much of modern America. So be it. We think that is a plus, not a minus. Having explored the application of these concepts, we are now in a position to engage in a bit of synthesizing to show how coalitions, elites, and masses fit together in contemporary America. We hope these generalizations will not induce the reader to reach, as Socrates finally did, for the deadly cup of hemlock.

In looking over the whole, we can see the magnificent strength of the system's foundations. The political culture as a unifying framework for all is muscular, perhaps the strongest anywhere. It is almost impossible to imagine an America without its Constitution and related values. Consensus really prevails. Yet for all its strength, the political culture is amazingly flexible. Conflict over the application of general principles is characteristic of Americans. A measure of lawlessness and violence is commonplace but rarely threatens the system. The nuclear family continues, in spite of stresses, to be strong. Great resources are expended on education and it has successfully indoctrinated generations of Americans. Religion remains strong for most people and heavily reinforces the system. Most of the population is affluent, even if most people are not as well off as they would like. And the population is "generally contented" with their personal lives—as distinct from the public sector. These attributes interlock to provide enormous support for the system. While these powerful reinforcements persist, the system's future is well assured. So also, probably, are its myths, George Washington and all.

Yet in celebrating the strength of the system and the good life available to most, we cannot forget the pervasive political apathy. The good life usually means one with low levels of political activity. Even the minimal form of participation represented by voting shows signs of declining. Most Americans are strivers who seek to achieve for themselves and for those whom they care about. Thus an individualistic privatism tends to divorce the private from the public sector. For most, the public sector exists on the periphery.

The system is at its best, then, in providing a stable, pervasive framework within which individuals may advance themselves as they see fit, a form of citizenship which joins the good life to a minimal level of public involvement. In a sense we have rights without politics.

Plural Elites and the Democratic Potential

A stable political framework does not resolve the question of control within the system. Some observers see the United States as dominated by a powerful single elite. From this perspective, the elite must then be assumed to be responsible for much of what happens, good or bad. But we have challenged this perspective and argued that America consists mostly of a vast middle class with much democratic potential and some real influence. Elites exist but are pluralistic and constrained.

The argument against the single elite theory is quite compelling when we add it up. The population is not only reasonably affluent and contented. It is pretty well educated. Furthermore, it is reasonably tolerant, especially as compared with a couple of decades ago. The system itself provides enormous opportunities for popular pressures to be brought to bear. Mass suffrage exists for almost everyone eighteen or older. The United States has more elections than the rest of the world combined. The fragmentation of government that prevails down to the grass roots worries critics but is more indicative of democracy than of elite domination. The polling of public opinion is intensive and varied, for both political and commercial purposes. These polls insure that much information is available about popular desires, in presidents and in toothpaste, for those who wish to know.

There is an enormous democratic potential and some of it is exercised. The electorate is more issue conscious and coherent than earlier research acknowledged. The grand scale of the New Deal and of the welfare state are hard to account for as solely the work of a benign elite. Supplementing the pressures of the electorate are those of a highly diverse interest group system, including those representing labor, blacks, and consumers.

To explain away this whole fabric of democratic structures and processes as devised and controlled by a single elite strains credulity.

When we turn from the public at large to survey the elite pinnacles of the system, we again find evidence of pluralism, not a single business-dominated elite. Critics typically single out gigantic business firms such as General Motors to argue for the concentration of corporate power and influence. As against this we found the system as a whole to be big. Government spends more than one-third of the Gross National Product and exerts much influence on the rest. Consumer spending accounts for about two-thirds of GNP. Employee compensation accounts for over three-fourths of national income and profits for well under 10 percent. The federal individual income tax brings in far more revenue than the corporate income tax. There is evidence that corporate profits are really rather low and so is the rate of capital investment over time. Military spending as a share of GNP has been falling for some time.

In looking at the automobile industry, perhaps the nation's biggest, we found much variety in the products available to consumers, as well as strenuous foreign competition. In addition there is considerable government pressure on behalf of safety, efficiency, and pollution standards. In this example of a concentrated industry we see a variety of checks and constraints that limit its power.

Related to this issue is considerable social mobility and specialization of elites, rather than an interlocking of elites. Studies have found these elites to be moderates, not hard-nosed reactionaries. As Watergate proved, the checks and balances still work. A media system that relishes its role as an adversary, and muckrakes accordingly, plays a significant role in these checks and balances. Added to these has been congressional curbing of the imperial presidency, not to mention a powerful and independent judiciary.

When we add up the evidence it points to a fragmented and diverse system of elites alongside a massive middle class. The latter does pretty well for itself and has plenty of opportunities to make its wishes known. Elites *are* constrained. They tend to avoid what is known to be unpopular. And in some respects at least, they do what they know the public wants.

We might press this line of thought one step further to argue that popular pressures can be excessive in some respects. The energy problem is a case in point. American consumers are used to cheap and plentiful supplies of energy. Most experts seem to be agreed that those days are passing and energy costs are bound to rise. Yet as the 1970s waned and the 1980s approached, the country had great difficulty developing a national energy policy. Political leadership was reluctant to impose upon the people the growing energy costs that the times seemed to require. While national leaders thrashed about, trying to devise politically acceptable alternatives, it appeared that the desires of the mass of consumers prevailed.

Undoubtedly the system is complex. In some ways the terms single elite and plural elite are inadequate. Elements of democracy and elitism intermingle and it is hard to sort out the resulting mixture. Perhaps those who wish to move the debate beyond to new concepts are right. But until such terms are available, we would insist that the United States system is better described as a plural elite than a single elite.

In this light it appears to us that mass indifference is more of a problem than irresponsible and exploitive elites. Many citizens are contented but serious social injustices still mar the country's domestic life. And global problems seem more complex than ever. Elites, no matter how well intentioned, cannot resolve these problems without public support. In a system as pluralistic as the one we have described, the public shares significantly in the responsibility for whatever happens.

The Passing of the New Deal Coalition

If the public and its opinions matter, then political coalitions matter as well. Although the old New Deal coalition seems to be on its way to extinction, it is really like the old soldiers who never die but just fade away. It has faded into changes in the political process, the issues of the day, and the components of the Democratic coalition of the 1970s.

The political process changed in part because society changed. As people became more affluent and educated they became less loyal to the parties. Voters became more independent, cynical, and demanding. People looked increasingly to the candidates and their issue positions, rather than to their party. A major consequence, often, was a split-ticket vote.

Party organizations weakened. Declining voter support contributed but so did other developments. Reform of the parties within and without did not help. Public financing of the presidential elections in 1976, for instance, forced the candidates to rely heavily on the media rather than party organization. The interest group system flourished, helped along by legislation that permitted formation of Political Action Committees. The number of committees formed and the money channeled into the political process virtually doubled in a short period of time. Even reform groups such as Common Cause tended to divert activists, who might otherwise have worked in the party system, into cause-oriented group activity and ad hoc coalitions. Increasingly the weakened parties lost control over nominations and general elections.

The role of the media in the political process also grew. The elite press led by *The New York Times* tended to serve as the national bulletin board or agenda setter for its elite readership. This press served as a conduit for information and provided a linkage in the process of exchanging ideas and opinions. It was muckraking reporters for the *Washington Post* who put Watergate, and other scandals as well, on the national agenda. Political reporters with this press served in effect as a "screening committee" that heavily influenced the determination of viable candidates for high office. In addition, the elite press consisting of the quality newspapers, the wire services, and the news magazines established a news consensus that pervasively influenced others. TV news functioned largely within this news consensus. And TV news reached perhaps two-thirds of the population, a large share of whom relied upon it almost entirely. It was not clear what effect TV newscasts had on political learning. There was a tendency for the news to focus on the horse race rather than the issues in a campaign. It might even foster "videomalaise" among those who found the news "bad" and were inclined to transfer these feelings to society and politics. But the people found the newscasters credible and tended to believe them much more than they believed the political parties.

With the parties seriously weakened, candidates increasingly turned to political consultants for help. They in turn created candidate-centered organizations that relied heavily upon professional skills drawn originally from marketing research. They also relied heavily upon the media, TV above all. For a price a candidate could buy an organization that brought together all the skills necessary for a successful campaign. To put a candidate on the public agenda was not easy, given the rather skeptical, cynical attitudes of much of the public. Paid TV political ads could be beneficial if well done. But it was usually better yet to somehow get the candidate into the news broadcast.

The political process has changed greatly from what it was in the heyday of the New Deal. We have dwelt upon these changes at some length to drive home a point. For if we are right, then the decline of the parties is no temporary thing. It is part and parcel of larger developments which add up to a significant long-term movement away from the parties.

The changing political process has altered the character of the Democratic coalition. A second change, and a major one, is the alteration of the issues. In its origins the New Deal reflected a struggle between the haves and the have-nots. What made sense then obviously may not do so in other times. By the 1970s the population was generally affluent and contented. Class differences had declined. The bulk of the population saw itself as middle class.

During this time a number of issues had come up to deflect concern from class-related issues. These included civil rights; the "social issue";

the Vietnam war; defense spending and détente; ecology; Watergate and trust in government; energy; and inflation. On top of this it was no longer clear that the old solutions to old problems, such as unemployment, really worked. Indeed, there was a growing suspicion that more government intervention might acutally make things worse. The "tax revolt" of 1978 was probably a compound of many things, including the media itself. But politically it was light years away from the issues and political divisions of the 1930s. Even the economic issues of the 1970s, such as taxes and inflation, were not those on which the New Deal focused. Nor was this complex mix of issues likely to disappear and allow the Democrats to focus comfortably on that old standby, unemployment. Any Democratic coalition in being would have to cope with a variety of issues, economic and noneconomic. And its leaders would have to keep in mind that the majority saw itself as middle class, not as workers.

So far, in describing changes in the Democratic coalition we have surveyed the political process and the issues. Third on our list of changes is the shifting composition of the coalition itself. In 1972 main-line supporters of the Democrats failed them. For the first time, union members and Catholics voted more Republican than Democratic. The Catholic and union margin for Nixon was small, and of course Nixon's landslide tilted the whole nation toward him in the voting. But that it occurred at all is surely significant. That it happened while Democrats retained large majorities in Congress is another indication of the times. Candidate-centered organizations created candidate-centered election victories, not party mandates.

Carter's election in 1976 can hardly be read as a resurgence of the old Democratic coalition. Authoritative observers, including the president's pollster, Pat Caddell, warn us against such conclusions. Blacks and union members supported Carter, it is true. But the big Catholic bloc was the "soft underbelly" of the Carter vote. Protestant-Catholic differences were less than in any previous election. There are indications that suburban Catholics favored Ford. In addition Carter drew upon the South, the suburbs, small towns, and rural voters. Big city support helped but did not matter greatly. Carter drew much upon nontraditional groups, and was not in the New Deal mold of people like Hubert Humphrey. His background was somewhat different, and in winning office he drew together a coalition that differed significantly from the old New Deal coalition.

The developments we have sketched warrant us in concluding that the old New Deal coalition is not likely to enjoy a rebirth. With so much changed—the society and the political process, the issues, and the components of the Democratic coalition—some fresh post–New Deal think-ing is in order. Neither the liberalism nor the conservatism that grew out of the New Deal struggle adequately addressed the problems of a largely middle-class postindustrial society. Much the same could be said of the aging socialist tradition.

When we add up the broad developments in coalitions, elites, and masses, we are left with a peculiar mix. We have the form of a constitu-tional democracy. But the reality differs from the ideal in perhaps unex-pected ways. The foundations centered on the Constitution and related values are about as secure as one could wish. This system appears to be so strong as to survive almost anything short of total annihilation.

Within this system we have a large, affluent population. The masses are not seriously exploited or oppressed by a single, dominant elite. Cer-tainly the people have ample opportunities to make themselves felt.

But an individualistic privatism prevails. And it is this which makes the democratic reality so different from the ideal. The system has the potential for far more public participation than most people care about. We have, as we have elsewhere described it, rights without politics. Per-haps we should congratulate the public for getting so much for so little. They have a good buy. But one cannot help wondering if the people, and the elites who profess to serve and lead them, will rally to the challenges of the times. The eminent American historian, the late Richard Hof-stadter, ended one of his essays with words that are fitting: "It is hard to think of any very long period in which it could be said that the country has been consistently well governed. . . . The nation seems to slouch on-ward into its uncertain future like some huge inarticulate beast, too much attainted by wounds and ailments to be robust, but too strong and resourceful to succumb."[1]

The Politics of the Post-Welfare Era

The future is uncertain, as always, but this analysis has some suggestive implications about the nature of political conflicts to come that are worth pointing out. The New Deal coalition is no longer totally workable, and perhaps the era marked by a fairly steady expansion of the welfare state is passing. In the first place, the New Deal was in part a reaction to the harsh economic conditions of the Great Depression. But by the 1970s most people were reasonably well off. A relatively small percentage were poor or unemployed, and women and blacks earned a good deal less, generally, than white males; but the welfare state had done much to alleviate the hardships of previous generations. Certainly it was no longer possible to justify further extensions of the welfare state on the basis of large-scale economic deprivation.

In the second place, in the 1970s there were no large concentrations of individual or corporate wealth that could be tapped to pay for sizable additions to the welfare state. Reformers might angrily reject such statements but the evidence certainly pointed in this direction. And if this be true, it means that the taxes paid by the middle class had become the major source of government revenue. A middle class largely resistant to increased taxes would stand as a major barrier to significant expansion of welfare state policies nationally. Indeed, the tax revolt of the late 1970s threatened even the existing level of services, not to mention possible expansion. In any event, in future it would appear that expansive social welfare policies would depend upon the support of a sizable chunk of the middle class, the group that would bear the burden. Political conflict was no longer a battle between the haves and the have-nots but was instead a struggle between segments of the middle class over the allocation of the burdens and the benefits of the system.

A third factor that could inhibit the expansion of the welfare state after the 1970s was the question raised by economists and others about the nation's basic economic health. In comparison with other industrial powers the United States now ranked extremely low in economic growth. And the continuation of this trend of meager economic growth into the future could threaten the nation's well-being quite fundamentally. It seems likely that only growth and the corresponding expansion of job opportunities can over the long haul significantly enhance the earning power of women, as well as blacks and other minority groups. Certainly a static economy would sharply curtail such opportunities. Concern with basic economic growth and with improved productivity might well become issues that could displace both environmental and welfare concerns.

Related to these issues are some that arise from the nation's drastically altered position in the world economy. In New Deal days the United States was relatively self-sufficient and could pretty well ignore economic events abroad. By the mid-1970s it was importing roughly half its oil, and this flow was absolutely vital to the operation of the economy. At the same time the cost of imports contributed heavily to the nation's trade deficit abroad and to a concern for the health of the dollar as an international currency. Oil imports exacted a political cost as well: the United States could not afford to antagonize those from whom the oil was imported. What this would mean in international politics over the long term was unclear. It *was* clear that the United States was no longer as independent and self-sufficient as before. And it almost certainly meant that the costs of the energy consumed by the American public would continue to rise. The American style of living, based upon cheap and plentiful energy, was under considerable pressure to change. This complex of problems, shot through with much that was confusing and uncertain, fell largely outside the kinds of concerns associated with the welfare state.

In many ways, then, in the last quarter of the twentieth century the nation was moving into an era beyond the welfare state. But the welfare state would not go away, in spite of the purple rhetoric of some of its critics. It had a vast and deeply rooted constituency in the tens of millions of people all across the nation who benefited from it. The erosion of some benefits may well occur, but it is hard to visualize a massive scaling down of the welfare state in any near future. Change in the American political system tends to occur slowly and piecemeal, and it tends to be accompanied by much traditional political rhetoric. We may expect debate over welfare state policies to continue, even as the nation changes and other concerns come to the fore.

But the times *are* achanging. The growth of the welfare state was a response to one set of problems. Much has been accomplished, even if imperfectly. The nation itself has changed in the process, proving again its adaptability as well as its volatility. Other problems have arisen much removed from the struggle between the haves and the have-nots. It is time for the nation to look at itself and its place in the world with renewed attention and a willingness to entertain novel ideas. Americans, whether leaders or followers, have much to work *for* and great talents to bring to bear in coping with new challenges. Over the long run, even if at times the process is slow, erratic, or contentious, the people can and will respond.

NOTES

1. Richard Hofstadter and Michael Wallace, eds., *American Violence* (New York: Random House Vintage Books, 1971), p. 43.

Appendix:
What Pollsters Do
and How They Do It

"Where did they take the poll?"

"Don't you really think the polls are rigged?

"I don't know anyone who's ever been polled. How do we know they don't just make it up?"

These remarks are more or less typical, not only of college students but also of most Americans who have anything to say about polls. When the questions come from students we reply with a question of our own: "How many people do you think polling organizations survey in order to reflect the views of the approximately 150 million Americans over eighteen?" Most answers to this question are guesses of anywhere from fifty thousand to five million. Given this range, it is easy to see why most who have thought about polling believe that if it were truly on the up and up, either they or some friend would almost certainly have been polled. But such figures are far from reality.

Established pollsters such as Gallup, Harris, Roper, Yankelovich, and others usually interview a sample of between 1,500 and 2,000 respondents, with occasional "quickie" telephone polls of about 750 and very infrequent large samples as high as eight thousand, such as Gallup used during the final stages of the Kennedy-Nixon race of 1960. Interestingly, the result of that poll was about one-half of 1 percent different from that of John Kraft, who surveyed 2,000 people.[1]

Since pollsters interview such a comparatively small number, it should not be surprising that few citizens even know anyone who has been polled. And what is difficult for many to accept is that a sample of only 1,500 (or even 8,000) can come close to mirroring the views of 150 million. But the evidence strongly indicates that it can.

The pollsters' magic method is "probability sampling," which employs a concept known as "random selection," in which every person in the "universe" (total population) theoretically has an equal chance of being surveyed. If the sample is truly random, it will reflect the characteristics of the universe. That is, both universe and sample will contain about the same percentages of Republicans, Democrats, independents, people under thirty, blacks, Catholics, Jews, Protestants, manual workers, males, females, rural, urban and suburban dwellers, college educated, high school educated, people with incomes over $15,000 per year, and so on. This makes it unnecessary to do "quota" sampling—whereby one actually attempts to interview X percent Catholics or Y percent blacks. What is important about a given sample is not size but whether or not it is truly random. Of course, true randomness is not always attained, and, as Michael Wheeler has indicated, theory and practice don't always jell. For example, certain people such as housewives, the retired, and the unemployed are more easily located than young working people. And on a number of issues, says Wheeler, "homebodies tend to have different opinions than those who are on the move."[2]

But since pollsters usually seem to be able to survey a representative sample, how do they do it? First they divide the nation into smaller units such as towns or counties, or election wards or precincts, and list these and their populations. They then choose some of these—the number depends on the size of the sample—and proceed to break them into even smaller units such as blocks and houses (example: third house from the east corner of a given block). The individual to be interviewed may be designated as the one over eighteen whose birthday falls nearest the interview date. The interviewers themselves are given as little discretion as possible regarding where and whom to interview.

The wording of questions is extremely important, and the rule of thumb seems to be "the simpler the better." To answer a question accurately, the respondent must first understand it. Questions used by professional pollsters have been previously asked of smaller test groups. Professionals believe that respondents will answer truthfully if they understand the questions, but the professionals still have trouble knowing what questions to ask and how to phrase them. The human mind is diverse, and complex attitudes often cause resistance to simple yes/no or agree/disagree choices.

Perhaps the major problem with polls is that many of those released to the media are not well designed or carefully done. So called "straw polls," in which people are accosted on a street corner or at a shopping center, or surveyed by mail, have no real validity. Nor do the informal surveys made by some politicians and later "leaked" to the papers. Even polls that use a very large number of respondents are not valid unless good sampling procedures are followed. The most glaring example of this is the old *Literary Digest* poll taken before the 1936 presidential election. The *Digest* mailed out millions of poll cards to people listed in the telephone books and on car registration lists. During the Depression, people with telephones and automobiles would tend to be of at least comfortable income level and therefore more likely to favor the Republican candidate. So what the *Digest* did was to poll a group in which Republican sentiment was considerably overrepresented. Poll result: a victory for Alf Landon. Election result: a Roosevelt landslide in which FDR carried forty-six of forty-eight states and exceeded 60 percent of the popular vote. In the debacle the *Digest* folded.

Unique among straw polls is the National Popcorn Poll, which uses the method of printing the Republican and Democratic candidates' names on popcorn containers in movie theaters and grocery stores. The consumer becomes a poll respondent simply by choosing one or the other. According to Bernard Hennessy, the "popcorn pollsters" have picked the winner in every election from 1944 through 1972.[3]

A point of contention is whether face-to-face or telephone interviews produce more accurate poll results. Most people assume that face-to-face would be best, and they could well be right *if the interviewers in the field would always make direct contact with the respondents.* But according to Michael Wheeler and others, this *if* looms large. Wheeler cites examples of people working for the Gallup and Harris organizations who simply concocted poll data rather than doing a number of interviews. Wheeler also quotes veteran pollster Albert Sindlinger about why telephone polls are more reliable: the polling organization can easily monitor the employees' work. Sindlinger told Wheeler that if field workers have "any intelligence, after the tenth interview they're going to sit down and make up the other twenty-five."[4] Needless to say, the Sindlinger organization relies on telephone polls.

Once all the data has been collected, there is the problem of poll interpretation. Even results of scientifically constructed and administered surveys can be deceptive, especially when accompanied by a misleading newspaper headline. Wheeler's interesting treatise offers the following graphic example: *The New York Times* featured an article in late 1975 headlined "California Poll Has Ford Losing Ground to Reagan." Actually, Reagan's lead was only one point, while the sampling error for the poll was plus or minus five and one-half points. Thus Ford might actually have been leading Reagan by ten points! Since this survey was made in

November, and a previous one in August had found the two Republican contenders tied, it was hardly accurate to say that Ford was "losing ground" to Reagan.[5]

What we need to keep firmly in mind is a check list of questions for use in determining the validity and meaning of any given poll:

1. Who took the poll?
2. Who paid for the poll?
3. How many respondents were there?
4. How many were interviewed?
5. How many refused to be interviewed?
6. How were the respondents selected?
7. What was the exact wording of the questions and how many questions were asked?
8. Does the interpretation in the article accompanying the poll follow from the data?

With this mental check list, we can look at poll results with the proper perspective.

NOTES

1. Bernard Hennessy, *Public Opinion*, 3rd ed. (North Scituate, Mass.: Duxbury Press, 1975), pp 66.
2. Michael Wheeler, *Lies, Damn Lies, and Statistics: The Manipulation of Public Opinion in America* (New York: Dell, 1976), p. 104.
3. Hennessy, *Public Opinion*, p. 51.
4. Wheeler, *Lies, Damn Lies and Statistics*, pp. 111–112.
5. Ibid., p. 298.

Index

ACKNOWLEDGMENTS (continued from page iv)

NBC Poll: Data from NBC Poll is reprinted by permission from *The Washington Post*, Jan. 9, 1976. © *The Washington Post.*

Norman H. Nie, Sidney Verba and John R. Petrocik: Reprinted by permission of Harvard University Press from *The Changing American Voter.* Copyright 1976 by the Twentieth Century Fund.

Thomas Patterson: "Press Coverage of the 1976 Presidential Campaign" from "The Media Muffed the Message" by Thomas Patterson is reprinted by permission from *The Washington Post*, Dec. 5, 1976. © *The Washington Post.*

Public Policy Research: "Trends in Party Affiliation" derives from *Public Opinion* (March/ April 1978, p.23). Published by the American Enterprise Institute for Public Policy Research. Reprinted with permission.

Robert Sherrill et al: From *Governing America: An Introduction.* © 1978 by Harcourt Brace Jovanovich, Inc. Reprinted by permission of the publishers.

Ben J. Wattenburg: Table from page 52 of *The Real America.* Copyright © 1974 by Ben J. Wattenberg. Reproduced by permission of Doubleday & Company, Inc.

William Watts and Lloyd A. Free: From *State of the Nation, 1974*, p.285, © 1974 by Potomac Associates, Washington, D.C.

Drawing by Weber: © 1976 The New Yorker Magazine, Inc.